D0536498

ATLAS
BIKER
Mountainbiking in Morocco

NICK CRANE

The Oxford Illustrated Press

Dedication
To the families and friends of the High Atlas who made us so welcome.

ISBN 1 85509 210 7

Published by:
The Oxford Illustrated Press, Haynes Publishing Group, Sparkford, Nr Yeovil, Somerset BA22 7JJ, England.

Printed in England by:
J.H. Haynes & Co Limited, Sparkford, Nr Yeovil, Somerset.

British Library Cataloguing in Publication Data:
Crane, Nicholas
Atlas biker: mountainbiking in Morocco.
1. Morocco. Atlas Mountains. Description & travel
I. Title
916.4045

ISBN 1-85509-210-7

Library of Congress Catalog Card Number:
90-80386

All photographs by Nick Crane unless otherwise credited.

Contents

Cast

Cast in order of appearance

Christopher Bradley	Biker and 2nd Unit Cameraman
Nicholas Crane	Biker
Mathew Dickinson	Biker and 2nd Unit Director
Annabel Huxley	Leading/Only Lady and Stills
Alan Ravenscroft	Director
Jeremy West	Chief of Support Crew
Andrew Flanders	Vehicles and Technology
Graham Smith	1st Unit Cameraman
Philip Millard	1st Unit Assistant Cameraman (Grip)
Stuart Bruce	1st Unit Sound Recordist
Abedelilah Latmer	Representative of Moroccan Production Services
Ahmed Echita (Mohammed)	Driver

Film Production (London)

Alan Ravenscroft	Producer/Director
Matt Dickinson	Associate Producer
David R. South	Managing Executive
John Gau	Executive Producer
Colin Luke	Series Editor
Julian Pettifer	Commentary
John Hackney	Film Editor
Chris Nixon	Assistant to Film Editor
Chris Trussler	Sound
Rebecca Perkins	Production Manager

'Blazing Pedals', the filmed version of *Atlas Biker*, was made by John Gau Productions in association with The National Geographic Society for Central Independent Television.

Mountainbikes, Tents, Rucksacks, Stills Equipment and Clothing

Derryck Draper at Best Layerwear
Errol Drew and Toby Howes at Madison Cycles
Paul Gates at Kodak Ltd
Mike Jardine at Europa Mountain Sport
Mike Longdon at Wild Country

Mike Parsons at Karrimor International
Mark Thackera at Olympus Optical Co.

'Atlas Biker' Maps and Altigraphs
Peter Williams

Geographical Bodies

The Royal Geographical Society – The Zanzibar Connection – National Geographic (USA) – Wrecks and Recces: The Birth of Atlas Biker – Jiving with Mr J – The Marrakesh Duress – A Test on the Tichka – To the Desert – The Biggest Sand Dune in Morocco

The Royal Geographical Society lives in Society's House, a solid, four-storey, Victorian stack of terracotta brick which watches over the wooded fastness of Hyde Park. From his alcove on the outside wall of the lecture theatre, Dr Livingstone presides over the traffic jams of Knightsbridge and – on Monday evenings – over the hurrying figures of the Fellows and Members who pour through the double doors to hear invited speakers deliver illustrated lectures on anything from the sandstone geomorphology of the Tibetan Plateau to the problems associated with kayaking the Zambezi. In recent years there has been a growing programme of lectures on such urgent subjects as ozone holes, acid rain, endangered species and rain forests.

There are 9,000 members of the Society and on a good evening as many as 700 will congregate for a lecture. The Society which despatched pioneers like Younghusband, Shackleton, Scott, Fuchs, Freshfield, Hunt and Hillary to cold, hot, dry or slimy corners of the world is now a focus not only for academics, explorers and travellers but for those who wish to play a positive role in the preservation of planet Earth.

Six miles from Society's House, behind a sign saying 'Private Function' in an upstairs room in the 'Cutter's Arms', a more modest meeting starts at around 7.30pm and continues until closing time. The room is small and the 10 or so chairs have to be moved to one side to accommodate upwards of 40 people who are likely to turn up. To keep the numbers under control, the dates of forthcoming meetings are not circulated; the 'event' has no name or committee and there is no apparent organiser. Gatherings are held on random dates, but always on a Tuesday and the season runs from around autumn to spring, leaving the summer free for travel. The mystery surrounding the 'Cutter's Arms' is compounded by its elusive location down a little-used lane somewhere in the City, and by its name, which isn't the 'Cutter's Arms'.

On an average evening, between one and four lectures are delivered, ranging in length from five minutes to two hours. It has been known for nobody to turn up, or for speakers to arrive and find the room occupied by a Rotarian darts tournament, or for there to be standing room only. Adventures presented since the meetings began in 1984, include simulated ice-climbing on the chalk cliffs of Dover, following the footsteps of the Japanese poet Basho, living on an Indian *ashram,* camel touring in the Sahara, steam engines in Rumania, North American Indian folklore, Antarctic pollution, Andean pottery, canoeing round Cape Horn, underwater swimming off the Galapagos, preserving Brazilian forests, Buddhism in Bhutan, tracing the Silk Route, running the Great Wall of China, running the Himalayas, running round the world, skiing in Norway, following the Incas, bussing in Korea, breaking the world land-speed record on a bicycle, horse-riding from Land's End to John o' Groats, ice-skating on the Baltic.

Chris Bradley heard about the Cutter's Arms from a man he met riding a camel in the Sahara. "You must come to this place. It's right up your street," the man had said.

Bradley came to the pub on 16 February 1988. After a Scotsman from Slough had finished describing a two-year trek around the coast of the Mexican Baja peninsula – surviving on a diet of cacti and rattlesnakes – Bradley fought his way over the bodies and introduced himself. Eccentrically dressed in a collar and tie, he was a compact, square-jawed man, with swept-back greying hair and a reassuring Lancashire accent. Bradley gave me two business cards: one was pale yellow with an ink drawing of camels leaning towards the logo of Explore Worldwide Ltd, while the other was Soho-grey and announced that the holder belonged to, or was, 'Zanzibar Films'.

Thirty days later I was pouring coffee down my throat in a desperate effort to find the words to describe the joys of paragliding in the snow in the Peak District for a magazine article when the telephone rang. "Matt Dickinson here," said a voice which assumed I would know who it belonged to. "You met my partner in Zanzibar Films, Chris Bradley, last month."

Dickinson told me that as well as being a part of Zanzibar, he had just started working as Assistant Producer with the independent film company 'John Gau Productions' who had been commissioned to make a new series of adventure travel documentaries. We arranged to meet in my flat on the afternoon of 3rd May, then adjourn to the Cutter's Arms in the evening to hear Hallam Murray describe his recent journey from Peru to Tierra del Fuego, by bicycle.

Bradley and Dickinson came into the flat as a team: Bradley first, with outstretched hand and case, then Dickinson, taller, electric-eyed, with road-worn brogues and a fishing jacket over a blue-striped shirt. "Hi! I'm Matt Dickinson!" he exclaimed, as he continued his forward surge to the wall of book-spines, round to the 9th-floor window, and finally to the table, where he pulled out a chair and said "Right!"

Bradley and Dickinson had an irresistible conviction that the combination of their personal backgrounds, of Zanzibar, and of myself, could form the basis of a team capable of making the adventure-travel documentary of the eighties. They needed ideas and proposals for exciting, interesting journeys.

"Doesn't matter how crazy," encouraged Dickinson, "Pogos through the Gobi, whatever . . . so long as you want to do it, and it's filmable."

Dickinson spoke with unnerving confidence for someone who was only twenty-six. He talked about his own adventures with the speed and enthusiasm of a DJ running through the pop-chart. From boyhood in Nigeria he had gone to school in England before setting off for Morocco at the age of sixteen.

"I went with a friend. We did everything wrong: ate 15 slices of melon in one sitting; ate *cous-cous* from the filthiest stall in Djemaa-el-Fna; were fleeced and caught dysentery. I deliberately put myself through it; I wanted to try *everything*." The next year, he travelled on his own to India, where he wound up in a doss-house in Delhi with advanced giardia. Looking for cooler air, he travelled up to Kathmandu and fainted on a rubbish tip. "Nobody bothered to pick me up for half-an-hour. The dogs used me as a lamppost."

After hitch-hiking around Iceland, and getting mixed up with Uganda's election troubles of 1979, Dickinson went to Durham University, where his archaeology-anthropology studies took him to the Sahara to record the rock-paintings of the Hoggar Mountains, and to the rain forests of Madagascar to look at lemurs. Over the next five years, he went east on the trans-Siberian railway; mapped an abandoned Touareg encampment in Niger; reported on the Paris–Dakar rally and then joined the adventure holiday company 'Explore Worldwide', for whom he worked as a guide on the River Nile, and in the Atlas Mountains of Morocco. Dickinson's television career began in 1985, when he joined TV-AM as a freelance journalist setting up sofa-interviews with celebrities like Suzi Quatro and the Dynasty stars. After two months, he was poached by the BBC to join 'Jim'll Fix It'.

Dickinson stood up and tore around my tiny flat, eyes alight: "I fell in love with 16mm camera work. It was the first time I'd been involved with film crews; till then it had all been studios and videos. With 16mm you have a language – 'Action! Cut!' and all that – you have a director; a clapperboard that goes 'Snap!'; you've got the personalities of the cameraman and the soundman. It was the most exciting discovery of my life!"

After behind-the-scenes roles on 'Wogan' and 'Jasper Carrott', Dickinson edged into travel documentaries by researching trans-Saharan trade routes for the BBC's 'Great Journeys' series. His current job, with John Gau Productions, was about to take him to China to shoot a film about two girls making a steam-engine odyssey through Manchuria and another about a man trying to ride the biggest tidal bore in the world on a surf-board.

Chris Bradley had been working on the Nile as the lead-guide for Explore Worldwide when Dickinson arrived to relieve him. The two had never met before, but found a common interest in travel, writing and television. Later, I was to find out that Bradley had at one time sold corn-dogs from the back of a van in Detroit, studied civil engineering at Liverpool University, played 'Hurricane' Higgins at League snooker, been Bedfordshire Schools' Cross-country Champion, and been something of a racing cyclist. As a tour guide, Bradley had led groups to North Yemen, along the Silk Road in China, on camel treks in Algeria, to Syria, Jordan, Guatemala and Belize, to Soviet Central Asia, Sri Lanka and India, and to Mexico. He had also written a novel called *The Ten Days of Osiris*, about an attempt on the life of President Sadat.

"I remember being really impressed," Dickinson recalled. "Chris was the first person I'd met who'd written a book; for every hundred you meet who say they're writing a book, you meet one who finishes."

Within months of meeting, the two of them had set up a production company called Zanzibar Films, and Bradley had begun training as a film cameraman.

Dickinson continued sprinting round the room: "The Third World, adventure, anthropology, people, places – anything which we can cover in a low-key, inexpensive, almost clandestine way, would be right for Zanzibar."

Over weekends and evenings, Zanzibar cranked into action.

Dickinson grinned: "We bought for £1,000 an old Arriflex ST. It sounded like a demented lawnmower. Our first take ever, was of a toy Panda in St Albans. Then, on Saturday, 24th November, 1986, we shot some gliders over Ivinghoe Beacon. We were so excited that we drove straight up to London and got it processed by Vis-News. We waited outside the labs like a couple of expectant fathers. When they gave the film back to us, we realised that we had no equipment for viewing."

We walked over to the Cutter's Arms.

The next morning I had a telephone call from the *The Sunday Times Magazine* telling me to "stop being so laid back" and to get on with the series of articles I'd promised them. I was trying to set up a series of five journeys by horse, canoe, bicycle, foot and sailing boat, all of which had to be completed in five weeks. By the end of the day I had all but forgotten Bradley and Dickinson and Zanzibar. The only evidence of our meeting was a note I found days later, penned on a sheet of typing paper saying 'Dickinson and Bradley, slightly mad, which is good'.

It was three months before I heard again from Zanzibar. It was Matt Dickinson who telephoned: "There've been some interesting developments; shall we meet?"

The 12th August was a Friday. At 8.30am Dickinson and Bradley arrived at my flat. We walked up Aldersgate, and on the corner with Baltic Street, turned through the plate glass front of the Regis Restaurant and ordered three breakfasts.

Dickinson started: "This series I'm working on for John Gau Productions; it's called 'Voyager'. National Geographic in the States, and Central TV here, are jointly funding a series of 13 films on adventure travel. Only 12 have been commissioned. It's a great opportunity. The final slot's still vacant and they're not sure how to fill it. Chris and I are putting in a 'Zanzibar' proposal to make a film about a mountainbike journey through the Atlas Mountains."

Dickinson enthused about his time leading adventure tours in the western mountains of the Atlas, where villages cling to cliffs and the Berber people are still blessed with an unspoilt tradition of hospitality. The previous year Matt had made a 150-kilometre trek with mules and local Berber guides, following in the footsteps of the great explorer Wilfred Thesiger, who travelled there in the fifties. While plodding along a mule track between passes, Matt had dreamt of returning to the Atlas, with a mountainbike.

"How long would we have to make the journey?" I asked.

"Twenty days. Thirty at the most. It depends on the filming budget. What do you think?"

I said that I had just started working full-time for a charity called Afghanaid who specialise in emergency relief for the civilian refugees of the war in Afghanistan. In four days' time I was due to fly out to Pakistan to prepare for an illegal crossing of the border into Afghanistan and thence across the Hindu Kush mountains by horse to the ravaged valley of the Panjshir.

"Interesting!" concluded Dickinson. "Give us a call the moment you get back."

I returned to the UK three months later, pleasantly surprised to be alive. One week later, on a Monday evening, I cycled down Kensington Gore to the Royal Geographical Society. An ex-soldier and a very short Portuguese woman had been giving a lecture on their trans-Saharan camel trip. Dickinson and Bradley were there. We ambled in the dark down Exhibition Road to the 'Daquise' a Polish café in Thurloe Street which has a conspiratorial atmosphere and serves subway sausages. The best tables were all filled. We wound down the stairs and jammed ourselves onto a bench seat in the basement. It took Matt 70 seconds to steer the conversation around to Morocco.

"It looks as if there's probably a definite commitment to make a mountainbike film," he said. "Central are keen, but Nat. Geo. are still hovering. They need a detailed proposal of the route and likely sequences. They're still not convinced."

It emerged that the immediate problem was how to turn 'Atlas Biker' into a story which could hold its own in a major TV series which already included 'Alligators Amok', 'Jumbo Jamboree' and 'Kangaroo Killers'.

"It's got to be Africa," added Matt. "All the other continents are covered."

In competition with Atlas Biker was another film which was also competing for the last slot in the series: a businessman-turned-adventurer wanted to make a journey through the Sahara Desert, linking Foreign Legion outposts by customised go-karts. There were rumours that he was prepared to introduce microlight aircraft in order to clinch his place in the series.

"Have you thought any more about the route?" I asked.

"Some of it I've already done on the Thesiger trip, but the basic idea would be to ride from one end of the High Atlas to the other, using the highest tracks we can find. There's a place called Midelt we can start at, which is right at the eastern end of the High Atlas. We can finish on top of Mount Toubkal, the highest mountain in the Atlas, which is at the western end."

"Who's going to ride the bike?"

"You!"

A tube of *wurst* split in my mouth. After three months of oily Afghan rice, every mouthful had a million flavours.

Dickinson leaned forward and explained that Atlas Biker would be a unique film because (he hoped) Zanzibar would be hired by John Gau Productions to provide a second film crew which would follow every inch of my journey. While John Gau's First Unit would be confined to road travel, Zanzibar's Second Unit would travel with me along the mule tracks. Incidents could be spontaneously recorded. Among travel films it would be unusually realistic. I asked: "Who are you going to use as this second film crew?"

"Chris and myself. We'll follow you by mule. Or on foot. Or maybe mountainbikes. We've experimented with carrying the camera and sound gear. It can't be carried in a pannier because the vibrations are too great. But we've found that you can take the camera to bits and carry it in backpacks."

"How much does it weigh?"

"Oooh, not much," said Dickinson, sweeping up his arm as if he were propelling a feather on an invisible cushion of air.

As I pedalled back to my flat through the smiling knots of people leaving the theatres along the Strand, I pondered Atlas Biker. After Afghanistan I needed a holiday; an adventure which would be frivolous, inconsequential and fun. Atlas Biker fulfilled all these needs but it lacked a 'hook'; that eye-catching tag so necessary for a TV journey that would be broadcast opposite 'East Enders'.

When I got home, I pulled my over-thumbed Philips atlas from the bookshelf and gazed absent-mindedly at page 122. The Atlas Mountains cut a deep shadow across the top of North Africa. To the north of the mountains was the green triangle of northern Morocco. To the south was a vast area of sparsely-labelled desert divided by the ruler-straight borders of Mauretania, Morocco, Mali and Algeria. At their eastern end, the Atlas crumbled into the Mediterranean; at their western end they tapered and dived into the Atlantic.

I stared. Shapes and lines moved over the map. I mentally overlaid the map with what little Moroccan history I knew, and with physical cross-sections. I looked at the rivers. Suddenly, I was looking at the answer. It was obvious: all we had to do was add a bit of the Sahara onto the beginning and end of the ride, and we had a journey 'From the Sahara to the Sea'. It was nicely alliterative; definitely difficult; it meant that televisually the route would include sand-dunes, rocky mountains, rivers, snow and ice and finally sea. It also sounded slightly mad.

On the basis that the distance from the tip of my index finger to the first knuckle joint was 250 kilometres, the total distance from an oasis in the northern Sahara, to the Atlantic Ocean, via the entire length of the High Atlas Mountains, was about 1,200 kilometres. Divided by the 20 days that were available, that would mean averaging 60 kilometres each day, which was just possible, allowing for the odd day lost through mishaps and allowing for the fact that we would be travelling on very rough mule tracks for most of the time.

The next morning I telephoned Matt.

"Great," he said. "We can start at Merzouga. That's where the biggest sand dune in Morocco is."

The date was 1 November 1988. If 'Atlas Biker' was to make the deadline for inclusion in the 'Voyager' series, the team would have to leave the UK in only ten weeks' time.

Matt and Chris decided that, if the film got the go-ahead, the most efficient means of transport for them – operating as the Second Unit camera crew – would be mountainbikes.

For Chris, this meant a revival of old enthusiasms: after retiring from cross-country running with broken toes, Chris had turned to cyclo-cross racing. He had competed in the yellow jersey of Luton Wheelers, been South of England Champion in 1970-71 and 71-72 and ridden for the British Junior Team in an international race in Belgium. He had once pedalled from Liverpool to Ravenna as a training ride, and had competed in the 'Three Peaks Race' – a massed-start race over the highest peaks in the Pennines, fought over by cyclists and runners alike. For Matt, bicycles – and mountainbikes in particular – were untried vehicles.

The telex from National Geographic confirming that 'Atlas Biker' had won the last available slot in the 'Voyager' series came through in early December. This prompted an attack of nervousness among those who now realised that they were about to be subjected to possibly the 20 hardest days of their life. I re-started my training runs along the Thames Embankment after dark, when nobody could see me walking.

To prepare for the Atlas Mountains, and to acquaint themselves with mountainbikes, Matt and Chris set aside a Saturday to traverse the entire length of the Ridgeway non-stop, in winter. It was months later that the full story emerged. The night before their big test, Chris, the Bolton-born cyclist, watched Matt's Home Counties approach to long-distance cycling with some incredulity: "I realised that I was biking with a yuppie when I saw Matt filling his water-bottle with Perrier!" he winced.

They set off from Avebury at 10am on a wet mid-December morning. It took them three hours to cover the first 15 miles; an average speed slightly above walking pace. "After that," Chris later explained, "it got slow!" By mid afternoon they were ploughing through the mud leading past the megalithic burial chamber of Wayland's Smithy when the rear derailleur on Matt's mountainbike crumpled into the wheel. Determined not to give up, they raced for the nearest town of Wantage with Matt freewheeling and Chris pedalling behind and pushing him. They arrived at 5.24pm, six minutes before the only bike shop in town was due to close, and bought the one set of lights in the shop and a chain-link remover. With the tool, they were able to shorten the chain on Matt's bike so that he could pedal gently in one gear. They then fixed the white light to the front of Matt's bike, and the red light to the rear of Chris' and set off in tandem. After the pedal fell off Matt's bike, progress was slowed even further, and they arrived at Streatley at 7pm, Chris pushing.

Also during December, Matt, in his role as Assistant Producer at John Gau, began the complex task of creating the logistics of a filmed expedition. A director – and his 'First Unit' consisting of a two-man film crew and soundman – had to be found; vehicles hired; a support-team recruited; permits obtained from the Moroccan government; insurance arranged and eye-catching bikes and rucksacks collected. Matt and Chris upgraded their Zanzibar 16mm film equipment by buying a broadcast-standard Aaton camera, lenses and a synchronised Sony Professional sound recorder so that they were fully-equipped to operate as the 'Second Unit'.

On 8th December, Matt telephoned, greatly excited: "Good news. We've got Alan Ravenscroft to direct. He's perfect; great sense of humour; he's good at documentaries that don't take themselves seriously; just back from the Antarctic. Everything OK? Good. Bye." And he put the 'phone down.

I called back: "Matt, I'm concerned about this sand dune. Until we know where it is, we won't know where to start the ride."

"You're right."

"I'm thinking of going out there next week to find it."

"Good idea."

On 11 December, I flew to Marrakesh with Annabel Huxley, whom I had met at the birthday party of *World* magazine, and who liked the idea of a quest in search of the highest sand-dune in Morocco.

From a cut-price rental company off Boulevard Mohammed V, we hired a white Renault 4 then rattled for three days over the Atlas and along the Saharan fringe until we reached the Algerian border, where we turned right. Dickinson had said that he thought the sand dune was at or near a place called Merzouga. Merzouga was a small oasis some 40 kilometres into the Sahara from the end of the tarmac road. Beyond Merzouga was a sand sea called the Erg Chebbi, which is about 30 kilometres long and 10 kilometres wide. The tallest dunes in the sand sea rose about 100 metres above the surrounding plain. The immediate problem was to identify which of the dunes was the highest. It was clearly not enough to start a bicycle journey from the Sahara to the sea on the *edge* of Morocco's highest sand sea; the ride had to begin right *on top* of the highest point.

Leaving the Renault at the edge of the sand, we hired two camels and the services of a local guide, a tall man in the flowing blue robes of the Touareg tribe. His name was Omar and he resembled the man who blew up the trains in 'Lawrence of Arabia'. Omar gave Annabel the best camel. Fifteen minutes after leaving base, my camel stood on its forelegs, reared its hindlegs, kicked its bottom and sent me soaring through the air. I landed on top of my 180mm lens, winded. When Omar and Annabel had recovered from their hysterics, and I had been reinstated on the hideous beast, Omar explained in French that it was the first time he had ever seen anyone fall off a camel: "*Incroyable*!" he exclaimed, his magnificent Touareg moustache tilting into a happy grin.

Over the next five hours we rode south east, lunched on eggs and peppers off a low round table in the mud-brick home of Omar's aunt, then returned along the gravel plain at the foot of the sand sea. No matter from what angle you looked at the dunes, one dune in particular presented itself as the highest. It looked to be about three kilometres into the sand sea. I took compass bearings from the plain, drew a sketch map, and we returned to London.

On 30th December I met Alan Ravenscroft. He was dressed in a beard and a briefcase, and his rounded profile seemed at odds with a man recently back from the Antarctic and about to embark on twenty days of physical deprivation in North Africa. As we filled in our respective backgrounds, Alan quickly revealed a likeable perversity: "After boarding school I worked for the Organic Food Society. At a time when everyone else was tramping round India with Leonard Cohen, I went to Ireland because it was a lot closer to home in case I got fed up." Alan is the brother of broadcaster John Peel, one of my boyhood heroes.

Alan's first role in TV had been with Rediffusion, where he had edited 'Take Your Pick' with Michael Miles. In 1968, he had gone off to Australia, then returned to join London Weekend Television's 'Aquarius' show, which was presented by Russell Harty. A period of making ballet films was followed by a job as a current affairs director on 'Weekend World', during which time he covered Northern Ireland, the Portuguese coup of April '74, and the Rhodesian war. The 'Pam Ayres Christmas Show', BBC's 'Nationwide' and 'Dave Allen in America' followed. "After directing current affairs programmes, I was thrilled to travel to places where something hadn't gone wrong," he added.

Alan made his first travel documentary with Robert Redford. It was called 'The Outlaw Trail', and followed the actor's horse-back pilgrimage through the badlands of the Wild West. Three films on the Titanic followed, and then Alan made an important discovery: "We went off to the Antarctic for National Geographic, to film Monica Kristiansen trying to reach the Pole. We were meant to be there for six weeks, but we got stuck in the ice and stayed three months. It was the first time I realised that I could enjoy things which were unpleasant. It was the first time I'd been with a camera crew who became part of the event themselves."

"I learnt from that film that when you don't plan things, it's often the best way. You have to trust that things will happen; that you'll get enough incident to make a film. The important thing is to *start* with enough ingredients."

As director of 'Atlas Biker', he was going to be responsible for shooting enough sequences of sufficient variety to make up a 25-minute film. The brief from John Gau Productions was precise: "Twenty days is going to be the absolute limit. The crews will have to get back on the plane on Day 21."

There was a pause, filled by the rumble of traffic on Aldersgate. Twenty days would leave no spare time for mishaps or delays. I said: "There's absolutely no chance that I'll at any time climb off the bike and join one of the vehicles. Not just because it'll spoil the journey, but because the film won't look authentic if there's any cheating."

"I appreciate that," said Alan thoughtfully. "So . . . what do you see as being the ingredients in this film?"

"Well, we start on the sand-dunes of the Sahara, move along a string of date-palm oases, through a huge gorge then turn left for the Atlas mountains. At first they'll be bare and arid, then we'll move up above the snowline, to visit the tribal castles of the Lords of the Atlas. Then we'll climb Mount Toubkal; then we'll rush down to the Atlantic and dive into the sea."

He looked pleased: "Bookends!" he smiled. "Bookends! Humphrey Burton – he was my editor at Aquarius – always used to say that a film needed bookends. It looks as if we've got them: the Sahara, and the sea."

But he still sounded uncertain: "Do you think enough will . . . *happen*? You know . . . there'll be enough interesting . . . *incidents*? It still feels a bit *thin*. I don't want to start influencing the expedition; there's always a narrow dividing line between making a film of an expedition and making an expedition for a film. But if nothing happens, it's not much of a film; remember its going to be broadcast at the same time as 'Eastenders'. This sort of film needs a strong cast." He paused. "How d'you feel about being the main person in the film?"

"It won't just be me. The film will be about the people I meet along the way, in the Berber villages, on the trail, in the tea houses, on the roadside."

Alan's frown remained: "I can see the historical sequences, and the action . . . but there's still something missing . . ."

Thirty minutes later, he departed reassured: he accepted that the bike ride could not be compromised by my hopping into support vehicles when the filming was dull, and in return, I was to ask Annabel Huxley if she would be prepared to play Helen of Troy for the purposes of providing the film with a fallback sub-plot: "You know the kind of

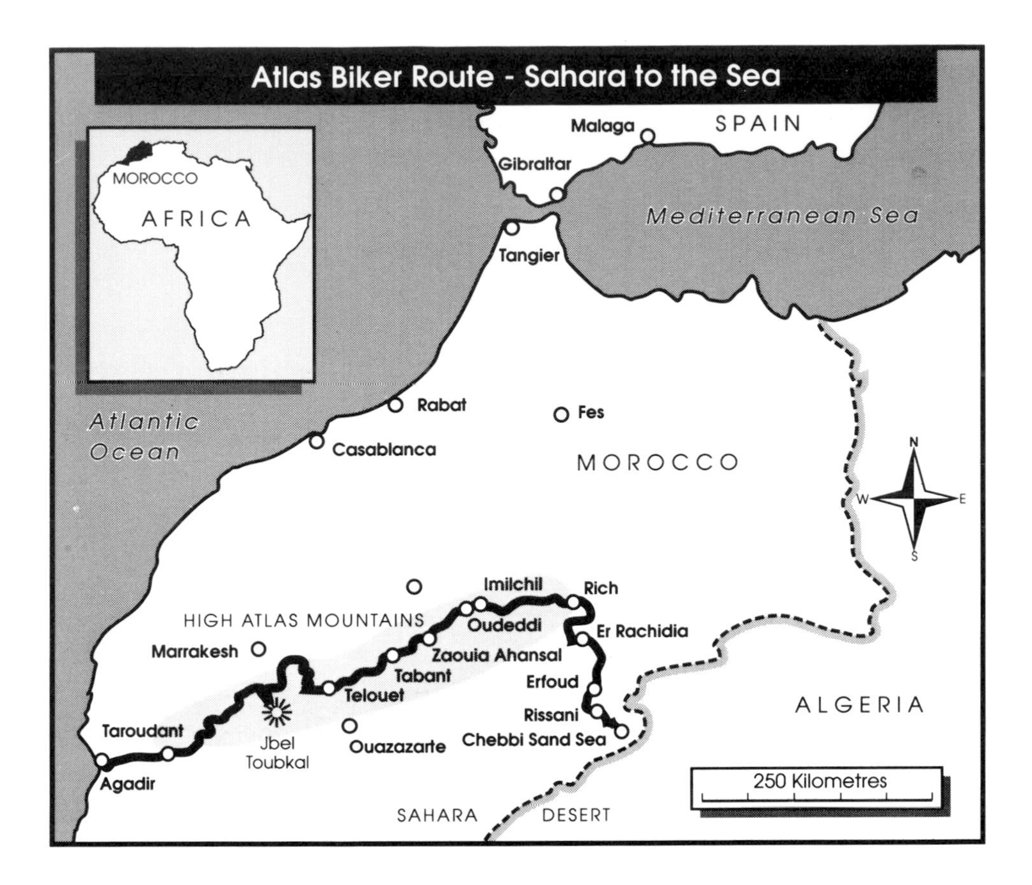

thing," explained Alan as he left: "the parting kiss on top of the sand-dune; the nervous wringing of hands when you go missing; the welcome arms in the sunset at the end of the ride."

"I suppose I could try *acting*," said Annabel doubtfully on the telephone that evening.

Annabel was used to diplomacy: in her real-life role as publicist for the book publishers Viking Penguin, her office was under siege from the Rushdie affair. She was also a traveller in her own right – eighteen months earlier, she had returned from a two-year trek around the Far East and Asia. Leaving Moscow on the trans-Siberian Express and travelling through to Japan and Hong Kong, she had taken the slow-boat to China and begun a long trek that eventually took her to the Gobi Desert, across Tibet and on to India. Her trip ended spectacularly, on the highest mountain in Tibet – Shishapangma – where she joined the base-camp team of a scientific/climbing expedition led by Colonel John Blashford-Snell. The two lead climbers, Stephen Venables and Luke Hughes, were forced back from the summit in deteriorating weather, and the subsequent storm ripped through the various camps, forcing a retreat

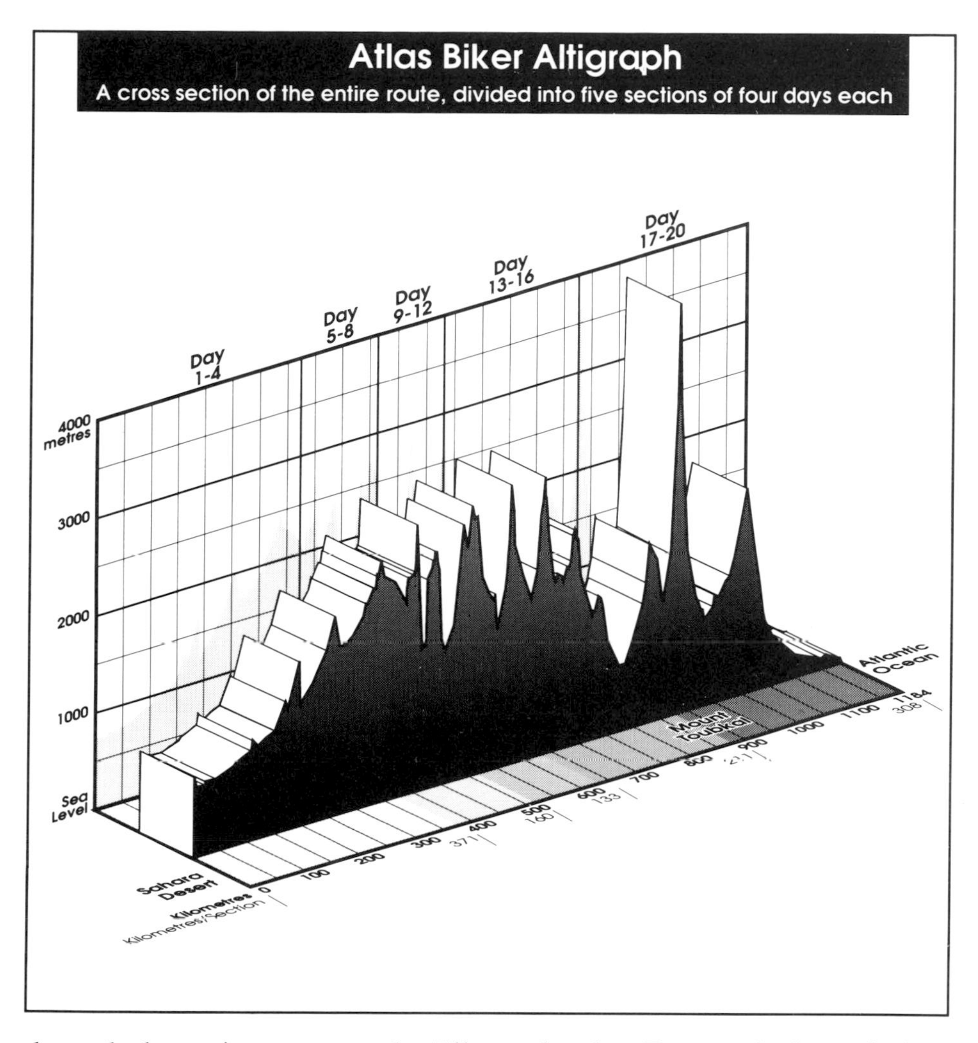

through deepening snow to the Tibetan border. Two weeks later, in late 1987, she was back in London.

By the beginning of January, 1989, two departure dates had been set: on 7th January an advance party consisting of two Land Rovers containing all the expedition equipment would leave London and drive the 2,500 kilometres to Morocco. On 12th January the First Unit camera crew and any expedition left-overs would fly direct to Marrakesh and rendezvous with the Land Rovers. Annabel, who was only able to take ten days off work, would join the expedition half way through. As well as providing romantic interest, she would also take stills photographs.

On 4th January, the final briefing was called at John Gau's headquarters in Putney. Assembled beneath the sloping glass roof of the Gau office, Matt Dickinson introduced his team to each other. In addition to

Alan Ravenscroft, Dickinson, Annabel and myself there were two of the First Unit film crew there: Graham Smith, the cameraman, and his 'grip' Phil Millard, a mountainbike enthusiast. Chris Bradley was away in Yemen. Strangers assessed each other; the conversation was polite; judgement reserved.

Sitting on a desk, Matt ran through the rules: "Temperatures on this trip could be extreme. As well as extra clothing for the high altitudes and cold desert nights, it may be a good idea to take protection against dust and heat for the film gear. The High Atlas frequently record temperatures equal to those of the Alps in winter. High quality sleeping bags are absolutely essential. The whole crew will be sleeping in tents; it's extremely unlikely that we'll be seeing any hotels. The support crew and film crew will travel in two Land Rovers: a 2¼ litre and a V8. There's a roofrack on the 2 ¼ which we can use for things like the spare bike.

"Cooking will be on a rota basis, though Jeremy West will be in charge. He's not here today, but he's travelled a lot in South America and Africa, and used to run safaris. We'll supplement food we take out from the UK with what we can find in local markets. Andy Flanders will look after the mechanics of the Land Rovers. He couldn't make it today either, but he's an expert with off-road vehicles and we shouldn't have any problems on that score. We'll all need a torch.

"Finally, this is a serious trip over high, remote mountains. There are many unknowns. Please! Nobody is to take any silly risks!"

The two Land Rovers had five days in which to cross France, the Pyrénées, Spain and Gibraltar, where they would take a ship to Ceuta and Morocco. In the Land Rovers would be Alan, Matt, Chris, Jeremy, Andy, the bikes, tents, food, clothing and the mountain of miscellaneous gear which always seems to accumulate whenever an expedition has the luxury of a vehicle. Fiona Dickinson, Matt's wife, had offered to provide a departure banquet at the house of her parents, part way between London and the English Channel.

I travelled down to Sussex on the evening of 6th January, with Annabel and Jeremy West, in the front of Jeremy's pick-up truck. In the back of the pick-up was Jeremy's equipment: a large, canvas sailor's bag, a sealed five-foot tube the diameter of a drainpipe, and an immense, wooden chest. "The tucker-box," he explained, as we heaved it over the tailgate.

It is tempting on meeting Jeremy for the first time to slot him into the category of post-hippy-wholefood-Zen-humanist, but that would be far too restricting. He divides his year between a terraced house in Wandsworth, and his second home, in Chile. "I *love* being with people, though for it to work, it's got to *jive!*" he announced as we threaded our way through the suburbs. Jeremy wore his corn-coloured hair in shoulder-length ringlets and had a voice which could reach every octave between tenor and *basso profundo* in one sentence. Of indeterminate age, his adventures have included a journey through the Spanish Sierra Nevada mountains on a horse called 'Earthquake', and a spell as a crop-duster in Texas and Sudan.

We arrived at 'Southern Heights' to find the area in front of the house strewn with bags and boxes, bits of bicycles, rope, rolled tarpaulins and a number of cardboard containers spilling everything from sparking plugs to Mars Bars.

A man in Army fatigues and glasses was tying a metal chest to the roof of one of the Land Rovers. Without climbing down, he shouted a cheery "Hello! I'm Andy!", and continued wrestling ropes around the chest.

The packing went on until the early hours, with a break for a four-course feast. Fiona's parents squeezed 20 people around the table, among them Matt's boisterous sons, Thomas and Alistair. For the team about to set off overland for Morocco, this would be the last English evening. At midnight, Chris arrived, having come straight from the airport on his return from Yemen.

At 7am the following morning, the Land Rovers left for the coast. Seven days later, we were in the foothills of the High Atlas.

The three Land Rovers grunted into life and lumbered like sleepy armadillos across the desert plain. Each time the big rubber tyres met a rock they compressed then crashed over the obstacle. Inside the swaying cabs, sitting three abreast, the occupants collided frequently as they were thrown from side to side. Shards of sun stabbed through a notch in the mountains, picking out in relief the rough knuckles of stone that had been our camp-site. It had been sufficiently cold in the night for Jeremy, who had declined to sleep inside a tent, to wake to find his Peruvian blanket coated in thick, white frost.

When the Land Rovers reached the road, they turned towards the rising sun and the warmth of a new day. We passed a signpost to Ait Benhaddou, chosen by David Lean for some of the locations in 'Lawrence of Arabia'. In front of us the infinite ribbon of tarmac slid beneath our wheels. On each side of the thin black line, mustard-coloured desert passed in a blur.

We had left Marrakesh 24 hours earlier. In Marrakesh, Matt's dream had finally materialised: all the components necessary to make a film about a mountainbike expedition through the Atlas mountains of Morocco had at last come together. We were ready to roll.

Dusty but intact, the two Land Rovers which had driven out from the UK had arrived in Marrakesh on the morning of the 12th January. At seven o' clock that evening, as Matt had led his troop of sticky travellers through the French quarter of Marrakesh to his old haunt, the 'Restaurant Jacaranda', a Boeing 747 belonging to Air Maroc had passed over Cadiz at 30,000 feet, then tipped its nose towards Casablanca and Marrakesh, to disgorge among the suits and briefcases on the plane three members of the First Unit camera crew (Graham Smith, Phil Millard, Stuart Bruce) and myself, not forgetting the 14 rucksacks and 27 aluminium crates of film equipment. I had spent the journey talking to the soundman, Stuart, a quiet Glaswegian who had been with Alan in Botswana. Stuart had also been in Antarctica, spending three months with a film crew recording the day-to-day existence of research workers on a Russian base. "It was dry," he said ruefully. "No drink."

"Like Morocco," I added.

Stuart tapped the yellow 'Duty Free' plastic bag under his seat. It clinked. He said: "Aye, I've taken precautions."

It was dark when the plane landed. It took 45 minutes to check all the film equipment through customs, and when we finally emerged through the glass doors of the airport building we found the car park deserted but for a single Peugeot taxi.

"There's nobody here to meet us," I said, stating the obvious.

"Typical," Stuart added succinctly.

Meanwhile, in the Jacaranda, as Matt was attacking the gateaux and Alan was pouring the wine, conversation was flowing freely: Jeremy West was telling a complicated story about an incident that occurred when he was working as a butler in a Scottish castle; Andy Flanders was describing to Chris Bradley how to unjam the differential lock on a Range Rover, and Abedelilah Latmer, the representative from Moroccan Production Services whom the Moroccan government insisted accompany the expedition, was telling Matt that as a qualified mountain guide he had climbed Mount Toubkal one hundred times.

Back at the airport, we were still searching for transport. When the one Peugeot taxi multiplied to three, we crammed ourselves and the luggage into them and joined the Avenue de la Menara – as wide and as straight as the Champs Elysées but fringed instead with a few stunted olive trees and the sporadic mounds of sleeping camels.

The address we had was in the French quarter of Gueliz. Hotel Smara occupied a corner site on Boulevard Mohammed Zerktouni. Its name, 'Smara', hung vertically down the modern concrete building in a stack of blue plastic lettering. 'Smar' is the name given to the picturesque rush lattices that keep the sun from thc alleys of Moroccan *souks.* I wished we could have stayed in the 'old town', the *Medina*, with its story-tellers and snake-charmers and orange-sellers and hustlers and tricksters; its air that smells like nothing in Europe, being a blend of spicy soups, spitting kebabs and the permanent warm aroma of evaporating urine and sweet tea; its sounds of honking cars, tinkling water-sellers' brass bells, screaming mopeds and the music of pipes and cymbals and small clay tom-toms. Instead, all I could hear was the muffled thud of a disco in the Smara's basement.

As I reminisced a knot of boys fell out of the disco on the street below and began punching each other.

The action over, I tipped the contents of my three rucksacks onto the carpet and began to categorise the jumble of clothing and equipment into piles according to usefulness. In order of ascending size, the piles were labelled: 'For me to carry'; 'For Matt and Chris to carry'; 'For hiding in the Land Rover' and 'Should have left in England'. Minutes before leaving London, I had suffered a characteristic attack of 'packer's paranoia' and had stormed through my flat packing every movable object on the assumption that 'it might prove useful'. Now, in Marrakesh, I was confronted by a mountain of miscellanea which included ten sets of spare shoelaces, a pair of running shoes with one sole partly peeled off, a 12oz pack of bran which had split, and a wad of photocopied pages from a dictionary of Persian. With the impending prospect of carrying my luggage on my own back, or bike, I re-discovered selectivity.

We were not – by nearly one hundred years – the first to embark upon a Moroccan bicycle journey. At the end of the last century, the Victorian traveller and writer Budgett Meakin set off from Tangier with his companion Dr Ruddock, with the intention of pedalling all the way to Marrakesh. In his book *The Land of the Moors*, Budgett Meakin wrote:

> "Not only has Morocco no road, it also has no inns or hotels after leaving the coast, and the prospect of unprepared native quarters was not exactly relished, especially as we knew from experience what they were like. So we schemed to carry what we could on our machines, which were rigged up with frames and carriers on which we were able to pack some sixty pounds apiece. Thus, indeed, we started, but soon relinquished our loads to a horseman whom we had engaged for the journey.
>
> "Nevertheless, from time to time I had on occasion to reload my machine – a 'Rover', which, with carriers, etc., weighed 40lb. – till it and I and the baggage together scaled 300lb., in which condition I rode it easily over pavements and stony roads, or up slight hills . . . A well-filled 18in. 'Gladstone' on the frame behind; a good-sized hold-all above the handles; a luncheon basket below, containing spirit lamp, kettle and tea- things; a packed valise inside the frame, with a sun umbrella strapped alongside; a water-can between the cranks, and a tin of oil below the seat, formed the full equipment: I found it enough."

The diminutive 'For me to carry' pile probably weighed no more than 20lb in total and I intended to cram it all into a single pannier and backpack. Unlike Budgett Meakin's luggage, mine was made from Goretex, Polarplus, nylon, aluminium and high-density plastic. My bicycle had 21 gears; Budgett Meakin's had one.

More pandemonium in the corridor announced the return of the overlanders from the restaurant. At last the team was together: two film crews, the support-crew, the biker, and Abedelilah Latmer.

The following morning on the pavement outside Hotel Smara, Jeremy and Andy supervised the packing of the equipment into the two Land Rovers. When both were full, there still remained on the pavement a waist-high heap of bicycles, boxes and rucksacks.

"We're just not going to get all of this clobber inside!" announced Jeremy, as he strode off with Abedelilah to rent a roof-rack which could be bolted onto the V8.

Twenty minutes later Jeremy returned with not just a roofrack but a third Land Rover. The garage owner had told Jeremy that if he wanted to rent a roofrack, the Land Rover went with it. Jeremy had winced as he foresaw his support-crew budget being whittled away. But the garage owner had not finished: if Jeremy wanted to rent a roofrack *and* Land Rover, then he would need to rent a driver too.

Ahmed Echita – or Mohammed as he preferred to be called – happened to be walking across the garage forecourt at the time. Mohammed normally made his living as a driver for the car-rental company based at the garage, driving tourists between Marrakesh and the airport, or on excursions over the mountains to Ouazazarte. Now the garage proprietor called Mohammed over, and two minutes later, he became the newest member of the Atlas Biker expedition. Mohammed was fortyish, had two sons, and a big heart. What became known as 'Mohammed's Land Rover' was an old, grey diesel, slightly lopsided, with an engine that rattled forebodingly.

To record and support one man riding a bicycle, the film industry had now provided 9 people, 3 small trucks, 4 bicycles, and 3 tons of equipment and supplies which included everything from Alka Seltzer to 4 miles of film.

"This is nothing!" said Matt on the steps of the Smara. "This is *lightweight!* And you'll see history being made tonight when the film crew crawl into their tents. Film crews *never* sleep *anywhere* but in 4-star hotels."

On the morning of the 13th, the convoy left the French quarter of Marrakesh and headed for the high pass which wriggles through a dip in the spine of the High Atlas mountains then plunges down to the northern fringe of the Sahara Desert. Driving non-stop, we planned to reach Merzouga and the start of our ride in two days' time.

Partly to stretch our legs, and partly to find out whether the bikes worked, Matt, Chris and I left Marrakesh ahead of the Land Rovers. Not even the Smara could hold us back from exotic Morocco; we launched ourselves onto our black and yellow bicycles and wove a euphoric path away from the Smara, away from French Gueliz, to mingle on Avenue Yacoub el Mansour with the workaday tide of mopeds and bicycles, buses and wallowing *grands taxis* – the fat Peugeots and Mercedes – heading for the big villages.

For three hours we flew west on the road to the mountains, dashing across the shadow-bars laid over the road by the avenue of eucalyptus trees. There was little traffic. When mopeds overtook us we pedalled demonically until we caught their slipstream, and then the shadow-bars flicked by so fast that fields beside us flashed on and off in a stroboscopic pattern of bright light and black. And so through Ait Ourir and a slower pace to savour the noon-day smells of new *tagines* (pots of stew) bubbling over charcoal braziers in front of road-side restaurants. A spice-seller stood by pots of cumin, pepper, saffron, cinnamon, ginger and paprika. Bouquets of fresh mint swayed in the breeze. We pulled up above a blanket spread on the dust and bought a half-kilo of peanuts, tipped them into our pockets and pressed on. Even the air could be tasted. At each café or restaurant we were welcomed by the oily miasma of *harira* soup and the aroma of *brochettes* being turned ten at a time over beds of embers.

Beyond Ait Ourir there was a hill. Enthusiasm for pedalling suddenly dwindled. The sound of an approaching truck crashing down a gear offered an alternative. Hanging onto various hooks and ropes we were towed up the first of the Atlas foothills. We were breaking rules which would be rigidly self-imposed once the ride started. The Land Rovers caught us up at the top of the hill. We had cycled 55 kilometres from Marrakesh, stretched our legs and breathed the air of Morocco.

The bikes were lashed to the roof of the $2\frac{1}{4}$, and for the next four hours we watched the landscape change from green to brown to white. We camped that night just west of Ouazazarte where we turned off the tarmac, and crept over a freezing, stony plain until we found some patches of smaller stones suitable for the tents.

Equipment spewed from the doors of the Land Rovers. Torchlit shadows wandered from pile to pile in a despairing quest for bits of personal gear which had been absorbed by the astounding sum of our luggage. Plaintive cries for a rucksack, or sleeping bag, could be heard through the cold, squeezing dark. Graham and Andy pulled out the generator and dug a pit to deaden the sound. Eventually the tents were erected and Jeremy and Abedelilah began preparing some food; Matt, Chris and Alan stood in a semi-circle on the desert plain, reading books by the beams of their head-torches.

Jeremy had built his 'tucker-box' for use in the bush of equatorial Africa. An Australian friend had helped with the construction, which was unusual in that they had first built a complete, sealed chest, and then sawn the top off it, thus creating a lid with a perfect fit. Inside the chest was an entire expedition larder. On top, there were three removable trays packed with herbs and spices. Stowed lower down were sacks of muesli and flour, sugar, rice and beans padded out with locally-bought produce such as dates, nuts, sultanas and cans of sardines. Everything was vegetarian. In the early days of the journey, it was not unusual for the lifting of the tucker-box lid to attract an instant audience who would stand with bowed heads and outstretched bowls muttering a psalm of thanks which took the theme of "More, more, more, more . . ."

Jeremy presided over the tucker-box in his evening wear: baggy green tweed plus-fours, a black oiled-cotton motorcycle jacket, a multi-coloured tassled scarf, Masi bracelet and a brown woollen hat which perched above the explosion of blond ringlets that ran half-way down his neck.

Andy and Graham failed after thirty minutes of ripping at the pull-start to fire up the generator. Without the generator the film crew could neither charge the batteries of their very consumptive cameras nor use the powerful lamps which they had brought for the night-time sequences. Alan looked at the lifeless 'genny' and said, "It worked when we had it in Antarctica."

Matt trotted past holding a bicycle wheel: "Try starting it when it's lying on its side." Andy tipped the machine over and gave the pull-start a condescending tug. The machine sneezed once, then settled into a contented chug. Disbelief crossed everybody's face but Matt's, who trotted on.

Ouazazarte is an old French Foreign Legion town bisected by a broad, ugly avenue that is punctuated by petrol stations and horrible hotels. Opposite 'Chez Dimitri', a cheerless restaurant favoured by travellers who prefer bad western food to good Moroccan food, is a small supermarket. Matt and Jeremy went inside. The bonnet of the diesel Land Rover was already up, the backsides of Andy and Mohammed jutting over its sand-scarred paintwork.

One by one, cramped limbs unfolded from the front seats of the station wagons and wandered across Mohammed V street. In the low sunlight we slumped on chairs at the rickety tin tables which stood white against the dark concrete, outside the Hotel Es Salam. Coffee arrived on circular, shiny trays, the sugarcubes wrapped in paper. The coffee was thick and dark, served in slender glasses. Abedelilah uncreased a copy of

Le Sport and leant back in his chair. The sun felt warm on our bare arms. It was a dry, comfortable winter heat. Ouazazarte sits at an altitude of 1,160 metres.

Andy, last to the table, pulled up a chair, and said something disparaging about air-filters. Matt handed Andy a plastic comb in a printed cellophane wrapper which Andy scrutinised intently for several seconds. "Reading the instruction manual?" asked Chris, "or seeing if you can connect it to the genny?"

Too soon we re-cramped and continued east up the valley of the Dades. Mud-walled villages drifted by; low brown brick walls set upon the piedmont of the Atlas. When we stopped for a picnic lunch beneath a clump of palms by Boumaine-du-Dades there was a chance to look to the mountains; to focus for the first time. Sixty kilometres away, hanging above the dun-coloured foreground that was part heat haze, part dusty ground, was a ribbon of shining clouds that seemed to stretch from one side of the horizon to the other. But unlike clouds, these did not shift. They were in fact the icy caps of the Atlas Mountains. Much of our route lay up there, above the snowline.

The man from Moroccan Production Services sat on his hams, washing tomatoes. Abedelilah had been collected from the Casablanca offices of MPS as the Land Rovers headed for Marrakesh. He spoke fluent French, was twenty-five years old and had worked as a guide in the Atlas Mountains since 1979. He had been born in Casablanca and had four brothers and four sisters. Two of the brothers worked in Saudi Arabia, one as a plumber, the other as a garage mechanic. Another brother did administrative work in the Polyclinique in Casablanca, and the fourth brother was an electrician, also in 'Casa'. Abedelilah also had fifty step-brothers and sisters because his father had four wives.

Abedelilah looked like Joe Strummer, the ex-guitarist of The Clash. He was good at handstands. Unlike the rest of the team, who – with the exception of Jeremy – were clad in anything from old climbing gear to Camden casuals, Abedelilah defined his sartorial standing by choosing natty black slacks, brown shiny shoes, a terracotta-chequered shirt, grey tweed jacket and plum-coloured tie. During the picnic he kicked a white plastic football from toe to knee to forehead to heel while holding a sardine sandwich in one hand and a large tomato in the other.

The ball's owners, four boys from the village a kilometre away, were unimpressed. The children from the village had walked across the barren no-man's land separating their permanent home from our lunch-halt. Apart from the four boys who had come close enough to pass the ball, the rest of the children stood in a tight, silent group just inside earshot, watching but not daring to come closer.

Through the afternoon, the $2\frac{1}{4}$ litre Land Rover led the way. Matt drove, singing to a crackly cassette of the Rolling Stones. "Just my imagination, running away with me . . ."

At Tinehir we passed the entrance to the Todra Gorge. From its bottom end it looked benign; a welcoming, shaded cleft in the mountain wall, almost encouraging. In maybe a week we would be up at the headwaters of that gorge, not sitting on sprung seats listening to the Stones, but having our bones rattled by the rocks of the Atlas.

In the afternoon the wind tore from the desert, so that by the time we had left the main road at Tinejdad and turned towards the oases of the Rheris valley, sand was beginning to blow across the road. Slower than its petrol companions, the diesel Land Rover kept trailing behind, though it was never allowed out of sight. In it was all the food.

We passed a small mountain, so perfectly conical that it looked as if it had been smoothed by a human hand. We watched it for a long time.

The wind strengthened until Matt had to slow to walking pace. The sun dimmed to a blob that you could stare at without hurting your eyes. Mustard-coloured dust blizzarded horizontally across the road. Fish-tails of sand formed on the patchy tarmac, in places obliterating the road altogether. Behind us the other two vehicles were invisible; swallowed by the fog of dust and sand.

As instantly as if a genie of the sands had thrown the switch on the wind machine, we drove through the window of the storm into the comparative calm of a valley pecked with the distant heads of palm trees. The road wound downwards, zig-zagged through the tight angles of Jorf and on to Erfoud. Here we turned right, to point due south. Coming the other way we passed men wrapped in *djellabahs,* their pointed hoods protecting them from the gritty northerly wind, sitting side-saddle on quick-stepping donkeys. At Rissani the road ended. A chipped roadsign on the outskirts of the oasis said: 'Merzouga 35, Haroum 10'. In one hour it would be dark. The desert track to Merzouga was indistinct, even in daylight. A kilometre outside Rissani, the road turned 90 degrees left and hopped over an irrigation channel. On the right a deeply rutted track dropped down between mud walls. We lurched off the road and threaded through the houses.

Beyond the last palms, we set the compass at 110 degrees south-east and skimmed over the solid surface of a dried salt pan. At the far side, the track dipped into a dried wadi. Soft sand enveloped the wheels. The track climbed a little, onto a plateau of compacted small stones. At a small pillar, three tracks diverged. We took the right hand track, our bearing now 160 degrees. Gravel desert vanished beneath the wheels. The light was fading fast.

A long ridge of sand-dunes followed us on our right. Behind them, we could see the distant crests of greying mountains. Forty minutes after leaving Rissani we came to a road sign. It said 'Chebbi 3km'. The dunes of Merzouga; the Erg Chebbi. The highest sand-dunes in Morocco.

In the last of the day's light they glowed rose-pink, a vast breaking wave of sand that seemed to be welling from the heart of the Sahara itself. Natural curves tapered into one another, honeyed hues and strokable tones converting every watt of daylight into a sensual continuum. They were impossible to look at with still eyes.

"Not bad, man," said Jeremy.

On the flat, infinite floor which wrapped itself round the northern fringe of the sand-sea, there was a solitary building. It was the 'Auberge Erg Chebbi'. The Land Rovers rolled to a halt beside the square, pink-painted inn. Between the two windows, the wooden doors bore the self-adhesive labels of previous tenants: 'Lucky Strike', 'Africa Queen 4 x 4', 'Métal 5'. Youssef, the teenager who had cooked Annabel and me a *tagine* the previous month came to greet us. He directed us to a sandy hollow a few hundred metres from the *auberge*.

Alan Ravenscroft called a planning conference in the lee of the V8 Land Rover. Matt, Chris, myself, and the camera crew gathered round. Alan started speaking in a way which indicated that the subject he was about to raise was one which had occupied his mind for some time: "Look chaps, before we start tomorrow, we need to make an important decision...". The wind rattled at our anorak hoods. It was cold. Alan looked at Matt, Chris and myself: "We need to decide who this film is going to follow. Is it about Nick? Or is it about the three of you making the journey as a team?"

This from the start had been the great unresolved question: as director and cameraman of the Second Film Unit, Matt and Chris would be responsible for all the filming on sections of the route inaccessible to the Land Rover-based First Unit. These wilder parts of the journey could add up to half of the entire route, and include some of the most dramatic scenery. For Matt and Chris, the first priority was to capture on celluloid the sensations of independent, wilderness travel. The problem we had to resolve was how to combine the sense of independence with the needs of the film-makers in a way that was believable on the screen.

Any adventures which befell me as a 'lone' traveller would be implausible since the TV viewer would immediately want to know how, if I was alone, I could have been filmed. I could not be both a lone traveller and a filmed one.

What if Matt and Chris were the subjects of the film too? A film about a film-crew making a film. It had the advantage of being honest, and the story would gain the extra dimension of 'human interaction': the fights and frictions – and camaraderie – that come with sharing a difficult challenge; three is the very worst number to travel with (one person invariably gets 'frozen out' by circumstance or personality) and therefore offered plenty of potential interest.

I sensed that Matt had no intention of missing the challenge of the bike ride; although he was really in Morocco as the Second Unit film director, I knew that he was planning to combine this with the physical challenge of completing the entire journey on pedals. Chris' plans were less clear, though he had already told me that his mother once sent him a newspaper cutting reporting a mountainbike climb to the summit of Kilimanjaro, and added the note "Why haven't you done this yet?" Which had stung him a little. So was Chris too planning to be both a film-maker and an adventurer?

As a threesome, we were an untried team. I'd never travelled with either of them, and had only known Chris and Matt in the suspended reality of London. There would be occasions over the next 20 days and 1,200 kilometres when our mutual safety would depend on like-minded heads and matched experience. Alan looked at Matt, then Chris, who looked at me. I had no doubts: "All three of us must do all of the ride on an equal basis. It's the only way the journey will look authentic. We start together, finish together, and we each ride or walk the entire route." Alan looked unsure. Matt said "Your decision Nick". Chris smiled, Alan moved on:

"OK chasps," (Alan had the endearing habit of slipping in an extra 's' when he was about to involve his subjects or his camera crew in something unbelievably inconvenient) "where are you going to start the ride?"

In the fading light I pointed towards the peak of the range of dunes. "The top. The highest dune. A dawn start tomorrow. The light will be fantastic."

The camera crew looked unconvinced.

"All right," said Alan "but how long is it going to take us to climb up to the top from here?"

Five minutes later Matt and I set off with a stopwatch. After a day's confinement in the vehicle, we were full of unburnt energy. It took us 30 minutes to scramble up the increasingly steep ridges of sand to the summit of the highest dune, a knife-edge ridge of sand curving like a giant melon slice lying on its side, with a huge view north over a ripple-bed of smaller dunes. The Land Rovers and inn were invisible.

Already the desert plain to the north was sinking into inky blackness and a half moon was climbing over the distant smudge of the oasis at Rissani. I set a compass bearing on the distant Land Rovers, and we turned back downhill.

By the time we arrived, the vehicles were drawn up in a semicircle, surrounded by thirty-foot dunes. The generator puttered quietly in a hole dug in the sand. Leads ran to a blaze of lights under which Graham Smith and Phil Millard were unpacking film cameras. Stuart was putting up his tiny one-man tent. Jeremy was squatting by the tucker-box chopping potatoes. Andy was on the roof of one of the Land Rovers, handing mountainbikes down to Chris.

The plan was finalised: Matt, Chris and I would leave after eating, and, carrying our bikes, a tent and sleeping bags, would climb to the top of the highest dune. Alan and the camera crew would get up at 3am, follow our footsteps, then film us emerging from the tent in the first light of dawn.

By the time the three of us were ready to set off it was solidly dark. Our packs seemed unnecessarily heavy. We wore the bikes around our necks. In one hand I had a torch; in the other a compass. It took 55 minutes of laboured plodding to return to the summit of the dunes. I was eager to pitch the tent on the crest of the highest dune. The sand on each side of the crest fell away steeply, but with our hands I thought we could excavate a platform in the sand, then belay the tent to the bicycles to stop it blowing away in the night.

"Stuff that," said Chris. "What's wrong with the flat dune just down there?"

"It's not the top."

"What's so special about the top?"

"It's the obvious place to be."

"Yes, but it'll take us an hour to pitch the tent, *and* it'll get blown away. It's crazy."

Matt chipped in: "Chris is right. Let's sleep down there."

For a few minutes we sat on the crest of the dune while the wind whipped sand about our knees. We could just see a pale glow coming from the main camp down below. Not quite ready to give in, I asked: "What if they can't find us in the morning. They'll never be able to see us camping down in that hollow. If we were on the top here, we could be seen by half of Morocco."

Matt didn't even pause before answering: "We'll bury this torch part way into the sand, pointing at the Land Rovers. It's got new batteries. In the morning all the camera crew need do is to head for the torch beam."

We slid down the face of the dune in silence, sand up to our knees, grit blowing in our ears and eyes. Below the crest there was no wind. It took just a few minutes to erect the tent. Chris and Matt squirmed inside and started unrolling bags and mats. It was 11.30pm. I scrambled up the slope behind the tent, and, leaning into the wind, followed the crest of the dune up to the high point. The torch was already buried by the wind-driven sand, its beam reduced to a pale yellow glow suffused through a drift of grains. Thirty-five kilometres away, a handful of lights twinkled in Rissani. Beyond that, about 50 kilometres away, it was just possible to pick out the glow of Erfoud. The half-moon picked out the contours of the dunes below, dunes that had seemed huge when we scrambled up them, but which now looked like ripples on the ocean floor.

The other way, southwards, the Sahara and the night merged in an awesome, black void. The air was unnervingly cold.

First Take

First Take (Day 1) – Mountainbiking the Sahara – Into the Oases – Bolton Wanderers (Day 2) – The Gorge du Ziz – Zap and the Art of Mountainbiking – Turn Left for the Atlas – First Frost (Day 3) – Unsound Recording – Past the Police Post – Long Shots (Day 4) – In Imilchil

Day 1 - 4

Chris woke first. It was still dark. It was his 35th birthday. In the world of cyclo-cross, this used to be a significant threshold. Until recently, when the age was raised to 40, racers of 35 and over were only allowed to race in the category called 'veteran'. The implication of premature dementia can sometimes be traumatic.

"I should be a veteran," announced Chris.

"That's interesting," replied Matt.

Out in the night, a whisper of voices was carried on the wind. We listened. Again, we heard an indistinct mutter, hardly decipherable from the slap of nylon and patter of sand grains.

"Must be the film crew."

"Shall we tell them we're here?"

"No!"

We drifted, dozed, postponing the dreaded moment of departure from our sleeping bags.

Chris cracked first, "Better go and see how they're doing."

The tent zip buzzed and Chris' feet slithered out of sight. Peace returned to the tent. Now and then, faint, disjointed snatches of far-off human voices were carried to us on the wind. The inside of the tent lightened. Chris returned.

"They're all huddled together in a survival blanket. All four of them. It took them an hour and 50 minutes to carry all the gear up here. They want us to get up."

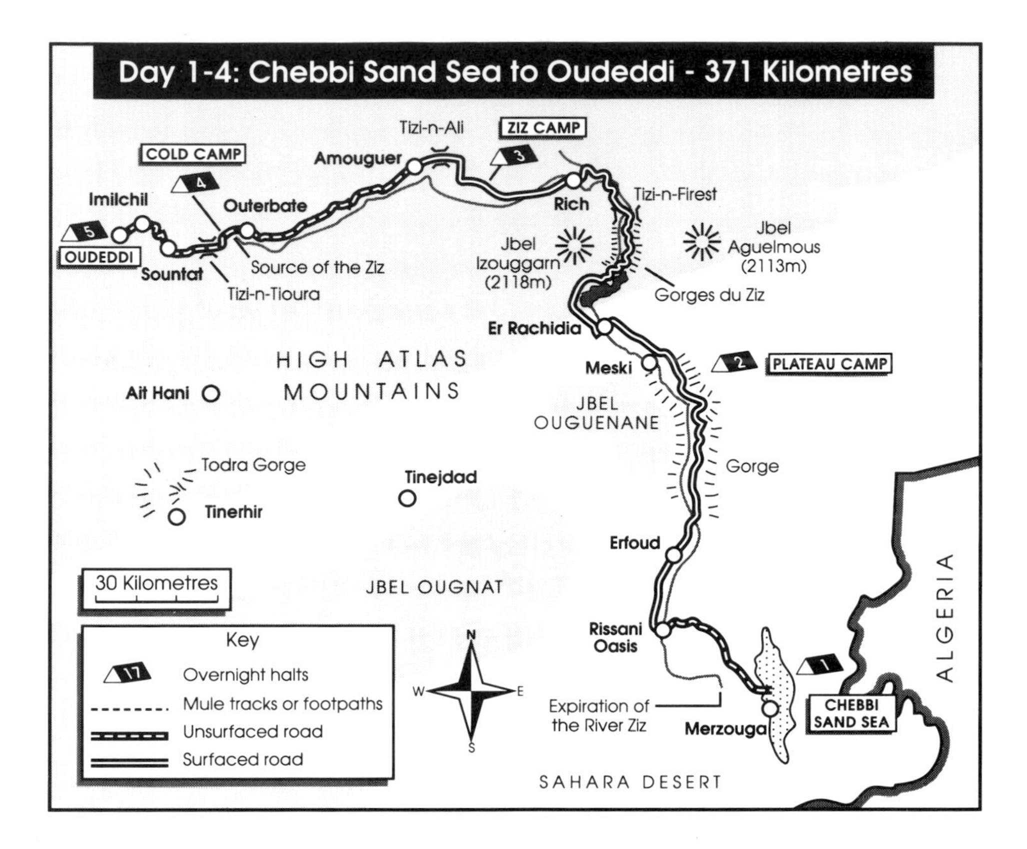

My watch said 5.30am. I left the tent, and holding my trousers up with one hand, climbed over the back of the dune and squatted contentedly.

"The tent!"

The distant shout was urgent enough to make me turn around. As I craned my neck upwards our precious yellow and green Wild Country Super-Nova rose over the dune and passed thirty feet above my head, borne on a powerful gust of wind. It did not take more than a second to calculate the likely destination of a lightweight nylon globe heading south into the Sahara at an altitude of thirty feet. Ouagadougou, 2,500 kilometres away in Upper Volta, was the location of the next hill.

Not for the first time, I made a snap decision to sacrifice personal dignity for the sake of an expedition. I sprinted trouserless down the dune after the tent. At 100 metres I was below the tent, which was tumbling in slow-motion through the air towards me. The tent did not appear to be either gaining, or losing altitude. It was travelling parallel to the ground. I ran, looking upward. My trilby blew off. Then the wind paused; the tent hovered, then sank; I leapt, hooking a finger round the elastic strap used for pegging the front of the tent to the ground.

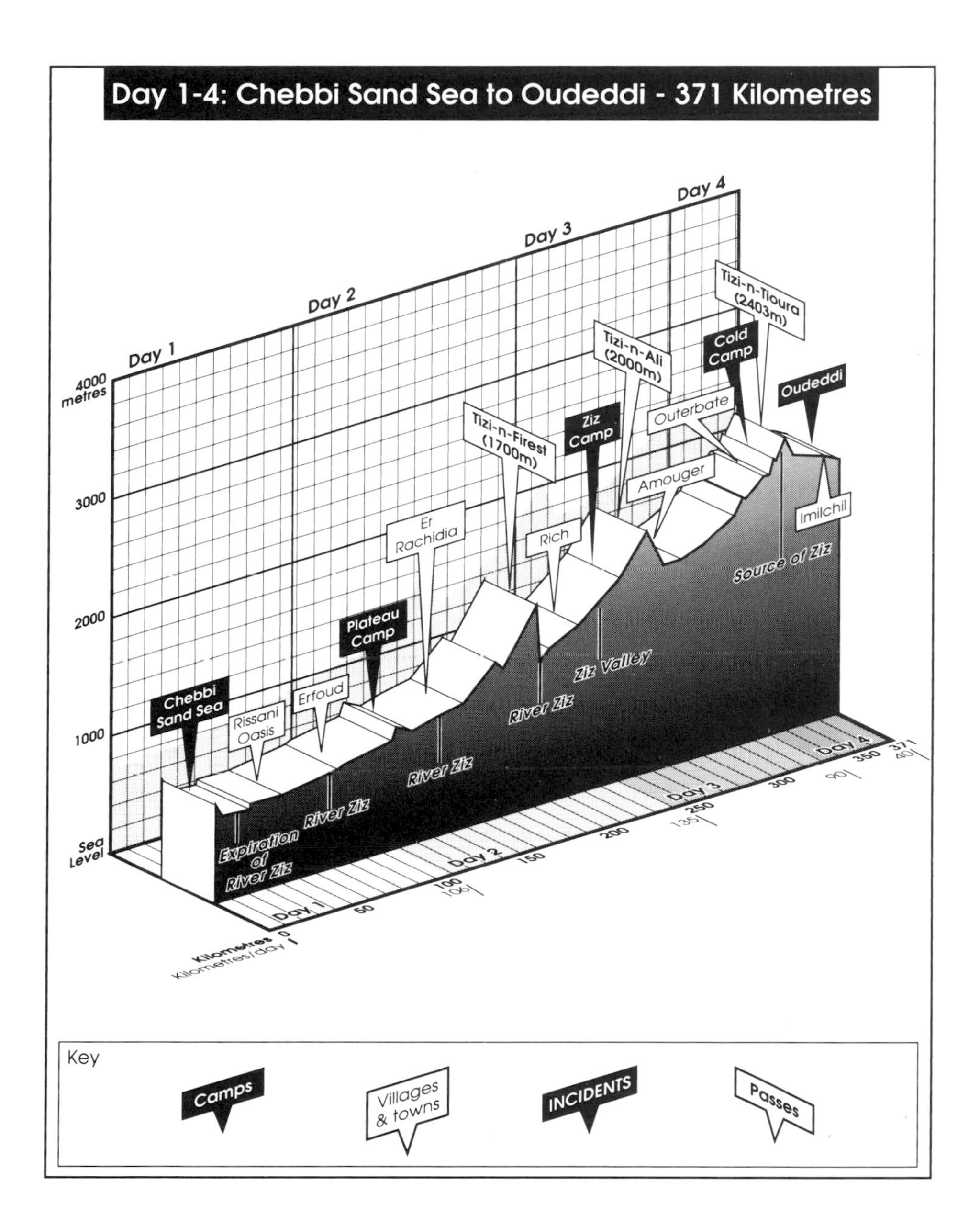

Matt and Chris were still at the camp-site, fitting panniers to their bikes. Chris looked up as I slid down the dune, towing the tent.

"Oh. You found it then," he said, adding by way of explanation: "Matt and I were taking it down and let go by mistake."

Matt put down his bicycle and hauled on a backpack: "Alan wants us up on the crest of the big dune. We're pitching the tent on the top and they're going to film us waking up as dawn breaks." To the east, the rays of an invisible sun were already suffusing the sky above the sand crests of the Erg Chebbi with a brightness out of all proportion to the slate-grey of the rest of the sky. The stars had gone.

Matt started up the slope, dragging the tent, with a bicycle around his neck.

On the knife-crest of the big dune, Graham Smith was leaning into the viewfinder of his Aaton camera. Alan Ravenscroft, swaddled in an enormous shiny blue duvet jacket, neck wrapped in an Arabian scarf, was standing legs splayed, holding a clipboard. "Over there chaps. If you wouldn't mind putting the tent about twenty yards down hill from the top. And we want to keep the sand clean, so don't walk between the tent and the camera. And if you could take the wheels off the bikes. All right Graham, how's that look?"

The tent was dumped at an absurd angle. There wasn't time to level a pitch. The camera wouldn't notice anyway. We crawled inside.

"OK chaps, when I give the word, we'd like you to come out of the tent, one by one, then walk to the bikes and begin assembling them. Remember you've just woken up."

"Who should come first out of the tent?"

We could hear a muttered discussion. The first rays of sun splattered onto the flysheet. In seconds, the temperature in the tent began to rise.

"Nick first, then Chris, then Matt."

Inside, the three of us lay against each other, torpid in the rising temperature.

"OK. Action!"

We tottered into the glare, rubbed our eyes, stumbled to the bikes, picked them up and began fitting the wheels.

"OK chaps. That was very good. We'd like to try it again with the tent facing a bit more to the sun."

We moved the tent through 15 degrees and crawled back inside. Filling in time, Matt mimicked our film director. Alan's voice pierced the walls of the tent: "Matt, we're recording. We heard that. OK out you come."

Outside, Chris picked up his bicycle frame and one of the wheels and said: "What are we meant to do with these? D'you want the wheels slotting into the frame, or the frame slotting into the wheels?"

It took twenty minutes to fit the wheels and panniers to the bikes while the lens of the Aaton scrutinised every twist of a quick-release and turn of a bolt. We bundled the tent into its bag and collected the tools and pegs, gloves and other oddments that had been strewn about our 'camp-site'. Chris said: "Well, we're off! Next stop the Atlantic!"

Alan held up his hand, "Not just yet. We've got to get the camera down there." He pointed to a spot near the foot of the sand-sea, a kilometre away. "We want a long shot of you leaving the high point."

After the crew disappeared, Matt, Chris and I were left standing alone on the summit of the Erg Chebbi. With us were three bicycles. It suddenly occurred to me that we were going to have to ride them. "We can't ride these on sand," I said. "It's impossible! The wheels'll sink in."

"Doesn't matter," reassured Matt.

A kilometre away an insect appeared to be waving at us.

"That must mean they want us to start."

We climbed on the bikes. They sank into the sand. Sitting astride the cross-bars with our feet pushing against the sand, we scuttled down the steep face of the dune. After ten metres I fell over the handlebars. Sweating beneath the weight of a backpack, and still wrapped in the warm clothes I'd needed for the night, I shuffled after the other two. Chris had found a stretch of harder sand and had managed a free run of five metres. He whooped with exhilaration. Or surprise. In the distance the camera tracked our progress.

When we got to the bottom of the big dune Matt said: "Thank God for that. We're out of sight. Now we can have a rest." We picked up the bicycles, carried them up the face of the next dune, remounted and slid on. Unaccountably the wheels did not sink. The sand was firm. It was so firm that we free-wheeled all the way down the face of this dune, up a short rise and down the next.

Alan was thrilled: "Wonderful. Let's get back to the Land Rovers. There are some close-ups I want to do."

We walked into camp, carrying the bicycles over our shoulders. Jeremy handed each of us a plastic mug of muesli.

"There you are chaps. I should think you're *jolly* hungry."

There was just enough time to lift the spoon above the rim of thc mug before Alan called from the far side of the camp: "Chaps. Could you come over here please? We need some foot shots."

The shot that Alan wanted was of a foot entering the toe-clip of a mountainbike and of that foot then turning one pedal revolution. At first glance it was the kind of shot which should have taken two minutes. It was not to be. First the sun was in the wrong place, then the sand beneath the bicycle was found to have someone else's footprints, and when finally Alan, Graham, Phil and Stuart were on hands and knees focusing on Matt's toe, ready to roll, an Army jeep roared into the camp. Stuart, the soundman, mouthed indescribable Gaelic obscenities.

In the jeep were two stern men in military dress. Abedelilah intercepted them, produced our papers and impressed upon them the need for complete silence while the foot was filmed. The soldiers looked perplexed.

After four takes of a 'leaving the dunes' shot, the expedition was not making fast progress. From waking up, it had taken us 5 hours to travel 2 kilometres, an average speed of 0.4kph; the speed attainable by a blindfolded man hopping backwards in snowshoes. On this basis, the 1,300 kilometres to the Atlantic would take us 3,250 hours – about 1 year and 40 days if we travelled for 8 hours a day.

Matt led us across the plain, the bikes skipping over the stones before the force of a benign southerly wind. The stones were small and dark, pressed into the sand by the weight of the sun and wind. Fifty metres from us the Land Rovers raced on a parallel course, the camera stuffed through the front window of the V8. By the pillar that we'd passed the previous night, Mohammed's diesel and the 2¼ veered inexplicably off to the left and disappeared into a wadi.

"It's an Abedelilah shortcut!" shouted Chris. "We should meet them again around Agadir!" The V8 vanished ahead of us, heading towards the distant green smudge of the Rissani oasis. We were left in peace.

I looked down at the blur of desert beneath my yellow and black bicycle, then roved over the fittings, following the two thin wires from the thumb-shifter gear-levers on the handlebars; the left wire connected to the small chrome cage above the three front chainrings, the right wire running the length of the bike to the long dog-leg of the rear derailleur mechanism hanging beneath its seven spinning cogs. If we failed, it would not be due to the bikes.

Our tyres tipped over the lip of a small wadi and we slithered down in soft sand, body weight well back. Sudden rains would fill this wadi with flash floods. This was the Ziz – the river which we would follow to its source in the High Atlas. Scrub occupied its bed. We wove a route across to the far wall, then pushed the bikes up the short slope to regain the platform of the desert.

We were following a track which was little more than two troughs pressed into the grit by infrequent vehicles. This ran into the baked clay of a bone-coloured lake bed. We skimmed across its surface, fried by the reflected heat and light, looking for the far side.

Suddenly we were at Rissani.

A line of low mud walls shadowed by palms marked Man's front line. Behind the front line: an infrastructure of wells and roads, homes and farms, lines of communication. In front of the line the desert: where lines are made by shadows and the time of day is felt by the height of the sun. Our track led us through the gap in the wall.

On each side of us, palms swayed in the stiff breeze. Water flowed swiftly in straight channels. A woman wrapped in black, her face covered, drifted by. We bumped round a corner and passed a small field of maize, the ears clicking in the wind. A bearded face beneath a baseball cap popped up from behind a wall: "I say chaps. You couldn't do that again could you? Riding on the other side of the track this time." We turned around, waited for the call and returned, on the left side of the track.

Rissani has the feel of a frontier town. It was mid-morning and the road was busy with chattering people, wailing transistor radios, the clop of mules and the asthmatic chug of tired diesels. Past the empty, tempting tables of a tea house we pedalled, threading our way through a herd of goats and past a scrum of men gathered at the yawning bonnet of a Bedford truck, and so to the main street of Rissani. It's hardly an imperial avenue, being about 200 metres long with a central reservation a metre wide, perhaps intended for the flowering of spring shrubs, now a battered concrete obstacle to the Land Rover taxis which like to U-turn from their dirt patch half-way down the street. At the far end, the street turns a mathematically-abrupt right angle and passes the fortified walls of the *kasbah.*

None of our Land Rovers were in sight, and after dithering at the roundabout on the edge of town we rode under Rissani's triumphal arch and turned north, straight into an appalling head wind. This was unpleasant. Head winds are physically and mentally the greatest difficulty a cyclist has to contend with. None of us had come prepared for exertion; it was a cruel blow. We were shocked into silence. I could hardly make my bike move. We had only fought the wind for about five hundred metres before the reassuring bumper of a blue Land Rover crept level with us.

"Phew. That's a relief," shouted Matt as the three of us tucked into the air-pocket behind the V8.

To be seen by an official of the Road Time Trial Council or British Cycling Federation 'taking shelter' behind a motor vehicle is a crime which commands instant disqualification. In British cycling races it is allowable to take advantage of the rush of air (a kind of suck-blow effect) caused by passing vehicles; this is done by edging out into the road and then speeding up so that you snatch maximum benefit from the passing vehicle. For several seconds you shoot forward as if pulled by an invisible strand of elastic. This is of course a highly dangerous, and universally-denied practice. But while it is tolerated, it is completely forbidden actually to move in behind a vehicle.

"This is cheating," I shouted to Matt.

"Who says?"

"The British Cycling Federation." Matt looked at me as if I had suddenly started talking Cantonese.

"Why's it cheating?"

"Because riding in the slipstream of a vehicle makes it easier."

"It makes sense."

We covered the 22 kilometres to Erfoud in one hour.

Erfoud is the main oasis town in the Ziz Valley. On the right hand side of the road as you approach Erfoud from the south is an hotel called the Salam. Outside it were the other two Land Rovers. Jeremy had rented two rooms for an hour. They had baths. I sat in a hot tub on a sandbank that had been rinsed from my hair and ears, hoping fervently that none of my companions from past trips would ever hear of it: bathing at midday, cycling with a support-crew, stopping in restaurants to eat rather than read the menu and ride on, slip-streaming behind vehicles . . . these were all heresies of the highest order.

At a long table in the restaurant the team worked its way through carrot soup, cheese omelette, baked potatoes, carrots, kebabs, crème caramel ("three please") and coffee. Within an hour I had an excruciating stomach ache.

Before we left, I collected our maps onto the table. So far, there had not been time to plan the journey. Unfortunately the only detailed map that we had of the entire Atlas range had been left behind on a café table in Spain. But we did have a series of six large-scale 1:100,000 maps produced by the French which Matt had used two years earlier when he had followed Wilfred Thesiger's route through a portion of the Atlas. These maps would be essential for the hardest part of our route, although one critical map from the series was missing; it covered the section of the journey between the mountain villages of Imilchil and Zaouia Ahansal. Mostly we would have to rely on local knowledge, a compass and common sense.

We had 20 days in which to complete our ride. We were half way through Day 1. The total distance we planned to cover was about 1,200 kilometres. We imagined that there would be four categories of 'road': tarmac, jeep track, mule track, mountainside. We made the assumption that we would be able to ride mountainbikes over the first three, and that we would have to carry the bikes on the fourth.

It looked as if the first 350 kilometres or so would be on tarmac and jeep tracks, but from then on we would be almost exclusively on mule tracks and mountain trails. Logically, it looked as if we should knock off the first 350 kilometres as quickly as possible so that we had time in hand to tackle the unknown sections in the High Atlas mountains. If we could average say 100 kilometres a day, for the first three days, we needed only to average 58 kilometres a day for the remaining 17 days. As plans go, it was about as detailed as we could make it; there were just too many imponderables.

"So, let's try and reach Er-Rachidia tonight," I suggested. "That leaves us well-placed to climb into the mountains tomorrow."

"Fine by me," said Matt.

The three of us left Erfoud at 3.25pm, pedalling gently up the long funnel of shop-fronts, past the barracks and out onto the open road. Beyond the town a bare ramp led up to a range of rugged hills. We pedalled slowly, winching ourselves up the sticky tarmac towards a nick in the skyline. The wind was still trying to push us back to the desert. It took 25 kilometres to reach the hills. When we did, the gradient steepened as we snaked through a palm-floored gorge. Children shouted to us from the villages: *"Bonjour, bonjour, bonjour!"* A medley of voices and thrumming of bare feet on tarmac followed us as little groups peeled away from the shade and dashed after the bicycles. Between the deep green of the trees, snatches of still, brilliant water tugged at the eye. Above the trees the far side of the gorge climbed vertically.

Different styles of pedalling were emerging: Matt liked to blast for one hour, then stop for a five-minute rest; Chris liked to keep going steadily, hour in, hour out. For three hours we pedalled into a wind which seemed determined to keep us down in the desert.

We came to a place where engineers had blasted a sloping shelf up the eastern wall of the gorge. A dirt track veered leftwards to continue along the bottom of the gorge. The Land Rovers were pulled up at the junction, Jeremy listening to a gesticulating man in a *djellabah.*

Jeremy called us over: "Guys. This man says it's not possible to take the Land Rovers through the gorge. There's been a landslide." We had planned to follow the gorge and camp at the next – and last – oasis, a place called Meski which was reputed to have a blue pool of well-known beauty. The light was fading by the minute. A good reason for pressing on down the gorge was that it avoided the tarmac road and led us to a string of isolated villages. It was a familiar dilemma: to take the interesting, or predictable option. I was sure there would be a way past the landslide but was outvoted. On the other hand, what was the point in going somewhere that couldn't be filmed? This wasn't a holiday.

Darkness was smothering the cliffs by the time we climbed back on the bikes. We zig-zagged up the tarmac, rising above the palm-tops; leaving the living banks of the Ziz and creeping up to a lunar plateau which basked starkly in the moonlight. Across the pockmarked landscape we could see distant puddles of light cast by headlights as the Land Rovers roamed about looking for a stone-free camp-site. They selected a spot about a kilometre off the road. It was a barren, cheerless site. The temperature was falling fast.

The sun had yet to take the chill off the rocks as we eased the bikes back across the pebble-dashed plateau to the road. We had arranged to meet the camera crew for coffee 25 kilometres further on, in Er Rachidia. The bikes seemed to find an early-morning momentum of their own.

We whispered down the blacktop in line astern, taking advantage of the wind-shadow of the rider in front.

Ten kilometres before Er Rachidia we began to mix with workers heading into town from the outlying villages. Most were walking; some were waiting for buses. We overtook a man wearing a brown bobble hat, a greatcoat and army boots. He was pedalling a new red and chrome racing bicycle. It was a French bicycle: a Gitane. As we swept past him, he hooked on to the tail of our column.

We were now a team of four: eight wheels articulating in harmony. The speed crept up. The surface of the great plateau began to blur; the metallic slap of flying chains changing gear marked every tilt of gradient. We crouched lower. The greatcoat flapped like a topgallant loose in a gale. Pedestrians stopped and stared.

By the time we were two kilometres outside Er Rachidia we were in top gear and travelling faster than the buses. With the coffee shop as the finish line, Chris suddenly swept ahead, Matt glued onto his back wheel. After a madcap sprint through the streets of Er Rachidia I found myself alone. I turned round: Chris and Matt were nowhere to be seen. But the Moroccan greatcoat was an inch off my back wheel, olive eyes grinning. I wobbled beside him, empty-legged, sucking draughts of crisp air. We introduced ourselves. He said his name was Abwiwa and that he cycled 12 kilometres to and from work, every day. He waved goodbye as he turned up a side street.

The Land Rovers were parked outside the Café Restaurant Sijilmassa. Alan welcomed us to a scattering of warm plastic chairs on the concrete pavement: "I'd like to do a Hopes and Fears piece, chaps."

A tray arrived with eleven glasses of dark coffee. The camera homed in on Matt. Stuart Bruce hovered like a slips player, off-view but recording every breath. His 24-inch muffled microphone – his 'woolly dog' – edged forward.

"So, Matt, at this stage, what are your main apprehensions?"

"My apprehensions are firstly snow – snow could stop us dead in our tracks. If we get more than about a foot, we're going to be absolutely unable to continue this journey. Secondly I fear that the bikes might break up, because we're really pushing them to their limits. And thirdly – and most of all – I fear the human limitations of this journey in that, you know, we simply may not be . . . be up to it."

The camera waddled over to Chris to find him with his ear glued to a radio, listening to the World Service: "Chris, what are your main apprehensions?"

"That Bolton Wanderers are going to get relegated to the Fourth Division!"

At three minutes past ten, we left the café and pedalled west up Avenue Moulay Ali Cherif. Beyond the outskirts of Er Rachidia we turned right onto the Meknes road. Ahead, we could see the Atlas Mountains: a grey wall blocking the northern horizon. The wind still blew hard from the mountains and on the exposed road outside Er Rachidia the pedalling became a monotonous treadmill.

Twenty kilometres beyond the town the road reared abruptly upwards. The scale of big journeys can be reduced by breaking them into manageable portions; leaving the sand-dunes of Merzouga; reaching the plateau above Meski oasis; and now, reaching the foothills of the Atlas, were all significant markers; like birthdays, or chapters in a book, they could be ticked off.

The road rose in a series of ramps, giving us glimpses of the Barrage Hassan Addakhil, an incongruous blue puddle occupying the dips in a landscape that seemed only to know shades of brown. To reach our start point for the Atlas traverse, we first had to ride against the grain of the mountain folds; only when we reached the centre of the range, midway between Morocco's southern desert and northern forest, would we bc able to turn left and ride with the grain.

Still being beaten by the wind, we turned into the massive Gorges du Ziz. The three of us were out of sight of each other. The scale of the gorge was made all the more dramatic by its contrast to the spacy landscapes we had lived in for the past three days. The road hugged the west wall of the gorge, contouring on a shelf that here and there crept close to plunging drops. Away in the haze on the far side of the gorge, sheer cliffs walled us in. I came upon the camera crew, parked in a layby. They were dithering: "Shame. The light's not right. We'd like to 'zap' you later, if it's not too much trouble."

Alan shaded his eyes, searching the serpentine road for Matt, who was somewhere behind me. Chris had disappeared ahead an hour earlier. Beyond the layby, the road turned away from the cliff and sank as true as a blade, into the guts of the gorge. Part way down the slope I hauled on the brake levers and, with tears blown across my cheeks from the eye-scouring flight, climbed the gravel bank and waited with my camera for Matt.

The Land Rovers were parked for lunch at a neck in the gorge. Chris had arrived half an hour earlier and was sitting off to one side, on a rock, rubbing his legs. Next to him was a litre-bottle of Sidi Harazem mineral water. I made for the bottle. Chris grinned: "Trying to make 'em work for this afternoon" he said. I looked closely.

"You haven't been shaving your legs have you?"

"Not since my last race." He paused with his massage, and added: "That was 12 years ago next Sunday . . . the National Cyclo-cross

Championships at Birmingham. . . Look at all these old cycling wounds. That one there, that was four stitches . . . that was sixteen."

"Those are the ugliest legs I've ever seen."

Chris massaged his calves lovingly. His fingers ran down a long pale cicatrice: "That was a knife in east Africa."

"Who stuck that in you?"

"The guy who was slitting the tent."

"You were sleeping in a tent and someone stuck a knife through it?"

"Yeah, in . . . what's north of Mombasa . . . Malindi? "

"It must've been a very long knife to have gone through a tent, sleeping bag and your leg all in one go."

"No, no, it went through the sleeping bag and I stopped the guy. We had sort of a bit of an argy-bargy outside and I suddenly found the knife in my leg." Chris slapped his calves sentimentally.

"Come on legs," he muttered. "Come back. Don't fail me now. It's the knee playing up. Four years ago I fell off a donkey in the Valley of the Kings in Egypt. Did in the ligaments. Hope this isn't the same problem coming back . . ."

A wide angle lens retracted from Chris' calf. In his caress-the-cameraman tone Alan murmured: "Thank you Graham. Nice."

Jeremy was emerging as a calming influence on a team which was by necessity driven by self-interest: the cameraman had to put his shots before all else; for the sound man, little else existed beyond the end of his microphone; the director had to concentrate on co-operation, on his sequences, budget and a deadline; Andy, who was probably putting more physical effort into the expedition than anyone, would get it in the neck if any of the vehicles broke down. And so on. Jeremy, our provider and mother-figure, had everybody's interests at heart. His generosity of spirit humbled everybody else into moderating their own selfishness.

The anxieties were building. This was going to be our last day on tarmac. Sometime tomorrow, the road would end. Then we would be on rough tracks. One and a half days of pedalling uphill into a headwind had served to place a scale between us and the Atlas. And we were getting smaller. There is, it seems, an inverse relationship between ego and altitude.

The frowns on the faces of the film crew were becoming more frequent; would they be able to get the footage they needed once we were on mountain tracks? How far would they be able to follow us in their cumbersome four-wheeler? What if one of us dropped out before they had enough in the can? To cover themselves they were filming every conceivable nuance of the day's journey.

Just beyond the neck of the gorge the road twisted along a short corniche then burrowed into the mountain. Two soldiers stood with guns at the entrance to the Tunnel Foum Zaabal. Inside, it was cool and dark; a moment's hiding place from the lens. Through the furnace door at the far end of the tunnel, the day burned.

We zoomed down to cross the River Ziz again, this time on a discoloured concrete bridge propped between the cliffs on either side of the river's shallow beds. It was the first time we had seen water occupying the riverbed of the Ziz.

Chris came past. He was cycling two metres behind the V8 Land Rover. Cantilevered from the back of the Land Rover on a cat's cradle of climbing rope and coloured slings was cameraman Graham Smith. From Graham's outstretched arms reached a long aluminium boom with a metal box attached to the end. The zap gun: a remote controlled camera which could be poked into places the bigger Aaton could not reach. The zap's lens was a hand-span above the tarmac, looking up at Chris' face through the spinning spokes of the front wheel. The Land Rover and bike were travelling at 30kph, over bobbly tarmac. As if he was gently drawing a spinner through a trout pool, Graham eased the boom upwards, so that the lens climbed up the bike's front wheel, past the brake calliper until, just above the handlebars, it hovered, staring at Chris like the Cyclopean eye of a myopic monster scanning its prey.

Chris, his two days' stubble bristling grey beneath his sun-bleached *Daily Telegraph* cyclo-cross cap, stared ahead as if he was entirely on his own. On the crest of a hill beyond the spa by the Ziz a road forked off to the left. We turned from north to west; the Atlas traverse had started.

The road sign at the junction read 'Imilchil 154'. So we left the Meknes road which continued north to cross the spine of the eastern Atlas, and followed the valley of the River Ziz, here broad and flat, and constricted by steep-sided barren mountains. Twenty minutes from the main road we came to the market town of Rich.

It had been market day in Rich. The lane leading to the *souk* was solid with traders heading home: bicycles weighed down with bags of potatoes; empty mule carts heading back to the farms; men with bulging sacks and chickens; pockets full of nuts. A man was trying to lead a tiny goat down the street, its rear legs as straight as chair legs, fighting every inch, skidding in the dust so that it left a pair of shaky tramlines down the centre of the lane. Rich pulsed weakly in the soporific afterglow of the day's excitement.

With the Land Rover parked half way down the lane and Graham standing on its roof, hunched over a straddled tripod, Matt, Chris and I wove our way through the throng, stopping part way to pretend to ask the way, then resuming our end-of-day meander through the vast pink-painted keyhole arch into the market. Inside, Graham got in a spot of bother filming a nut-seller, and had to beat a tactical retreat: "They didn't like the camera," he said, slinging the heavy Aaton into the back of the vehicle.

There was maybe one hour until dark.

Beyond the town, the River Ziz crossed the road in a ford about 500 metres wide. It was too much for Alan to resist: "Wait here chaps. We'll get set up on the far side."

The Land Rover wallowed into the water, which looked deep enough for our feet to go underwater with every revolution of the pedal. We waited with a gathering crowd of onlookers, then splashed through, resenting the wet socks which would not now dry till the next day. We emerged grinning, for the camera: "Once again please chasps, with the donkey this time."

Beyond the ford, the road unwound westwards along the centre of the flat-bottomed valley. A maternal wind patted us on towards the sinking sun. Low huddles of mud houses caught the last glow of day, their warm ochre walls drawing ant figures in ones and twos along the pale veins of the valley's smaller routeways.

We camped that night on a stony hill a kilometre from the road. Jeremy cooked a chicken that he'd bought in the *souk* at Rich. We ate under a puddle of electric light cast by the bulb wired to the back of one of the Land Rovers, fingers skidding on casseroled legs in our haste for protein. Warmed by mugfuls of greasy stock, Matt and I stripped the heavy knobbly tyres from the bicycles and replaced them with light-weight racing tyres.

By the light of a headtorch in our tent I spread out the Michelin map that we had been using for the road section of the ride. We had cycled 241 kilometres in two days. So far we were just on the safe side of our required daily average.

This was the eve of our first real test: tomorrow we would leave the tarmac. In the next couple of days we would find out what kind of speed we could manage over rough tracks. If we could not average our required 50 kilometres a day, then our route would have to be modified; we would have to use more jeep tracks, at lower altitude. The film then ran the risk of looking too 'soft', and the journey itself would miss the wildernesses and the remoter Berber villages.

At 7am the alarm sounded, for a 7.30-am start. I rolled onto my stomach and felt under the pile jacket, that I'd been using as a pillow, for my contact lens container. I scoured each lens clean with my tongue and flipped them onto my eyeballs. For the first few blinks it felt as if a handful of gravel had got stuck under each eyelid. I sat up, and let the sleeping bag fall to my waist. The air had frozen in the night. Salopettes then pile jacket, scarf and trilby. I checked that my gloves were in my jacket pocket. Each side of me, Matt and Chris were lying prone, looking the other way. A snow shower of frozen condensation scattered off the zip as it shrieked open. The morning was already bright. In the tent porch my leather boots had partially frozen so that they would only bend a little, like thick plastic. With the laces flapping I clumped round the outside of the tent, ripping at pegs with frozen fingers. Jeremy was already up, crouching over the gas stove. The milk had frozen, falling onto the mug of muesli in fractured lumps.

Matt pulled the sleeping mats from the tent. "Revised departure time 7.45."

Andy helped pass the bikes down from the roof of the Land Rover. We had tied them there for safe-keeping during the night.

"Any of you guys like coffee?" called Jeremy.

Tent pegs, bicycles, jerrycans were dropped as outstretched arms made for the kettle. The prospect of arriving at the kettle too late on a morning cold enough to freeze the milk was a horror too awful to contemplate. I found my mug in a climbing boot. A piece of chicken skin had frozen to the bottom. Coffee grains, a slosh of steaming water, a scoop of sugar and an iceberg of milk knocked the remaining muesli off the inside of my mug, so that a miscellaneous flotsam of rolled oats, toasted wheat flakes, half a hazlenut and a long bran-like extrusion swirled in the whirlpool of brown fluid before settling in the centre of the vortex and lodging on the sandbank of sugar when the mug was finally emptied. I was keen to leave; if we could not manage a disciplined start to the day when life was cushy, what would happen when we were alone, up in the mountains? I checked my watch again: "OK let's *really* try and get away by eight."

By the time the sleeping bags had been rolled from their patches of sun where they had been spread to dry, and the panniers had been packed, it was 8.03am. Then there were water bottles to fill. And Chris decided to pump up his tyres.

It was 8.15 by the time we pushed the bikes down the stony slope towards the road.

The sky was empty. There never seemed to be any clouds.

We rode gently upwards on smooth tarmac, the road no wider than an English country lane. On each side of us, the hillsides were thinly covered in dull, spiky grass, growing in clumps four feet apart. The whole landscape had been ravaged by goats. Soon it steepened. This was our first pass: the Tizi-n-Ali. It wasn't much of a pass, but it kept us occupied for an hour. Chris danced upwards. He was so light and lithe that his body and bike seemed to flex in a single web of muscle and tendons. Matt came last, fighting the bike upwards, swearing to himself. We tipped over the crest at 9.20. The road scythed through a fifty-foot cutting that had been sliced through the top of the col. A kilometre post read 'Imilchil 94'.

Parched, barren, desiccated mountains filled the eye. Exposed strata caught the sun like so many lips, grinning at us from every angle. Matt and Chris were wearing lurid pink windproof trousers: "Kinky but photogenic" Matt had rationalised as he had pulled them from the manufacturer's box in London.

We flew, frozen, down the west side of the pass onto freshly-laid tarmac. The road only just fitted between the cliff face and the river bank. The cliff face bore the scars of recent blasting; rock which had never seen the light of day stood exposed, its surface dry and brittle. The mountain had lost its natural gradient. Part of the cliff had already collapsed, dumping a cone of boulders onto the clean tarmac.

Another kilometre post edged by: 'Imilchil 92'. We approached the village of Amouguer through wispy trees, thinking wistfully of hot tea in the first café. As we topped the hill by the village's mosque a familiar voice called from the midst of a knot of children: "Once again please chasps: from the last bend of the river. With passion!"

We stopped thinking of tea, turned around and cycled back the way we had come.

The village was in the middle of a traumatising metamorphosis. The dirt track which had served the valley for centuries was being tarmacked; a faster surface for the trucks and tourists. In the centre of the village a huge yellow road scraper was advancing west, grinding the inconsistencies from the street and meeting place that had looked the same for generations. As the scraper passed the village's only bar, its exhaust fired a dragon-roar of black breath through the chipped, blue doors. There was nobody on the street.

Outside the village, the tarmac suddenly ended. This was the moment that we had been waiting for. The bikes dropped over a lip and on to old, worn gravel. Now the handlebars shuddered; we had to look where we were going; the tyres made a sound like slowly ripped paper. We passed a kilometre post. It read 'Imilchil 100'.

We were in a narrowing gorge of the Ziz. The river snaked from one side to the other of the gorge, licking the rock-walls at every bend so that the Land Rovers had to wade through the water with each new curve. The water was too deep to cycle through. To avoid the river, the three of us were forced, at each river bend, up onto the cliff. A goat-width track edged along the cliff, which was occasionally reduced to loose rocks and slippery pebbles, forcing us in places to hook the bicycles onto spiky scrub while we inched forward to the next foothold.

Stuart Bruce, the sound-recordist, was standing in the middle of the track . "Mind if I wire you up lads? We'd like to get some wild-track of the kind of things you say to each other when you're cycling along." Stuart attached a clip-on microphone to each of us, threaded the lead through our clothing and plugged it into the small transmitters wedged in our back pockets. "Just talk normally," he said, "as if you're not on tape."

Stuart ran back to the Land Rover. We rolled forward. Matt started talking: "Nick, yesterday lunch time, did you see that big yellow-billed stork stuck in the middle of the river?"

"Massive great thing. Must have been about three feet high." Chris added.

"I'm very disappointed that we missed the desert fox this morning."

"Well, if you will hang behind."

"I get confused with these packs of desert foxes. In February these hills are just covered with them. They go west and when they get to the cliffs at Agadir they launch themselves into the sea." David Attenborough he wasn't.

"Chris, you have made a mistake. Some day you'll see the error of your ways and you'll be using racing tyres. They go over these boulders effortlessly."

Chris accelerated away, to a commentary from Matt: "Chris Bradley. Look at him go. The man who has done for mountain-biking what Mao Tse Tung did for hang-gliding." Matt paused for reflection, then continued: "I had this dream about Rolf Harris last night. He was sitting on top of Toubkal at 13,690 feet and was cooking a big bowl of spaghetti when we arrived there."

"D'you know what that means? Dreaming of Rolf Harris on mountain tops?"

"Can't hear."

"You're going track crazy."

We came to a levelling in the track. The V8 Land Rover had stopped. Stuart Bruce walked towards us. He took the microphones away without saying a word. I don't think he was impressed.

At 1.20, we came upon the Land Rovers nuzzled into a green corner of the gorge. Sprawled in the sun we picnicked on French 'Laughing Cow' processed cheese and triangles of bread ripped from discus-shaped loaves. Abedelilah manufactured one of his Moroccan salads using two cans of sardines, some tomatoes and onions, and then did a handstand.

We left, wondering how close to Imilchil we could get before darkness would force us off the trail. Two hours on, we came into the village of Outerbate and found our way blocked by a police post. At the end of an avenue of large eucalyptus trees with white painted trunks was a barracks. Abedelilah took our passports to the officer inside and we waited in the shadowed compound while two woodpeckers darted between the branches above our heads. A painted board outside the police post read 'Imilchil 42'. We had to sign a book, and were allowed to leave.

The pass started from the corner outside the police post. A meandering dirt track took us up a desolate valley, beside a chasm filled with old snow. An icy breeze cut down from above. A dull glow still lit the western sky – embers from the sun – drawing us on towards Imilchil. Now we were racing against the dark: the hill that we were climbing was one of the markers of the journey, for somewhere on these barren slopes was the source of the River Ziz. When we crossed the watershed, up there in the greying day, we would descend into the valley that would lead us to Imilchil and the High Atlas. I desperately wanted to peek over that watershed.

I found myself alone, the other bikes and the Land Rovers separated from me by the ascent. As the gradient eased, I speeded up. Two dogs detached themselves from a shepherd's hut and tore after me. I speeded up a little more. Suddenly I was on flat ground, and moments later tilting down. I had reached the top. My eyes strained into the gloom. Ahead, a lightless range of peaks and troughs disappeared into the gloom. I turned back to find the others.

The Land Rovers had called it a day, and were grumbling in bottom gear across the untracked mountainside looking for a flattish patch of ground. They settled on a bleak slope, just up from a dry riverbed.

It was so cold in the night that Jeremy slept in a tent.

The film crew were up early. Matt, Chris and I managed to get away from the camp by 8.45. Behind us, Andy and Jeremy quietly stowed gear in boxes and roped the rucksacks to the roofs of the Land Rovers. Mohammed was making clinking sounds inside the bonnet of the diesel.

It took twenty minutes to return to the highpoint that I had peered over the previous night. When we got there it was clear that it was not the top of the pass: beyond the high point, the road dipped then reared up again. The V8 chugged past, looking for a vantage point.

The road continued in a straight line. Ribs of solid rock ran diagonally across the surface of gravel and broken chips. The low sun bored straight into our eyes. The gradient steepened and the road began to cut shallow Zs. The corners were steepest. At the top, the film crew were waiting, zooming in on Matt's face, a mask of studied ambivalence. But his lips were moving, and as his wheels trembled towards the summit, Matt's mantra was borne upward on the wind: "You bastard, you bastard, you basta . . ." The words revolved in perfect synchronisation with his pedals.

A few metres to the north of the summit a crooked-armed gully branched into a fan of short fingers. It was the source of the Ziz. There was not a drop of water to be seen, but snow banks lay in the hollows.

The film crew were capturing every conceivable angle; Alan was convinced that he would never see us again after Imilchil and that he would have to construct an entire film from the footage he had shot between the Sahara and the end of the jeep track. We were filmed flying down the pass ("One more time chaps please, a little closer together, not *too* fast") and then we escaped. We left the film crew waiting on the pass for the other two Land Rovers, which had mysteriously failed to appear.

We bounced down into a broad, light-filled valley. Somewhere in this dusty trench was a stream – the Asif Melloul. It was a river which was critically to shape our forthcoming days. In the centre of the trench was a road junction. One track turned left, to follow the main valley south. The other pointed north. A sign read 'Ait Hani 60 km'. Ait Hani was a village half way between the point where we stood and the Todra Gorge; the narrow funnel which opened onto the Saharan slopes of the Atlas.

We turned right, curving up a narrowing valley. The heat was building by the minute. As the road hugged a mountainside of black rock, a village slid into view. It was too beautiful to pass by. In the midst of this saw-toothed aridity was a community; an island of homes and fields drawn from the soil that fringed the banks of the hidden Asif Melloul.

The village was separated from the road by an irrigated strip of fields 300 metres wide and one kilometre long. The fields were small and square, fringed by low mud banks to contain the water. Each field shone with pale green light. Between the fields and the village was a thin line of saplings, marking the course of the river. And beyond the saplings, the village itself: a mud Manhattan of cubes and towers climbing the lower slopes of the mountain. Two defensive *kasbahs* dominated the roofs, each *kasbah* towering three storeys high and each topped at their corners by four tapered watch-towers. There was nobody in sight.

"Amazing!" Matt was standing, transfixed.

"That's the most beautiful, most perfect Berber village I've *ever* seen in the Atlas. Alan has *got* to film this."

Matt and I sat on the bank above the road, watching Chris wheel his bicycle along the ridges separating the fields. Five minutes later, we saw him climb up the slope on the far side of the river and disappear between two houses. We lay and watched the day stand still.

Chris returned. "Some people call it Mazal. Some call it Sountat," he said. It would still be several days before we moved onto our large scale maps, and until then we had no way of knowing precisely where we were. The only help we had was our 1:4,000,000 Michelin map covering the whole of North Africa.

Just then the V8 Land Rover arrived. Sountat (for this was probably the real name), was indeed a perfect Berber village, with a romantic mountain backdrop, accessible furthermore by Land Rover. The sequences fell quickly into place: "If you could take the bikes up that mountain (Alan pointed to a distant peak) then cycle down that track (his finger followed a diagonal whisker down the face of the mountain) we can get a long shot of you arriving in the village. Then we'll come across and do some shots of you meeting local people, asking the way and riding through the houses. OK chasps?"

We set off for the peak.

By the time we reached the first house, everyone in the village knew that we were there. It was the children who came closest. Small girls decorated with earrings and necklaces pulled at each others' shoulders. The boys pulled at the brake levers and kneaded the tyres and cried, "*Conduire votre bicyclette!*". The 21 gears were viewed with disbelief. While we were filming, the other two Land Rovers crept down the far side of the valley. They were connected to each other by a length of rope.

Imilchil took ages to arrive, although it was in fact just an hour's bumpy riding beyond Sountat. The valley broadened at a corner and we passed a loose agglomeration of houses which finally found some form of nucleus at the T-junction below the high wall surrounding the *souk*. Imilchil lay at a crossroads of tracks in the centre of the High Atlas. Running through the village from north to south was the track linking the Todra Gorge south of the Atlas, with the main Fès-Marrakesh road to the north. East from Imilchil was the track we'd come along from Rich. And running west, the smallest track of them all was our way to the heart of the mountains. Each year, in September, Imilchil plays host to thousands of Berber tribes-people who migrate to this sheltered valley for the annual marriage fair. A sea of tents surround the town as young men and women from far-flung villages circulate in search of the perfect partner. It is an impetuous tradition, defused only slightly by the opportunity to back out of a marriage after a three-week trial period. I looked at the stubbled chins of my two companions and it occurred to me that, in the Atlas Mountains, three weeks can be a long time.

Looking over the deserted rectangle of the *souk* was the Café Hotel Haut Atlas. Running the entire length of the south side of the café was a broad, sunny terrace, roofed and fronted with welded railings. Four solitary formica-topped tables gathered mid-point along the terrace, close to the café door. Above the door, a fox skull had been pushed over the light fitting jutting from the wall so that the electric bulb protruded from the animal's gaping jawbones.

We lifted the bikes up the short flight of steps onto the terrace, propped them against the bare cement wall and flopped onto the chairs. Over coffee and omelettes we reviewed the game which we were now committed to complete. We were nearly four days into the journey and had covered 370 kilometres. So far on Day 4 we had only travelled an estimated 43 kilometres. We could not afford to hang around at Imilchil, yet whether we liked it or not this was not going to be a normal, quick lunch halt. Here, on this café terrace, the expedition had to shrink from 11 people and 3 Land Rovers, to 3 people and 3 rucksacks.

At Imilchil, our expedition was going to be prised apart by the steepening terrain: we expected that the track west, which had become steadily rougher since leaving Rich, would now deteriorate to the point that it would not be motorable, even by Land Rover. So it was to be a parting of the ways: the three Land Rovers would have to find an alternative route around the mountains, while Matt, Chris and I pressed on west using mule tracks.

For the first time on the journey we would be out of reach of the First Unit. Alan and his highly professional crew would be unable to film whatever happened to us over the next section of the ride. Matt and Chris would now step forward as the Second Unit. On our backs we would carry 16mm film and sound equipment. We would film ourselves. This was the section of the ride for which we had no adequate map. All we had was a page torn from a French mountaineering guide. We spread it over the meal debris in front of us.

West of Imilchil, the map showed an indistinct collaboration of greens and browns threaded by the thin indigo strand of the Asif Melloul. North of this river wandered the drunken pecks of what could be construed as a mule track or footpath. The next place west from Imilchil was a tiny black dot called Zaouia Ahansal. Historically, a *zaouia* was a sanctuary; a focus for Islamic life and a place where tribal disputes could be resolved. In a region as wild as the High Atlas, Zaouia Ahansal would have been an important centre. Matt left his chair and crossed the verandah to the café-proprietor who had been watching the debate from his vantage-point propped against the door-jamb. The camera peered over Matt's shoulder as he spoke: *"Monsieur? . . . Il y a une route à Zaouia Ahansal? C'est á combien de kilomètres?"*

The man threw his arm towards the distant mountains and said: *"Oui, il y a une route . . . quarante kilomètres."*

Forty kilometres at the kind of speed we had managed over the previous days would only take us half a day. But most of it would be on rough tracks. The man added that the jeep-track from Imilchil ran west for another 14 kilometres, then stopped. We turned back to the map. North from 'Z.A.' a thin red vein twisted through the mountains to the northern plain. Zaouia Ahansal was clearly the next possible rendezvous which we could make with the Land Rovers.

"How long's it going to take to get to this place?" asked Alan.

"The soonest we can make it will be tomorrow evening. Maybe tomorrow lunch. The longest will be about three days."

"Right, so we'll drive north from Imilchil to the plain, then along the Marrakesh road, then turn back into the mountains again. We'll be at Zaouia Ahansal from tomorrow midday onwards. We'll just wait there till you arrive, though we do seem to have some kind of problem with the Mohammed's waggon. Andy says it's severely broken."

We dispersed, each of us to our own chores. Chris had a puncture to mend in his back wheel. Matt went to fetch all the Second Unit film equipment from the Land Rover. I was charged with organising what little equipment we would carry over the mountains to Zaouia Ahansal. The First Unit hopped around, filming the preparations. The only person with nothing to do was Jeremy, who for the first time since leaving Marrakesh was neither driving nor needing to feed people. He sat bemused on one of the metal chairs watching the expedition disintegrate: "This is great, just great," he mused to nobody in particular, "out in the bush at last."

Out on the slanting dust-patch beyond the café, Andy and Mohammed were bending over the gaping bonnet of the diesel Land Rover. "Split head," pronounced Andy. The engine had vomited oil onto the ground at his feet. Mohammed looked very miserable. Andy elaborated: "Last night it was so cold that the diesel froze. Down at about minus 12 degrees it turns to wax. So this morning Mohammed couldn't get it started. First we warmed the diesel, then found that all the core plugs had popped out of the engine block. No anti-freeze. I told Mohammed that he had to drain the engine each night to stop it freezing. Now the head's cracked. We had to tow it all the way here. Mohammed's going to get a real bollocking if he takes this wreck back to Marrakesh."

Molehills of minutely scrutinised equipment multiplied across the verandah. On two of the tables which he had pulled together, Matt arranged Zanzibar's Aaton camera, 2 rolls of Kodak 7291 64 daylight film (each roll providing about 10 minutes worth of filming), one magazine, one 10-200 zoom lens, one fixed 12mm lens, a Sony Professional tape recorder with its little 'sync' add-on box, and the clapperboard. I picked up the clapperboard. It weighed a ton: "We're not taking this," I protested.

"This goes *everywhere*. It's part of the Zanzibar tradition."

"There isn't a Zanzibar tradition."

"We're making one now!"

By comparison, my little pile hardly filled a pannier pocket: compass, the map, a small medical kit comprising a roll of sticking plaster and some antiseptic cream, a basic bicycle tool kit, one puncture repair kit, one bicycle pump, one watch, my Olympus OM1 camera and three lenses, a two-bladed Swiss Army knife, sunglasses, a whistle, notebook and biro. Each of us would carry our own survival blanket, sleeping bag and clothing, which included a set of thermal underwear, windproof jacket and trousers, gloves and balaclavas. The only food we would take would be a handful of chocolate bars.

Because the film equipment was fragile, we would have to carry it on our backs in the rucksacks, wrapped in the protective folds of our sleeping bags. Clothing we were not using, and the bits and pieces, would all go in the single pannier we would each carry on our bike.

Andy arrived having abandoned his efforts to mobilise Mohammed's Land Rover: "We'll have to tow it out of the mountains," he said unenthusiastically. "Anyone want any help?" I gave Andy a chain-link removing tool and asked if he could lighten it by removing the handle. He returned ten minutes later. The handle on the tool had been sawn off, and he had drilled out the small key which would normally be used to revolve the tool's spindle. "Look; saves a lot of weight," demonstrated Andy. "Instead of the key-handle, there's now a hole big enough to take one of the Allen keys which you are carrying anyway."

With precious time running out, and the sun already sinking, we oiled the bicycle chains and gear mechanisms and checked the tyre pressures. We were ready. Alan led the film crew down to the signpost below the gate to the *souk*: "We'll get an arriving and departing shot," he said. "Arriving first."

We cycled a hundred metres back towards Rich, turned and rode obediently into the camera, chatting excitedly as if we had just arrived in Imilchil after a long day in the saddle. "OK, thanks chaps. Now we'll film you going."

We set off in the opposite direction, westwards, towards Zaouia Ahansal. A hundred metres down the lane I said: "Let's go back. They're bound to want another take." We stopped, turned and rode back towards the camera. Alan waved us away: "What've you come back for? We got it first time. You can go. Bugger off!"

We rolled westwards out of town with dust spouting from our tyres along a thinning trail into the sinking sun.

House of Said

Beneath a Berber Moon (Day 4) – The Second Unit's First Take (Day 5) – Up a Gorge Wall – Accident – The Woodcutters' Cottage – More Mistakes (Day 6) – Which way to Z.A.? – Bivouac! – The Stone Desert (Day 7) – Cliff Climbing – Zaouia Ahansal – "Gentlemen: we should rock on!" (Day 8) – Chris Disappears – Crunch Time

Day 5 - 8

We left Imilchil at 5.15 pm on Day 4. At last we were alone. The process of shedding was now complete. From an incomplete proposal which had existed in the heads of executives, film makers and bureaucrats in Putney, Washington and Marrakesh, 'Atlas Biker' had been mobilised by a budget of nearly £100,000; this had been translated into film crews, plane tickets, permits, support personnel and bags of muesli, which had then mutated into a caravan of three Land Rovers in North Africa. The final, ultimate turn of the focusing ring had now taken place: we were now just three cyclists and a film camera. It was the image we had been straining towards for weeks.

"Great. I'm looking forward to this," said Matt, as we left Imilchil suspended in the dust-cloud of our departure.

The track was wide enough for a four-wheeled vehicle, yet showed no tyre tracks as it undulated between ragged stone walls into the sunset. The honeyed walls of a village drifted by over to the right. The light was fading fast, but it was too early to stop. We needed to distance ourselves from Imilchil; perhaps even reach the end of the road before nightfall.

"Stop at the next village?"

We all agreed. The track turned to the left then braided into footpaths on a dry rise crowned by the blank walls of a village. Which of the footpaths to take was unclear. The village was sinking into twilit gloom.

There was nobody in sight. At the edge of a dustpatch at the top of the village, we climbed off the bikes. Choosing a direction at random, I wandered through an alley and out onto a path which skirted the hilltop between an overgrown cemetery and the walls of a row of small houses. I thought I caught a glimpse of a face at a door, but it had gone by the time I turned.

I followed the path and took a left turn up another alley to return to the dust patch. Matt and Chris had opened negotiations with a clutch of children who were leaning around the corner of a wall. A woman with a galvanised steel bucket balanced on her head slipped into a doorway, face averted. I left Matt and Chris, and set off along the same five-minute circuit I had just completed. This time I could hear the soft patter of feet on the dust behind me. With exaggerated slowness I stopped by the cemetery and looked out across the valley. The pattering feet stopped too. The echoes of shepherds drifted across from the mountainside beyond the river, and as I stared into the dark face of that mountain two sparks of light flared brightly near its summit. Somebody was lighting fires above the far cliffs. Quietly I turned to look behind me. At the bend in the path, fifteen children were standing statue-still, looking. Quicker than it took me to smile, the mortuary silence of the village was shattered as the children rushed forward, shouting and laughing, climbing on the wall; experimentally nudging my elbows. Laying my head on my hands, I mimicked a man falling asleep. More laughing. A young man with a thin, neat moustache and a brown woollen hat pulled to his ears emerged from the back of the bunch and beckoned me to follow. In an unruly procession we ambled back to collect Matt and Chris, who by now were also surrounded by a small crowd. In a mixture of Berber, French and Arabic, Matt explained to the young man that we were looking for somewhere to stay. We were led away from the square.

At the end of the cemetery, the young man tugged aside a tree trunk which held a sheet of corrugated iron across the gateway to a small straw-strewn courtyard. We leant the bicycles against the wall. A bullock shuffled into the corner of the courtyard as the man bent into a doorway. At the end of a black tunnel, a door creaked and we stepped one by one into a room about four metres long, three metres wide, stacked with sacks at one end and with an uneven mud floor occupied by old cans, straw, stones, bits of rope and wood. A soft puddle of light fell through a tiny, barred window. We cleared a space on the floor and the man spread out a blue and white blanket. We gave him some money and after we had taken off our boots he told us to come with him into the adjoining room.

The family room was bigger than the store room. It had no windows but it was lit by a paraffin lamp hanging from a roof beam and a

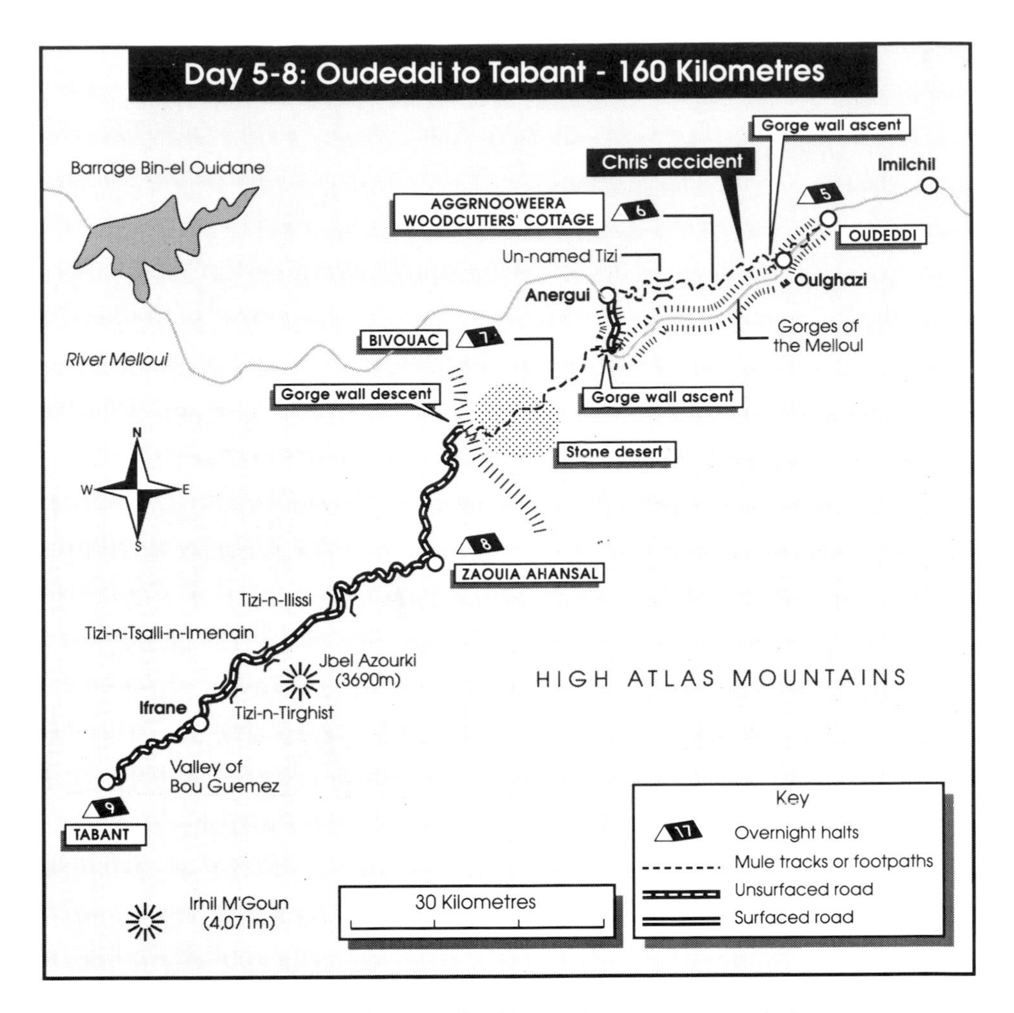

portable gas-lamp squatting on the floor. In the centre of the room was a tall stove made from an oil-drum. From the side of the oil-drum, an elbowed metal pipe led up through the flat roof. The shadowed back wall of the room was occupied by dried firewood. Sitting cross-legged round a rug spread in front of the stove were four people: two women, and two men. We were asked to sit at the rug. The room was warm and friendly and safe, and in anticipation of an entire evening confined to this small corner of rug my limbs and mind began to relax.

Already the old man was making the tea and warming the glasses by tipping the tea from one to the next, then returning it to the pot. The young man introduced himself as Said Amgoul. The old man, his father, was called Hassan and the village which we were in was called Oudeddi. We explained to Said that we were going to travel to Zaouia Ahansal. He nodded, and said that the route was very difficult – there might be snow – and that it passed two villages: Oulghazi and Anergui. I wrote their

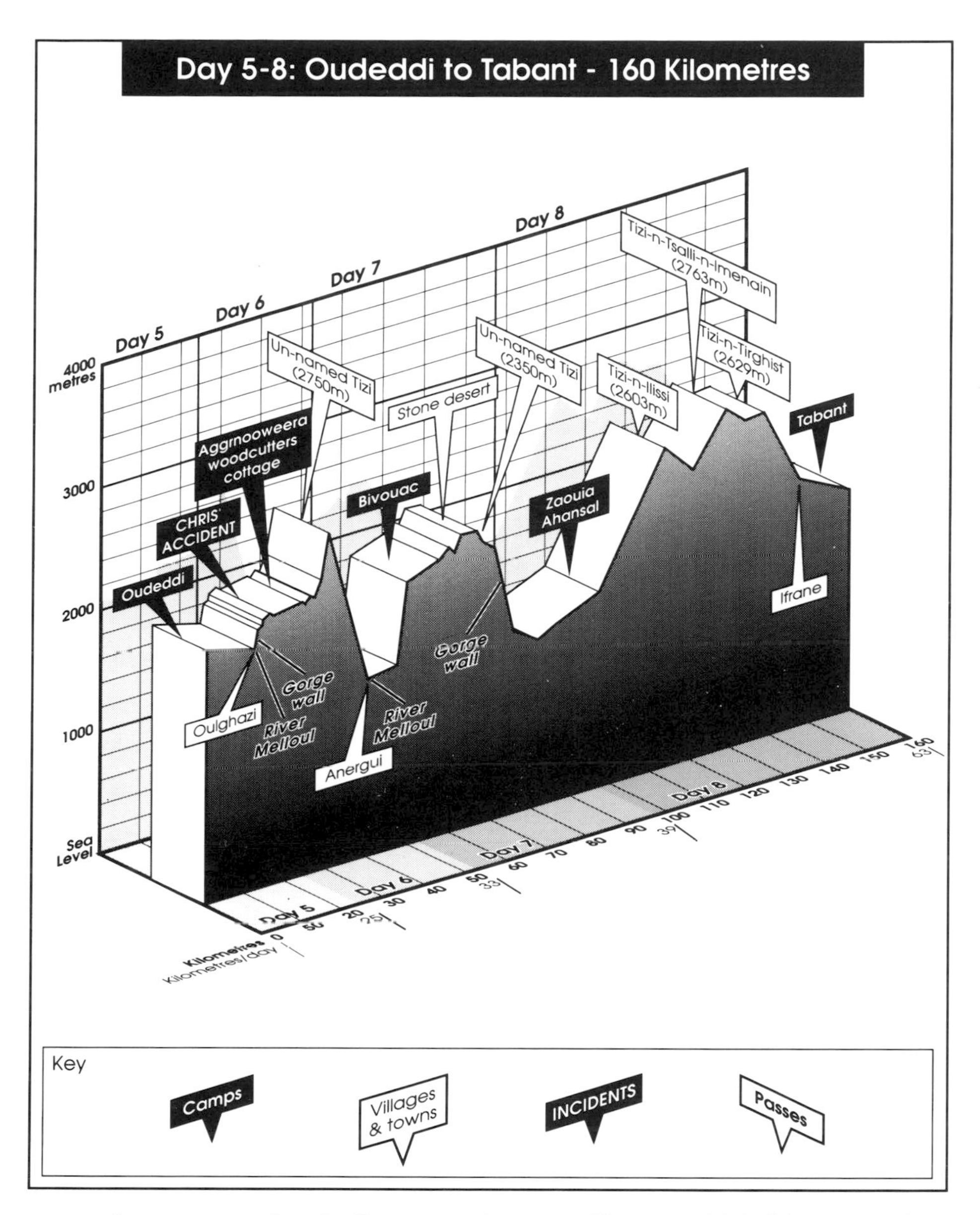

names into my notebook. Between the two villages, said Said, was a high *'Tizi'* or pass.

On the far side of the rug, the daughter sat cross-legged, pulling wool from a small cardboard box and spinning it onto a thin, tapered stick which was embedded in the dust. We watched hypnotised, as the wool was wound onto the fattening waist of the stick. Next to the daughter, the mother (whose name was 'Berri', said with rolling 'r's), sat wrapped in the heavy folds of a deep plum blanket, rocking occasionally on her haunches and holding brief, quiet conversations with her daughter.

The first brew of tea was poured into a row of seven small glasses. Berri and her daughter shared a glass. The custom is for visitors to drink three glasses, and as we sipped the syrupy, minty tea, we watched the glow at the bottom of the stove. The air in the room was still. By the light of his tiny torch, Matt was reading the instruction manual to the Aaton camera; before him on the rug were spread large bits of camera. "We haven't used this type before," he said casually, picking up the two largest lumps, "I always wondered how these two bits fitted together."

I drew a little map in my notebook, illustrating the day's progress. Tomorrow would be our first real test. By the end of the day, we would have discovered how feasible it would be to mountainbike along Atlas mule tracks. Chris subsided into the darkness.

The sounds of returning goats and the sharp yelps of the shepherds permeated the thick mud walls. Said explained that the fires on the mountainside had been lit by the shepherds to drive the goats back to the valley.

Sometime later Hassan poured the second pot of tea. Sitting next to Said's younger brother, Matt was sewing up the split seam of his pink overtrousers. Said himself was hunched over a massive plastic Sanyo radio-cassette player exploring the stations. Bursts of static alternated with Elton John, the news in Arabic from Casablanca, and a wailing Egyptian singer. Chris appeared to have fallen asleep. Beside the daughter, the sausages of spun wool had grown.

Eventually the mother carried in an earthenware pot with a conical lid topped by a small button-handle. The pot was placed in the centre of the rug, and Hassan passed a pile of dinner-plate sized loaves of unleavened bread around the circle of rosy faces. With a conjuror's flourish the lid was lifted from the pot and a cloud of steam erupted above the rug. When it had cleared, we all leant forward to savour the sight and smell of the heaped potatoes, carrots and onions of a huge *tagine.* Black olives floated in the channel of vegetable juices around the rim of the bowl. Hassan tore off a strip of bread, and, holding it between thumb and forefinger, used it to pick a piece of carrot from the top of the pile. "Do the same," he indicated.

By the time the third pot of tea had been brewed, the swaddling warmth of the room had set a glaze over everyone's eyes. When the pot was empty, we lurched singly along the tunnel to the small wooden door and the abrupt cold of the moonlit courtyard. The sky was studded with stars and the mountainside, which earlier had been lost in the shadows of dusk, was now brightly illuminated by the moon.

We were woken by Said standing astride our sleeping bags as he wrenched open the small wooden shutters covering the barred window.

Icy light penetrated our homely cave. We hopped about, tugging at trousers; getting in each other's way. Next door, the family room was glowingly hot from the stove. Berri and her daughter were sitting in the shadows. Said placed a low, three-legged table in front of us. On it were a stack of flat breads, three glasses and a bowl of yellow liquid. The bread was still hot from the oven; we dipped it in the warm, melted goat's cheese.

Said came to the bridge below the village, to show us the way. He walked fast, his hands jammed into the pockets of the thick brown *djellabah* which flapped around his ankles. It was so cold that he had an extra blanket wrapped around his shoulders and head. The sun still lay below the mountain ridges. At the bridge over the stream below the village, we stopped. Said pointed up the steep hillside opposite. A small path zig-zagged its way into the distance.

We pushed the bicycles up the slope, and joined a thin mule track which followed the left bank of the River Asif Melloul. It was just possible to pedal, and Chris, with his cyclo-cross skills was soon ahead of us, leaving Matt and me to clatter along at the back, bouncing off rocks and skidding on the gritty inclines. It was along this section of track that Chris took a fall; it was nothing dramatic, but he was dumped heavily on the track. He had also fallen six days earlier, when we had been playing in a ditch on that relaxed ride from Marrakesh.

In our enthusiasm to prove ourselves on this first day on our own – on real Atlas mule tracks – we rushed headlong past the narrow opening to the gorges of the Asif Melloul and, with ignorant enthusiasm, pedalled up a side-valley which eventually trapped us between the deep water of the river and a cliff face. "This can't be right," shouted Chris, who was edging along a sloping shelf at the foot of the cliff.

Below him, Matt and I were crunching through a forest of reeds and waist-high scrub. There was no sign of anyone having used this route before. The track which had led us there was nothing more than a goat trail. It was an annoying mistake. "We'll have to go back. Maybe the track went up that other valley we passed ten minutes ago."

We returned to the meeting place of the two valleys. It was clear where we had gone wrong: on a rock five metres above the riverbed the track turned a bend; if you stopped at the bend, and looked over the edge of the rock, you could see a narrow footbridge hopping across the mouth of the side-valley on a series of boulders.

"Great place to film. We'll stop here. It'll only take twenty minutes," announced Matt. Of course we had to stop and film; it was the reason we had come to Morocco. But mid-morning was already creeping up on us and we had travelled hardly any distance from Oudeddi. We'd lost valuable time up the side valley.

"Got the mag, Nick?" Matt had already pulled the lens and Walkman from the folds of his sleeping bag; Chris was pulling the camera from his rucksack. Lens and body met with a soft click, and the heavy magazine was snapped onto the back of the camera. Finally the sculpted wooden hand-grip with its finger trigger was screwed into place.

"Just got to check the gate, Chris." While Chris held the camera to his shoulder, Matt removed the lens then peered into the Aaton's innards with the small pencil torch. The beam played across the stamp-sized aperture in the recesses of the body: "The gate opens and closes 24 times each second as the film slides behind it. If the thinnest hair, or tiniest flake of emulsion from the film gets lodged in the gate, every frame will be ruined." Matt plugged the microphone cable into the Sony Walkman and looked around him: "OK. Let's see what it looks like from below."

We all three scrambled down the rock to the shingle below. It was a pretty little corner: from below, the short rock face looked vertical, and just five steps across the shingle from its foot the long, thin bridge skipped across the surface of the churning river to the backdrop of a vast sunless cliff wall below which our track ran west. The bridge had three layers: resting on some boulders either side and just above the river were treetrunks laid lengthways; on top of these was a layer of flat boulders and above these some strips of turf packed with handfuls of mud and small stones. Icicles fingered the freezing water where the turf stalks draped low.

Matt was excited: "Do you *realise* that this is going to be Shot 1, Take 1 for Zanzibar Films? Right, we'll do three shots, first one from the bottom of the rock looking up as we come down." He thought for a moment, then added: We'll hide the sound gear on the ground out of shot. That way we'll get two of us coming down the rockface. Chris and I'll take turns to do the shooting; so that it's not always Nick and me in the shot."

Chris braced himself against a rock, with the Aaton on his shoulder. Matt balanced the Sony Walkman on a stone and unwound the microphone cable. He knelt down and pressed the red 'Record' button on the end of the Walkman and said into the microphone: "Testing, testing, and what did you have for breakfast?" A man wearing a long, dark *djellabah* stopped half-way across the bridge and stared at Matt. Matt pulled on the earphones and rewound the tape. "Sounds good," he said.

The man walked on. Matt led the microphone cable across to the bottom of the section of the rock down which we planned to climb and rested the microphone in a thin undercut. "OK Chris, ready to go?"

"Ready!"

Matt and I climbed back up the rock. On the way, I piled a few small stones onto every foothold so that I could kick them off again on the way down; the sound of falling stones would make the shot sound suitably wild. At the top of the rock, we slung on our lightened packs and lifted our bicycles onto our shoulders. Out of sight of the camera, we waited. Chris called: "OK. Action!"

We walked forward, one behind the other. At the top of the rock, I slowed and peered down. The rock looked much steeper than it had done earlier when we had scrambled up and down unencumbered by bikes and packs. I went first. To descend facing the rock would have been the normal, safe procedure, but it would also mean that the camera would not see our faces. Feeling with my heel, I stepped downwards and scraped my foot along the first ledge. A satisfying clatter of falling stones told me that I had hit the right target. Two thirds of the way down I stepped onto a stone-strewn ledge which I'd failed to clear properly. I shot down the rest of the rock with nothing to slow my fall but the friction of my backside on the remaining ledges. I landed right in front of the camera with my left shoulder all but ripped off by the weight of a mountainbike decelerating from freefall to static in hundredths of a second. I stumbled with throbbing buttocks and a dislocated shoulder towards the bridge, conscious of the camera still following me. At the far side of the river Matt and I walked a further twenty paces and dropped the bikes: "What was that like?" I shouted.

Chris' voice mixed with the tumble of water: "One more time. Closer together." This time I did not pile stones on the ledges. During Take 3 of this shot I was struck by the notion that this journey was not going to need any embellishment; we were losing so much time that it was likely to end up wilder than anticipated anyway.

For the second shot Matt and I walked across the bridge with the bikes on our shoulders while Chris walked behind, holding the camera at foot level. It took two takes to get it right. The third shot was a close-up of an icicle hanging from the bridge being buffeted by the current. "*Great* sequence," announced Matt. The three shots had taken us an hour and a quarter.

In an attempt to make up lost time, we pedalled frantically above the Asif Melloul on a difficult track which had been cut into the foot of the canyon wall. Rubble from the overhang above had fallen down on to the track, creating a carpet of fist-sized rocks, through which a smooth, path had been scuffed by the passing of mules and men. The wall was stratified into horizontal rock-bands and sealed by a river of sky above our heads. Two desert foxes ambled across the track in front of us. They had tails as big as squirrels and seemed unconcerned by our noisy stone-crunching flight. I stopped to take a photograph. Even the 50-mm lens could not contain the scale of the cliff. I squeezed the shutter release as a tiny pink cyclist crept along a rectangle filled entirely with grains of stone.

By the time I had replaced the lens cap, stuffed the camera back into the top of my rucksack, heaved it on my back, fastened the waist strap, pulled on my sunglasses, replaced my hat and picked up the bike, then reversed the whole process because I suddenly realised that the gorge which had been fringed with ice two hours earlier was now cauldron-hot, the pink cyclist was out of sight. In the distance I caught sight of Matt, climbing back onto his bike and moving on below the cliff.

The village appeared quite suddenly. It occupied a flattened spur which sat in the crook of an elbow in the gorge, one hundred metres above the river. The river was out of sight and earshot in the dark cleft below the few houses. Locked by its pitiless geography, the village had neither the dash of a passing stream nor a patch of living vegetation; it was entirely colourless.

On the approach to the village the track parted, one overgrown trail slanting up the scree slope, the other descending towards the roofs ahead. Neither Matt nor Chris were in sight. The unmistakable tracks of mountainbike tyres led along both tracks. I chose the upper one. The track was too steep to cycle, and I hitched the bike across my shoulders and began tramping upwards. Matt was standing in the shade of a gully fifty metres above me. Shouting, I asked where Chris was. Apparently he was in the village.

I plodded on upwards. By the time I reached the spot where Matt had been standing, he had gone. The track looked otherwise unused, with a few thin weeds, which the goats would normally have eaten, sprouting from occasional crevices. It was, however, the only obvious way on from the village. Was this Oulghazi, the village which Said had told us we would pass through? If it was, the upward course of the track made sense, since it would lead up to the pass he had told us to expect. Beyond the village, the gorge tightened its grip on the river. There were no pale veins of scuffed footpaths leading west from the village. The only way on appeared to be up.

Two hundred metres above the village, I caught up with Matt. He was standing, looking down on the flat roofs below. The houses seemed glued to the spur. We could see Chris now: he was pinsized, standing beside his bike on the bald patch at the top of the village, talking with two dark figures, attended by several children. We watched for several minutes, then Chris detached himself from the group and moved slowly towards the base of the cliff. Fifteen minutes later, he joined us. He was soaked by the exertion required to climb the shadeless gradient. When he reached us, he dropped his bicycle to the ground and said he'd have to put it in a lower gear next time he carried it up a steep hill.'' Matt looked at him, and asked what the villagers had said.

"That's Oulghazi all right. One of the guys is a relief English teacher. He's been there two years. He says you two are already on the path. I asked if this was the way to Anergui and he said it was 8 hours' walking. I said we'd manage that today, but he said it's not possible."

Chris paused for breath. I looked at my watch; it was 12 noon. He continued: "They say that Zaouia Ahansal is one day beyond Anergui."

If the people in Oulghazi were right, then we would arrive in Zaouia Ahansal two days after we had told the support crew to expect us. It seemed easier to believe that the people in Oulghazi were wrong than to accept the implications of spending 3½ days on a section of the route for which we had allowed only 1½.

Above us, the scree climbed steeply to the foot of the cliff, unbreachable but for a shadowed cleft far over to the left. We stepped up, making height fast on a track which climbed laboriously upwards in acute S bends which were buttressed against the slip of the scree by the remnants of retaining walls. It was an old route, which now looked little used. Three hundred metres below us, the square roofs of Oulghazi baked beneath the overhead sun. All the people had gone back indoors.

At the top of the scree, the path met the bottom of the cliff, hesitated for a moment, then squeezed between the ascending rocky shoulders of a darkened gully. The bicycles kept catching on the rock. We emerged into sunlight to find ourselves on a thin ridge which looked for a moment as if it would carry us to the top of the gorge wall. But at the last moment it swerved left to join a groove which slashed horizontally across the face of the adjacent cliff. Instead of continuing upwards, the track-builders had excavated one of the softer bands of rock strata to create a smooth-floored terrace with an overhanging roof which ran for two hundred metres above a fearsome drop. The roof was only five feet above the floor; by bending low over the handlebars we could just cycle along this open-sided cave-tunnel. At arm's reach to the left, the lip of the terrace ended in clear space.

"Got to film here!" cried Matt.

For forty-five minutes we rode to and fro before the bemused gaze of a boy who had climbed up from the village to graze his goats. Looking out from our slit in the cliff we could see a wild Arizonan panorama of canyon-slashed plateaux. It felt as if we were about to emerge onto the roof of the world. Oulghazi had completely disappeared. Matt and Chris dismantled the film equipment and divided it into three burdens. "A third of the film is used up," Matt announced, "We've got enough film left for about another 6 minutes. Which is hopefully OK since we can't expect anything more dramatic than this!"

We rode to the end of the terrace. The track ahead started to lose height. This was worrying: we had expected to emerge onto the plateau, then climb the pass. To be going down now, meant that we had yet to climb up to the *'Tizi'* – the pass separating Oulghazi from Anergui. The bikes rattled down a boulder slope. It was nearly too steep to ride, and the three of us became separated when we climbed off the bikes to lift them down rock steps. Climbing back on again, we slithered down a path thick with small rocks which spat and skidded beneath the tyres. The track plunged down towards the miniature flat roofs of two houses.

The weight of the rucksack pushing us forward made it harder to hold the handlebars on a true course between rocks which, when touched, snatched the front wheel from under the bicycle. The rear wheel, loaded with a pannier and locked by a permanently-applied brake, shuddered and crashed continuously. Just above the houses, I saw Chris fly over the handlebars.

He lay still, face down on a slope of large rocks, with the bicycle on top of him and one leg pushed crookedly through the frame. Matt and I unthreaded his leg and lifted away the bicycle. "You all right, Chris?"

Through strangled moans, gasps and grunts we heard: "It's . . . my . . . knee . . . my knee!" As an afterthought, he added: "Be . . . careful . . ."

We rolled Chris over, and with one of us lifting him under his arms, and the other cradling his legs, we swivelled him through 180 degrees, then unclipped and pulled off his rucksack. He sat up straight away, clutching each side of his knee joint. In the middle of his kneecap was a small red gash. The knee was already swelling. Supporting Chris' knee from underneath I asked him to move it. With some difficulty he swung his lower leg through 30 degrees. No sharp bits of bone or lumps of gristle suddenly broke the surface of his leg, and there were no crackling sounds coming from inside. "Well," I assured him, "there's nothing broken."

I looked at Matt and mouthed the word 'Film?'

"Chris," announced Matt, "How would you feel about us filming you?"

Chris did not look up, but said "All right," and continued to rock gently forwards and backwards over his injured leg. "Just going too fast. We simply cannot afford to ride over stuff like this", muttered Matt as he pulled the camera from Chris' rucksack. He seemed mildly angry. I handed over the film magazine and clapper board, and rummaged through the small pocket on the top of my rucksack, looking for the first aid kit. With water dropped onto a piece of bandage cut with Matt's Swiss Army knife, I swabbed the dust and grit from the area around the cut. In the background I could see Matt collecting bits of camera and running out the microphone cable. "OK Chris. Just hold the clapper-board will you?"

Chris detached a hand from his knee and accepted the clapperboard. Moving a stone beside Chris, Matt concealed the microphone and scurried away. Heaving the Aaton onto his shoulder, he bent to switch on the tape recorder and crept forward, dropping to one knee not far from Chris' face. "OK Chris, tape recorder's on!"

Chris looked up, his face contorted with pain. Matt shouted: "Right! Action! Chris, the clapperboard!"

Chris turned to the lens, raised the clapperboard, and let its arm drop with a sharp 'clack'. With commendable clarity he said "Shot 1, Take 14," then hid it behind his back. Matt zoomed; I swabbed. "Moans Chris, we need some moaning!" The camera ran for 15 seconds observing the scene before Matt asked "OK Chris, what happened?"

"I was coming down the hill, and the front wheel caught something and disappeared in front of me. I went over the handlebars and landed on my knee, on this sharp rock. It feels as if the whole mountainside has passed through it." The cut on his knee was not deep, but the impact must have badly bruised the cartilage behind the kneecap. It had puffed up with fluid. "It's the same knee I injured before," muttered Chris.

"Cut!"

The first consideration was to find some shelter. Three hundred metres further down the mountain were two houses.

"Chris, can you make it down to the houses?"

"I suppose so."

Matt led the way, carrying two rucksacks, a bicycle and supporting Chris with his spare arm. I followed, wearing my own pack, a bicycle balanced round my neck, and Chris' bike in my hands. It was a slow descent. By the time we reached the levelling in the track near the houses, one and a half hours had elapsed since the accident. We stopped near a small tree. A man came out of the nearest house and asked if we would like any tea. Ten minutes later he returned with a tall pot and three small glasses on a tray. He left the tray with us and returned to his house.

"Chris, d'you think you can walk?"

"I reckon so. Slowly. It would be easier if I could ride the bike. It's the weight on my knee that's killing me!"

"We can't ride here. It's too rocky."

"Well, I'll walk then."

"All right. Next thing is, do we go on, or go back? If we go on, we've probably got at least another day's travelling, maybe two, before we meet the road again. If we go back to Imilchil, the Land Rovers will have already left. We've no way of letting them know what's happened. We know there's no phone in Imilchil because Alan tried to find one."

"We'll have to go on."

"Well, look, let's go on and see how we do in the last couple of hours of daylight today. We know these two houses are here if we have to come back, but we're bound to run into another hamlet or shepherd's home."

The man who had provided the tea refused to accept any money. We removed the pannier from Chris' bike. Matt tied the pannier onto the top of his own rucksack. I took Chris' rucksack and tied it to the top of my own. Matt grinned at Chris, and added, "Your bike'll do as a rolling crutch."

Gently, we stepped on towards the softening sun. It was going to be a beautiful evening.

From the site of the accident we walked for just over two hours. The track climbed gently back up the right-hand side of the gorge. Chris limped, in silence. As we gained height, the track moved through stands of stunted pine; trees with thick trunks of rough, splintered wood and top-knots of spiny foliage. After the denuded views of the past five days the trees seemed chummy. We were level with the top of the gorge walls on the far side of the valley; they glowed with the warmth of Thames valley brick. We saw no-one, nor any sign of habitation. At 4pm we paused, and agreed to stop at the next house or shelter we came to.

On cue, and with about thirty minutes till darkness, the roofs of two houses crept into view on the mountainside below the track. Ahead of us the track curved across a dry field, then dropped out of sight. The temptation to press on a bit further; to notch up a few more valuable kilometres, was too much to resist. While Chris and I waited, Matt pedalled across the field to see what lay round the corner. Maybe there would be a village.

While we rested, four girls ran up from the houses, shrieking hysterically. Leaning on his bike, Chris joked with them in scraps of Arabic. The girls wanted us to come down to the houses. Matt returned with the information that the track disappeared into a freezing chasm. "It doesn't look very appealing," he said. "We're better off staying up here for the night."

The tallest of the girls wore a patterned green cotton *djellabah* tied at the waist; she had an odd flattening across the bridge of her nose and a foot that was so twisted that she could only walk by swinging her leg in swift semicircles. The girl led us past a lone tree and through the gap between the two houses. The houses were built side by side, looking out across the valley, and had been constructed with their backs into the mountainside so that they only had a front wall, and two tapering side walls. You could walk straight down the mountainside and onto the roofs. The walls were made of stone picked from the slopes, and the earth roofs were trampled by goats and sheep; if it were not for their man-made symmetry, the houses would have blended invisibly into the valley-side. In front of each house was a scrappy patch of earth hemmed in by a tangle of thorns. We turned towards the house closest to the sun. A few chickens scattered as we passed through an opening in the thorns. The ground was speckled with fresh wood-chippings. The girl pulled aside a blanket and led us through the low door.

It was so dark inside that at first we hovered at the doorway, unsure of which way to go. The room smelled of smoke. As we blinked in the gloom, the perimeter of the room slowly began to emerge. It was about six metres by three metres, with a rug occupying the right-hand half. The girl ushered us to the rug and left the room. Chris lowered himself painfully. With our feet sticking beyond the edge of the rug, we pulled off our boots and contracted into our indoor-resting positions; backs against the stone wall; cross-legged; straight-legged; knees-to-chin. Nothing in this world could have matched the flood of appreciation we felt stepping from the trail into the sanctuary of a stranger's home.

Through one of the two small windows on the front wall slanted a shaft of sunlight, trapping in its beam the suspended motes of seed and straw and dung and earth; the dust of a day's labour. While the day lay down, we rested numbly, staring ahead; occasionally shifting to ease an aching limb. Chris kneaded his leg. Just before the light disappeared altogether, a man emerged through the blanket at the doorway. He was wearing a white turban and pale *djellabah.* He shook our hands; his hand felt as dry as the bark of a tree: *"Salaam aleikoom".*

"*Aleikoom salaam!*"

He smiled. Our host was called Mohammed Hadri. The girl was his daughter. Within a few minutes his brother, who looked alarmingly like Bruce Forsyth, arrived. Mohammed's two sons, Abdul and Said, came into the room and greeted us, but like their sister, they did not stay.

It was good to be indoors. Matt leant forward and handed Mohammed 100 dirhams to cover the costs of our stay. Mohammed tucked the worn brown notes inside his *djellabah.* The tea-making increased the smoke-emission from the stove so much that the crack of light around the doorway was extinguished. Darkness came within a few minutes. Mohammed lit the paraffin lamp and placed it on the floor in front of the rug.

We were in a place which sounded like 'Agrrnooweera' a woodcutter's camp. We told the story of Chris' accident, to cluckings from Mohammed and 'Bruce'. Mohammed gave us the roll-call of places between his house and Zaouia Ahansal: "Agrrnooweera! . . ." he said, then inclined his flattened hand like a launching ramp; "Anergui! . . . (another launching ramp) . . . Tiroogirrt! . . . Zaouia Ahansal!"

"Sounds like quite a hike."

I pulled the map from the rucksack I was leaning against. "And two more passes to go over before Z.A." Matt was scrutinising our hopeless map by the light of the miniature torch. "How's the knee, Chris?"

"It's OK. Let's see what it's doing in the morning. At the moment it's seizing up."

Chris was sitting in the corner. From the oil-drum stove beside the door, Mohammed drew off a teapot's worth of boiling water. Silence returned, each of us pursuing private thoughts. We were in a mild predicament: the immediate post-accident crisis was resolved by finding shelter; now we had to decide what to do about the remainder of the journey. If Chris could not move in the morning, Matt and I would have to leave him at Agrrnooweera and press on to Zaouia Ahansal and arrange a rescue-party. If he could move, we would continue west as fast as his leg allowed, an option which would jeopardise our chances of reaching the Atlantic on time. It was obvious that it was more sensible to continue on towards Zaouia Ahansal – even if it meant crossing two more passes – than to return to Imilchil; the support crew was now in front of us and there was nothing at Imilchil to help us. Moreover, to turn back now, would be to end all dreams of a continuous bicycle journey from the Sahara to the sea; we would never be able to regain the lost time. What, I wondered, was Chris thinking?

For the present, the tea-making ritual provided an absorbing distraction. From a small, decorated wooden box divided into a grid of nine compartments, Mohammed lifted five glasses and arranged them in a row. Beside the main stove, on top of which was a kettle of boiling water, stood a small three-legged brazier filled with glowing embers scraped from the bed of the adjacent fire. The teapot containing the leaves and water rested on top of the brazier. After about ten minutes, Mohammed lifted the pot and dropped into it two rocks of sugar which he had smashed with a hammer from a solid white cone. He filled one of the glasses, then a second. He then tipped the two glasses back into the teapot and poured an inch of tea into a third glass, which he sipped. Lifting the lid off the teapot, he added another, smaller, rock of sugar, then filled all the glasses.

Later, much later, the five of us sat around a large dish of steaming *couscous* and mutton, then unrolled our sleeping bags and fell asleep on the rug. At intervals through the night, more wood was stuffed into the stove.

We woke on Day Six to fresh clouds of woodsmoke as Mohammed stoked the stove. Coughing, Matt and I stumbled sockless for the door. The sun had yet to climb over the ridge behind the house and the air was milky and frost hard. Inside the house, Chris was coughing away a night of smoke. Mohammed brought bread and olive oil, which we washed down with glasses of sweet tea. Breakfasts are always quick. "How's the knee, Chris?"

Chris rolled up his trousers. Matt and I peered; a mixture of curiosity and concern. Chris' knee was soft and puffy. "I'll try it," he said, "see how it goes."

We drained our glasses for the last time. Mohammed picked up a small skin bag and slung it over one shoulder. We pulled on our boots, picked up our rucksacks and followed him outside. As we stepped out, the sun exploded over the ridge behind the house. We said our farewells to Mohammed's family and pulled our bicycles from the wall of his house. Following Mohammed, we pushed the bikes back up to the main trail and walked gently west. Behind us, Chris was hobbling beside his bicycle, his jaw locked with discomfort. He was carrying his own rucksack, but we had fixed his pannier to the rear of my bicycle.

When we reached the brink of the chasm down which Matt had peered the previous evening, Mohammed pointed downwards and said, "Anergui!" Then he turned and walked back home. Matt and I waited, kicking our feet against the cold. "How's it going, Chris?"

Chris did not reply. Slowly, we descended the chasm. It was sunless and chilly and filled with the twisted trunks of old stunted pines. The path zig-zagged steeply down to meet a dried streambed. The large, bleached stones gave no hint of which way the stream ran, but there was some dung lying a few metres to the right. We turned right. Twenty minutes later a track veered out of the riverbed and climbed back up through the trees. It had to be our track.

It took half an hour to reach the top. Chris carried his bicycle cyclo-cross style, with the frame resting on one shoulder, front wheel down, a technique which allowed the hand of the other arm to prevent the handlebars from swinging. Matt and I had opted for the less conventional method of lifting the bike over the head then gently lowering it so that the down-tube rested across both shoulders. This technique spread the weight of the bike across the shoulders equally, but had the serious disadvantage that a slip whilst carrying the bike would drive the sharp teeth of the front chainring deep into the carrier's neck.

At the top of the climb we met a man with a cream turban and a sack round his shoulders. He was carrying a small, battered metal water container the shape of a milk-churn. We asked: "Which way to Imilchil?" The man pointed back the way we had come. "Which way to Oulghazi?" The man pointed in the same direction. Having established his accuracy with two directions we could verify, we then tackled him on the 'big one': "Which way to Anergui?"

The man pointed obliquely down the mountainside to the valley we had just left. We thanked him. "Well, that's just *brilliant!*" muttered Chris.

I pointed to three different parts of the horizon and asked: "Anergui?"

The man selected the middle option, a nick in the distant, snow-dusted mountains, and nodded: "Anergui!"

"*Tizi?*"

He inclined his hand and nodded again: "*Tizi!*"

I turned to the other two: "Looks as if we have to go over that col with the snow, which must be the pass Mohammed told us about. Unfortunately it also looks as if we shouldn't have climbed up here from the stream; this man says the route follows the valley."

Matt was already walking away; Chris was looking displeased. Following Matt, the two of us started cutting across the rocks and earth of the mountainside, aiming to cut off a corner rather than retrace our steps to the stream. Chris soon opted for a lower route. I stopped and got out the compass from the pocket of my salopettes. The col that we were now aiming for lay south-west; close enough to our general heading of west.

Catching up with Matt I passed two shepherd boys. One of them was knitting a tube of blue-green wool onto four copper rods about 5 inches long. "A sock?" I asked, pointing at my own royal blue Lakeland stocking. "Waha!" he laughed, then explained by lifting his trouser leg and pointing at a bare foot slotted loosely into a huge plastic shoe. The boy asked where I was going. I told him Anergui, and he shook his head, pointing down into the gorge.

Matt had disappeared. I climbed down a horrible cascade of tilting rock. Near the bottom I heard the crunch of falling rock, and saw Chris lifting his bicycle down through the scrub. "All right?" I yelled.

"Would've been better if we hadn't wasted time climbing up here."

Just before reaching the level ground of the gorge floor, Chris slipped. All his weight shifted to his injured leg and he sagged on to the rocks. He sat beneath his bike for a few moments to catch his breath, then slowly got to his feet and continued downwards.

The three of us met again in the mean defile that marked the final narrowing of the gorge-funnel. A thin, freezing wind barrelled down the defile, but there were signs on the riverbed that this was a regularly-used routeway: driftwood sticks broken by hooves; a trough of footprints through a bank of soft gravel; a footstep in a patch of snow. Parts of the bed of the defile had been scoured clean by spring torrents, and in dips on the smooth, bare rock, lay transparent sheets of water-ice. They were nearly invisible. The consequences of being flipped upside down on one of these while wearing a bike round your neck, and a film camera on your back, hardly bore thinking about.

It was a long, steady, rhythmic plod, broken part way up for two-thirds of a Spanish 'Twix' bar each. The higher we climbed, the narrower became the defile. We scrambled up a number of waterfall steps on footholds which had been worn shiny by the passage of centuries of feet and water. Finally the defile widened into a broad V-shaped valley, its left, northerly slope pale with snow. There were no trees; just isolated clumps of heathery grass set in a cold desert of loose stone. After two false summits, we emerged onto the col. It was too cold to rest for more than a few minutes. We pushed on into the wind, to the brink of an enormous drop.

We leaned over the edge; it was very steep and the mountain had been cut away to reveal slightly tilted layers of strata. The harder, more prominent layers had collected a coat of snow, so that the mountain face beneath our feet was striped with white as though it had been swiped with a giant paintbrush. We looked over the edge, searching for the tell-tale zig-zags which would mark our escape route. But there were none. Then we could see it: much further down the mountain, and far over to the left beneath some crags, we could just make out the pale angles of a man-made track. Instead of zig-zagging up to meet us, the track had been etched into one of the rock bands, which ran from the foot of the crag right across the face of the mountain to meet our feet. From above, this wild 500-metre slipway was nearly invisible.

In the fast-freezing wind we folded ourselves over our ridiculous map and tried to ally the vague green and brown blotches on the paper with the topography around us. With generous allowances for the cartographer's imagination, it was just feasible to believe that the indistinct smear reaching down from the north, to touch the blue wriggle which was probably the Asif Melloul, was actually the mountain on which we now stood. If it was, then we were not even half way between Imilchil and Zaouia Ahansal; the adventure was getting a little out of hand. "This is where we are!" I announced, with my fingertip on an area of at least 100 square kilometres. "Anergui's got to be down in this valley."

We stepped down the rocky notch onto the start of the slipway. For the first time that day, we climbed onto the bikes. One by one, each of us let go of our brake levers and flew like arrows, straight across the face of the mountain, helped by gravity and a little bit of madness. Beyond the slipway we joined a tall stack of zig-zags and jigged on down, kicking the bikes' tails through bend after bend; in twenty manic minutes we tore down a slope which would have taken us two hours to climb.

At the bottom there was a warm, sunlit, rocky cleft. I hauled on the brakes and spreadeagled myself on the grit of the trail. Ten minutes later Matt appeared. "Where's Chris?"

"Coming slowly. He's fine."

We rode the last hour together, freewheeling safely down towards the trees of the valley bottom. The track twisted and turned through stream gullies then eased onto the shingle floor of a wide riverbed. Behind us, impossibly high and far away, was the vast orange cliff down which we had just plummetted. On the streambed we started to see signs of life: a ruined building, some women in the distance; then a man and wife, balanced on a mule. They eyed us incredulously. We rolled straight from the riverbed onto a vast dust-patch on the edge of a village: "Anergui?"

"Got to be."

"Let's see if we can buy some food. We'll stop here for long enough to eat, then press on for Z.A. We may still have a chance of getting there today."

The village looked deserted. We pedalled a lap of the dust-patch. A man in a brown and cream striped *djellabah* appeared. He had a neat, manicured moustache. We asked him where the shops were. He led us through a gateway into a rectangular compound. Instead of being chock-full of traders, mules and piles of produce, the *souk* was absolutely empty. "What day is it?" asked Matt.

"Thursday. No, Friday."

"Friday! That's the Moslem day of rest. No shops open on Fridays."

It was another mishap to add to the ever increasing pile: the accident; our useless map; our massive underestimation of the difficulties of the route. Now we had arrived at the only village between Imilchil and Zaouia Ahansal which had shops, on closing day.

The man led us across the depressingly bare compound towards one of the shuttered shop-fronts. Unlike the 70 or so blank shutters which surrounded it, this one was half-ajar, propped open by a dead branch. We bent underneath the wooden flap and looked inside. The shopkeeper – a very old man – was sitting cross-legged on a shelf surrounded by small, dusty pyramids of soap, tins of milk powder, torch batteries, plaits of string and a hundred other categories of hardware. We stared, silently, probing with our eyes for something – anything – that looked edible. We bought three cans of sardines, a packet of Moroccan biscuits and four small tins of condensed milk. The shopkeeper had more sardines and milk, but refused to sell them, presumably because they would be needed by other villagers.

Our guide led us out of the *souk* and down the street to a house whose main door was all but obscured by a brushwood sun and dust screen. Inside, his wife, a smiling woman dressed in a pretty print skirt and strawberry cardigan, with a red scarf tied close round her forehead and chin, waved us to the rug spread against the wall. A huge metal key – the kind used to open castle doors in Crusader films – was produced. It was the family's sardine-can opener; it ripped off the metal lids as though they were cardboard.

The man's wife tipped all our sardines into an enamel bowl, and brought out a piece of the morning's bread. The children who had been quietly filtering into the room since our arrival, giggled continuously as our tea-glasses were filled.

The conversation drifted around to the interesting question of our location. This was, said our host, Anergui. Grins all round. He asked where we were going. 'Zaouia Ahansal,' said Matt. "La, la," said our host; Zaouia Ahansal was too far he added. We were much better to ride north from Anergui to Tassemit on the *piste,* then leave the mountains and return south again on another *piste* to Zaouia Ahansal. It was, he said, a loop of some 75 kilometres – all of it on jeep-tracks. It was the first time that we realised that Anergui was linked to the outside world by a motorable track. Our host could not understand our insistence that we had to travel to Zaouia Ahansal by the direct route, over the mountains. It was a day's journey, he said. It was already 3pm.

More consternation was caused when we asked which track we should take from Anergui. "It's too late, too late!" our host said as he tapped his watch. We should stay the night with his family, and then leave early the next morning. "No, no!" we insisted, "We must leave now." We felt incapable of explaining the rationale behind our turning down a sensible offer of accommodation in the comfortable home of a Berber family in favour of an arduous trek over the mountains just to keep a film schedule dictated by a man in a suit in America.

Patiently, our host drew with his finger on the floor a map of our route between Anergui and Zaouia Ahansal. In five kilometres, he indicated, we would have to climb steeply and cross a flat-topped mountain. We tried to leave some money for the bread and tea, but it was rejected with a dismissive wave of the hand and much good-natured laughter. I took a photograph of the family lined up against the outside wall of their home, the man holding my bike, the mother waving both arms in the air, Chris and Matt in the centre.

We rode like crazy; we had to: now there were only four hours till dark. Chris found that the fluid in his knee was preventing it from bending fully and that each time he stopped pedalling for more than five minutes, the knee seized up. The *piste* was wide enough to drive a jeep carefully, and it followed the edge of a broad valley on the floor of which were hamlets and empty winter fields. In one village, a horde of children all but blocked the way. As I drew level, they shouted 'Ahansal' and shrieked with laughter.

At the last village in the valley, the track narrowed to foot-width and dived down to cross three fields. Then it clambered across a cantilevered bridge made from tree-trunks and flat stones. On the far side of the bridge, a young boy joined us, running beside the speeding bikes calling *"stylo!"* and *"l'argent!"*. The track continued with the river, but now the valley had turned into a gorge, and we were forced off the earthen banks onto the stones of the riverbed.

The boy led the way. Now and again, he dropped back to lean on the pannier of one of our bikes, pushing it up the hill. I pulled from my pocket the tiny tape-recorder which I had been using to keep notes:

"20 January . . . I'm recording this at 5.24 on Day 6. We must have made 1,000 feet in the last hour. I can look backwards above the stunted trees to an extraordinary sight: the facing gorge walls are pink, mountains piled up beyond. The gorge walls are layered with horizontal trees. The trees run round the walls in lines separated by 100 or 200 feet. The lines of trees look only 10 feet thick. There are as many as 20 lines on each gorge wall . . .

"It's quite a misty evening. Snow fell last night on the mountaintops. Don't know how high we are; maybe 6,000 feet, 5,000 feet. Still climbing . . ."

Below me, out of sight through the trees, I could occasionally hear snatches of conversation as Chris and Matt shared the hill.

"The little boy has been with us since the last village we went through, four kilometres after Anergui. He was running with us when we were cycling fast along the gorge floor. We were trying to fend him off thinking that he wanted to be a guide. Now it turns out that he was coming our way anyway, and that he lives up here on the gorge side . . ."

The boy disappeared. One moment he was there, pushing on the back of my bike. Then he was gone.

"Day 6. 5.31 in the afternoon. We've been climbing for 1¼ hours. Incredibly beautiful evening. Not a breath of wind. There's a bird crying in the trees. Walking through sparse pines that have been hacked and sawn for firewood; ravaged by weather and man. Above and to the left is a gorge wall which is not as steep as the rest; there's snow sticking to it. Above our heads, rising 300 vertical feet, there is a sheer rock face. To the right is a patch of blue sky and feathery clouds towards which we're heading, on a path zig-zagging through enormous boulders. Rocky underfoot; big tree roots; steep climbing; gentle plod. I'm still carrying Chris' pannier; I've drunk all my water. One pint. Probably going to climb above the tree line in the next 500 feet. Passed a woman in a blue kind of sari, baby tied on her back in a strip of cloth; topknot of hair, heading down to Anergui before dark. Mule dung on path. Reassuring. Quite a mist . . .

"5.45 Day 6 . . . we've just reached the foot of the rock wall and we're traversing round on a ledge about 5 feet wide which is one of the layers of rock which is jutting out. Gorge rearing above us, parts of it overhanging. The track is slightly descending, which isn't very pleasant since we've only just laboured up such a climb. Looking for somewhere to sleep . . .

". . . Unfortunately we have no matches. Or lighter. Which is a serious mistake. There are plenty of rock overhangs around, corners to make a shelter, stacks of dead wood. We could have been roasting warm all night if we'd got some matches. I can't imagine how I managed to leave the lighter behind.

"5.52 Day 6 . . . we have just crept through the notch in the head of the gorge, like a doorway to the hidden world of the plateau. Where's the path . . . ?

"5.59 Day 6 . . . Light fading rapidly. We're on a compass bearing heading roughly south, slightly east of south. Only slightly.

"6pm Day 6 . . . Having thought that we were merely going to contour round the gorge, we're now zig-zagging up the back wall of it. So we're already 100 feet above the notch we came through.

"6.21 Day 6 . . . And we have crested a high point about half an hour after sunset. Full moon. We're trying to keep up with a man and his wife and a little baby and a mule, who say there's somewhere to sleep an hour from wherever we are. But they're probably going to get a bit ahead of us. There's a camp fire on the mountainside opposite. Or a goat-driving fire. And dogs . . .

CHRIS . . .! SHOUT IF YOU'RE OK . . . CHRIS . . .!"

"Did you hear anything, Matt?"

"No."

"I'll shout again . . . CHRIS! . . ."

My voice drifted into the night. There was no answering sound. Matt and I stood silently on the path. We waited for ten minutes till we saw the pale, swaying form of Chris move slowly towards us. "OK?" we asked.

"How about stopping soon?"

"Let's go on a bit. It's a good night for walking. We're doing well."

Following in each other's footsteps, we walked for another hour. Although the moon was bright, it was very difficult to see the details of the track. For Chris, trying to protect his knee from slips and trips, it was both tiring and excruciatingly painful. Above us to the right, we passed the outline of a building, and for a moment thought we might have found shelter, but our shouts were met by the massed howling of a pack of dogs.

By a snow bank we stopped and scraped ice-crystals into our water bottles. We came to a broad valley. There was a huge mound of stones, and a low concrete wall. We circled the wall, climbed the mound of stones. The mound was hollow; steps led down to a shiny black mirror. It was a frozen well. Beside the wall there was just room for three people to lie down. The wall would offer token shelter from the wind. It was a miserable place.

"I'm going on up the track for ten minutes."

I walked up a gently-rising desert of stones trying to work out whether it was better to press on in the moonlight or stop and sleep. The path, which had been well-defined lower on the mountain, was now hardly visible. It was too dark to notice if the track split. Maybe the track had already split. Maybe we had spent the last hour walking in the wrong direction. It was even possible that in the dark we would walk over the edge of a cliff, and even if we did manage to cross the plateau without losing our way, we would never manage a safe descent off the plateau to the gorge holding Zaouia Ahansal. All these gorges seemed to have vertical walls. Much better to stop and rest now, then start moving again at first light. By the time I reached the black tree-stains which I had seen from the well, the idea of a prompt bivouac had gained in appeal. On the side of the valley there were a few, solitary, enormous trees. Each was about 50 paces from the next. I moved from one to the other, till I found a tree with branches which dipped low over a carpet of soft pine needles. The trunk was so fat that it would protect us a little from any night wind. I walked back to the well to tell Matt and Chris.

We spread three silver foil blankets on the ground below the tree and slithered fully-clothed into our sleeping bags. I pulled mittens over my feet and jammed my trilby over a green down balaclava which I had found fifteen years earlier on the slopes of Cader Idris. "What's for dinner, Matt?"

In front of Matt's sleeping bag, we piled any scraps of food we still had. It looked like a feast: 1 Mars Bar, 2 'Snickers' bars, 1 wholefood fruit bar, 5 incredibly small tangerines, 1 packet of Moroccan biscuits, 1 small tin of condensed milk and three-quarters of one of Jeremy's healthfood carob bars. Matt divided the bars into precise thirds; we kept the carob for the morning. Lack of water was a problem: the ice we had collected earlier still rattled undrinkably in the water bottles. Matt stuffed his frozen bottle down into his crutch, hoping it would melt by morning. So long as it did not snow in the night, we would be fine.

There was ice on the sleeping bags in the morning. Looking around, it was interesting to see where we were: our bivouac site hardly matched the mental landscape which we had created in the black of night.

We were lying under a congenial pine on the edge of a broad, sloping valley bordered by tree-covered hills. Away to the east – the direction from which we had come – there were distant mountains. To the west, our valley sloped progressively upwards until it met the rim of surrounding hills. When the sun finally burst over the horizon, it could not reach our bags. The tree was in the way. I fished in my rucksack: "Anyone want any carob?"

"No thanks, it'll spoil my breakfast", grinned Chris.

Matt sat up and looked around. He was wearing a navy-blue woollen hat pulled down over his ears and had several days' growth of beard: "We must film this. It'll make a great bivouac sequence."

With clumsy, gloved hands, we pulled out the various camera parts from the rucksacks. "OK, three shots . . . waking up, and then sitting up and looking around, then a long shot of the plateau." Matt would be director and soundman; Chris the cameraman; I would be slumberer. It was a good deal.

While Matt unreeled the microphone cable, Chris hobbled around in the sun with the Aaton perched on his left shoulder, experimenting with angles. "It's not going to work; we need the bivouac site ten feet to the left, where it's in the sun."

Outside the sleeping bag, it was cold enough to stiffen every joint. Matt and I dragged the site ten feet east and rearranged the bikes. I squirmed back inside my sleeping bag; "How's it look now?"

"Great, terrific. Right, go back to sleep. Clapperboard Matt! . . . OK, rolling . . ."

"Action!"

I lay still, then opened my eyes, then grunted. "Great. OK. Shot 2 . . . sitting up."

It was an hour after sunrise by the time we had re-packed the camera and jammed our sleeping bags back into the rucksacks. Our panniers were empty; we were wearing every piece of clothing we had. From the tree, we cut across the valley to join the line of the track which had passed the well. But the track seemed to have petered out. Somewhere back down the valley, in the dark of the previous night, there must have been a fork. We had taken the wrong one. On a westerly compass bearing we headed for the tree-clad hill bordering the valley. At the top, there were two houses. From one of them came an old lady, stooped and ill, mucus shining on her thin, lined, parchment face. She was joined by another woman from the adjacent house. The second woman was heavily pregnant, and asked us for medicine. We had no medicines. Neither of them appeared to have heard of Zaouia Ahansal.

Still on the compass bearing, we descended the far side of the hill, which had now taken the shape of a ridge running down from a high plateau to the north-west. At the bottom, there was a level, grass-floored valley about 100 metres wide. We hopped on the bikes.

"I've got a puncture," Matt yelled.

While Matt inserted the spare inner tube into his back tyre, I sat on the grass, in the sun, mending the punctured tube. We were as completely lost as it was possible to be; we had no food and no water (the two women had told us that they had no water), our map was no help and we had lost the track. Yet everything was still under control: Chris was making good progress, and if we kept heading west we would ultimately hit the brink of the gorge running north from Zaouia Ahansal. All we would then have to do would be to travel north or south along the lip of the gorge until we found a breach safe enough to descend. In the warmth of the sun, the rubber solution dried quickly.

We pedalled slowly up the grass of the valley. I felt unsettled by the two women: their difficult circumstances had suddenly put our frivolous game in a more realistic perspecitve.

The valley carried us up to a plateau of stones which ran west as far as the eye could see. At the beginning of the plateau we passed a lone shepherd: *"Labas!"* I greeted him.

"Labas."

"Imilchil?"

The shepherd pointed to the east.

"Anergui?"

He pointed east again. "Zaouia Ahansal?"

Without hesitating, the shepherd pointed along the track, westwards. *"Shokran, shokran.* Thank you."

"B 'slama. Goodbye*"*

"B 'slama."

It took us one and a half hours to carry the bicycles across the stone desert. There was no shade; in fact there was nothing growing at all. Directly overhead, the sun seemed to bore into the soul, prise apart the head. I felt cocky about the sun; between the three of us we had travelled across the Sahara, the Gobi, Arabia, the Mexican Plateau . . . Then I worried about being cocky, and two minutes later I was fearful of the sun. In places the trail was hardly visible; only where little patches of red grit had formed could we be sure that we had not strayed from the route. Mule droppings, the imprint of a shoe heel, a bent horseshoe worn as thin as a credit card were our reassuring signposts in a little-travelled wilderness. The trail twisted and turned over desiccated rock, dropping into gullies, but trending generally upwards. If it had snowed even a centimetre the previous night, we would have had to steer across the plateau by compass. The light was intense.

The sporadic narrative of our labours led to increasingly disjointed communications between the three of us. Each time the path narrowed or steepened, we caught up with each other and for a few minutes we would be dragged from personal reveries into sequels of conversations that had been running for hours. Over the days, Chris had been telling me by instalments the life story of his great grandfather, a private soldier with the Lancashire Fusiliers who had miraculously survived an extraordinary number of wars. J.J. Bradley (both his Christian names were James) served in Bombay, Karachi and Quetta before being shipped to Egypt to join Kitchener at the Battle of Omdurman and the Relief of Khartoum. He was wounded during the Boer War, and, at the start of the First World War, he was wounded again at Gallipoli. He then served in the trenches of Flanders and eventually died of old age in 1947. "Statistically . . ." concluded Chris as he lifted his bicycle onto his shoulder for the hundredth time, "it was amazing that he survived."

About two-thirds of the way across the stone desert we came to a cairn; it was on a high point; a slight incline in the wasteland of locked rubble. Old, crusty snow lay in the crevices. Ahead, the rock dropped away and we could see through the midday haze the profiles of mountains on the far side of a vast valley. Was that the gorge of Zaouia Ahansal?

The trail dropped and curved, skirting a distant precipice as if it could not pluck up the nerve to go near the edge. We came to a pocket of grass. There was a well. The water was filthy with animal muck. Not worth the risk. We were thirsty and lay on the grass. I was getting a little concerned about the water situation; we had drunk only one pint of water each since leaving Anergui, 22 hours ago. And we still had to descend the gorge walls to Zaouia Ahansal. The lack of food was just a discomfort; we'd had a couple of chocolate bars and tangerines each the night before, and each of us had a good stone or two of fat to burn yet.

We rested at the well for three minutes. The track was now clear to follow, and it began to descend more steeply over small crags towards the top of the tree line. Three days of carrying the bicycles was by now beginning to have a deleterious effect on our morale; initially it had been mildly amusing to see three state-of-the-art mountainbikes being carried up and down gorges but now it was nothing more than a pain in the back.

With each downhill step, the metal tubes of the bicycle pressed onto the bruised flesh of our shoulders, while the weight of the bicycle and the luggage centred so high meant that even a slightly misplaced foot threatened to tip us out of balance. These discomforts were compounded by the facts that we did not really know where we were, how much further it was to Zaouia Ahansal, and that we might arrive at the edge of the plateau and not be able to find a way down the cliffs to the village below. Limping along at the rear on a knee like a melon with a bite in one side, Chris had an extra worry: would anyone in the Land Rover remember to tune into the Saturday evening BBC World Service and note the Bolton Wanderers score?

"I'll be sick if they don't," he winced.

Forty-five minutes after leaving the well we spotted the roof of a house settled into the rock and pine of the mountainside. As we climbed down, we saw there were three houses. They were all brand new, built with Inca-like precision using stone blocks hewn from the plateau. The houses had thick roofs made from tree trunks and earth. The first two houses were empty. Playing in the dust outside the third house were two children who burst into tears and ran indoors when they saw us. A smiling woman stepped out into the sunlight. She had a blue tattoo on her chin: *"Salaam aleikoom . . ."* She drew me towards the door of her home.

The house had a single room with a rug against the long back wall. The lower stones of the back wall had been rubbed and polished by resting, sweaty backs. From a crude wooden chest at the end of the room nearest the door, the woman fetched some bread, and sugar. The tea was already hot. We gave her 20 dirhams.

While we savoured, sip by sip, the first glass of tea, the woman flipped open a small mat and knelt facing east, silently mouthing her noon-day prayers. Then she broke a handful of eggs into an enamel bowl, stirred in a dollop of water, and tipped the mixture into a pan of hissing olive oil. We ate the eggs from the pan, with the bread, appreciative of her simple dignity and unquestioning welcome.

We asked the woman how far it was to Zaouia Ahansal. She said two hours, maybe three. We asked her which way we should go; she took us out into the sun and pointed to a thin track curving away through the trees; then she asked if we would like her to send her son with us as a guide. "No," we said, thanking her; the track looked clear enough.

Shortly after leaving the woman's house, the trail divided into two, one track disappearing uphill, the other descending to the bed of a ravine. We descended. Not for the first time, we were about to be led astray. Carrying the bicycles along the clean stones of the ravine, we became increasingly uneasy as the blank walls began to close in and shut out the sun. The ravine ended in a vast picture window through which we gazed to a view that had preoccupied us for three days.

Far, far below, and cooking in the midday heat haze, were the scrubby levels of the valley which – we hoped – would lead us to Zaouia Ahansal. The ravine ended in a ten-metre drop. By climbing up onto a ledge, it was possible to skirt the drop. But the ledge merely ran horizontally out of the ravine mouth and onto the face of the gorge itself, where it tapered into thin air. Unaccountably there was a plastic jerrycan full of water, with some old, frayed rope around the handle, standing in the centre of the ledge. We were clearly on a route to somewhere. We stood with our toes sticking over the edge, looking down through 60 metres of warm, rising air, to the top of a steep cone of scree. It was a spectacularly exposed situation, with no apparent way off. There were still 80 feet of film left. We re-enacted our arrival at the gorge face, and simulated part of the descent by filming a bike being lifted down onto the ledge and then being pedalled towards the camera above the fearsome drop. Matt was excited: "Nobody will believe this when they see the rushes." (He was right; they didn't.)

The film stock ran out after five shots. Matt was beside himself with anguish: "All this way to find a location like this and we run out of film? I can't bear it! There's no way the First Unit will climb up to a spot like this."

By the time we had disassembled the camera, the sun had slid out of sight, leaving our corner of the gorge in chilling shade. As we were packing our rucksacks a small figure came into sight on the far side of the ravine mouth. We watched the girl walk along a ledge several layers below our own, which seemed to cut right across the face of the opposite cliff. Presumably she was coming back for the jerrycan. Then she disappeared among some huge fallen boulders. Passing the bicycles to one another we climbed down from our ledge onto the floor of the ravine, and then up a few metres to the girl's ledge. The ledge took the form of a huge gallery, wide enough to drive a car and roofed by the overhanging cliff. We walked between waist-high boulders across the face of the cliff. In places where the way ahead was confined to a narrow squeeze, the rocks underfoot had been polished by hundreds – thousands – of feet. Like the last ledge, this one tapered into the cliff, leaving no option but to climb downwards. We were still 50 metres above the top of the scree slope, but there was a regularly used rock-ladder: footholds had been cleared of loose stones, and, above a vertical piece of cliff, two tree-branches formed a bridge over a section of cliff that had avalanched away.

As I waited while Chris picked his way across the logs, I looked down. The scree below was now speckled with goats. The goats were milling about a bush which appeared to be moving, as if it had legs. We met the bush at the bottom of the cliff. *"Labas,"* said a voice from deep inside its foliage. As Chris and I picked our way down a series of off-camber ledges strewn with stones which shot out from under our boots, the bush began the rock-climb up the face of the gorge.

Matt had disappeared from sight, charging ahead along a narrow, shabby track which cut across the screes at the foot of the cliffs. Zaouai Ahansal – presumably – was down in the forests below us. Would the others have already spotted us in their binoculars? Maybe the First Unit were part way up the mountain, waiting to film the last metres of our mini-adventure? One thing was certain: we would be back with them in the next couple of hours. For the first time in 48 hours it was possible to start thinking again of the overall aim of the expedition; we had just 'lost' two days up on the plateau; now the challenge was to see whether we could regain the lost time.

The three of us became separated as first Matt, then I, took off in an undignified race for the valley. At a corner in the track, a spring bubbled from the rock. I lay face down, greedily sucking in icy draughts to quench my thirst, then stamped on down. In one place, a huge avalanche had torn away the track. Trees had been ripped from the earth and tossed like broken matchsticks 200 metres down the mountain. We were clearly not on the main track. Two villages as important as Anergui and Zaouia Ahansal would be linked by a maintained track – or at least one which bore the prints of passing men and beasts. Nobody had been down this track for months. I caught up with Matt: "This track doesn't look right . . ."

"No, I asked the man with the bush whether this went to Zaouia Ahansal and he said 'Yes'. And 'No'. So God knows where it goes."

The lower we got, the worse the track became. Every few metres fallen trees blocked the way. We soon left it and slithered straight down the mountainside. Matt and I met the track again at a stream gully. We had descended about 600 metres from the top of the gorge. We stood still, listening. There was no sound of anyone following us. Matt knelt and drank from the stream. We shouted for Chris. There was no reply. Leaving my bicycle with Matt, I started to climb back up the mountain.

I met Chris on a section of zig-zags in the old track. He was walking slowly, leaning over his bicycle. Impatiently, I said, "Here, let me take your bike."

"No, no, no," insisted Chris. "It's all right."

"Chris Bradley, stop being such a hero, we haven't much time." Chris looked completely exhausted, but held on to his bike.

The stream took us down gentler slopes where we could ride the bicycles again. I could almost smell the *tagine* which we were going to share that night; I was already rehearsing the tales which we had to tell: the accident; the bivouac; the woodcutter's cottage, the gorges . . .

We came out of the trees onto a dirt road.

"We've done it!"

"Where's Chris?"

We waited. A man in a small field between the road and the trees told Matt that Zaouia Ahansal was an hour away. Fifteen minutes later Chris emerged from the trees. "Streuth. That was horrible. Awful," he said, nevertheless managing a grin of relief.

I checked the compass for a final time; at last we were heading south. "It's all road now. Easy."

After one hour of furious pedalling there was still no sign of Zaouia Ahansal, or the Land Rovers. Instead, it got dark. For the half hour between sunset and moonrise it was difficult to see through the gloom. The prospect of spending another night out was too depressing to dwell upon. The road was following a narrow valley – a tributary of the Asif Melloul. There were several short, unpleasant climbs. By the light of the moon it was possible to see the pale band of the road ahead. A village came in to sight, shuttered for the night. As we rode past, sparks from a chimney hovered like fireflies above the road. It could not have been Zaouia Ahansal; the team would have left one of the Land Rovers on the road – or at least some marker – which we would recognise. Zaouia Ahansal was turning into a fantasy; an unreachable goal.

Some time after the village I saw a sudden flare of light as a pair of headlights swept the mountainside. The Land Rover? A tall tower slid by. Then I caught the smell of woodsmoke. At a bend in the road I stopped and peered over the edge. Down below the road the wall of a house was lit up by the flames of a large fire. I yodelled. A woman's voice rose up on the smoke. A black shape detached itself from the fire. I yodelled again. I started as a figure leapt out of the night and gripped me round the shoulders in a huge bear-hug; felt an unshaven chin kissing both my cheeks; heard the uninterpretable, frenzied greetings of a familiar voice. "Abedelilah!"

With Abedelilah's help I skidded down the dirt slope towards the fire. Faces turned; the light of the fire was suddenly dulled by the white blaze of a camera light. There were people up on the roof of the house, and the First Unit camera, mounted on its tripod. "We thought we'd lost you for good!" said Andy. "Where are the others?"

"Coming, coming. Just down the road!"

"Have a *chai*," said Jeremy as he stepped round the flames and handed me a white enamel mug of tea. I leant the bike against a low wall, and perched beside it, blinking at the familiar faces, too thirsty and tired to talk. Matt skidded to a halt in front of the fire, lifted his leg to dismount, and fell sideways to the ground. Jeremy disentangled the legs and bicycle. As Matt climbed back to his feet – his face darkened by a week-old beard – he said: "That just about sums up today, doesn't it?"

Someone handed him tea: "What a day! That was truly horrific. I honestly don't believe that anybody who gave us a direction today knew where he was. Impossible. Everybody said that it was two hours and it turned out to be ten."

Chris rolled into the light. He was leaning over the handlebars and wore a dazed expression: "So is this Zaouia Ahansal. Or is there more?"

"No, the village is a little bit down the road but . . ."

"How many kilometres?"

"I don't know. Two? One? . . ."

"Dear God . . ."

"It was never coming, was it . . ."

"No . . ."

Alan Ravenscroft appeared. He was wearing his baseball cap and thick down jacket. At his left elbow was the snout of an Aaton, sniffing for emotional breakdowns. Alan and the lens zoomed in on Matt : "You feel in good shape?"

"Yeah, I feel OK . . . my . . . you know, in terms of fitness, I feel absolutely fine . . . we've just got to sort our route out . . . get a good map. We've . . . we've carried the bikes for 99 per cent of that journey. Over 70 kilometres."

The camera swung round to Chris' stubbled face. He didn't need a prompt: "Good grief. When we were coming down the mountain I thought: that's one of the hardest days I've had; now we've just ridden for another three hours. Today's been one of the hardest weeks I've had! That wasn't fun. Oh . . . good grief. The people on top of the mountain have *no* idea where anything is. They sent us completely the wrong way. We've been miles away. I mean this last stretch of road has been . . . uh . . . hideous. There's no way we should have been this far out."

Chris looked around at the semi-circle of intent faces. For the first time in three days, he managed a laugh: "I'm knackered."

As the hubbub subsided we settled into a circle around the fire. There were logs and rocks to sit on, and important news to share: the accident; the hospitality of the Berbers; the scenery of the gorges; the bivouac; the 23 hours without food and water. And their news: the First Unit's filming plans; the adventures of the support crew in their drive round the mountains; Andy's foot-patrols to see if he could find us.

Chris sat, mostly silent, his injured leg out straight in front of him. His only consolation was that Bolton Wanderers had drawn 1-1 with Reading.

After the two teams parted at Imilchil four days earlier, Andy had towed Mohammed's broken diesel Land Rover for 12 hours through the mountains to Beni-Mellal, where they got it mended the following day. Mohammed had been extremely relieved, and the three vehicles had then made the 150-kilometre journey back through the mountains, on dirt roads, to reach the Zaouia Ahansal rendezvous on time.

The wall by which we were sitting belonged to the chief of Zaouia Ahansal – a man called Mccadam. The chief's house was on the outside of the village, and when the Land Rovers had arrived just before midnight on Day 5, this had been the door that Mohammed had knocked upon. Mccadam had provided the crews with enormous evening meals and had allowed them to use his house as a base while they waited for our arrival. Phil Millard, the Assistant Cameraman, had spent the entire day on the roof of the chief's house with the camera ready to roll at a moment's notice. Alan had wanted to capture, 'live', the moment of our arrival.

While we sat basking in the warmth of the fire, the chief returned from the village. Greetings were quickly followed by a delicious *tagine.* Afterwards, Jeremy led Matt and I down darkened mountain paths to the river, where we stripped off and slid beneath water so cold that it would have been iced over had it been still.

The room in the chief's house was insulated with thick, coarse carpets. It was a long, thin room; so full of sleeping bags that it wasn't possible to find foot-space between them. In the corner, under the yellow pool of a paraffin lamp, I tried to calculate what proportion of the ride we had covered. But it was too late. And it had been a long day.

I woke up at 5am, heart thudding. The pint mug of sweet coffee and huge wedge of Matt's mother's chocolate cake, which I'd munched in my sleeping bag five hours earlier, had condensed during the night into a cocktail of caffeine and blood-sugar so that brain and body broke surface like a man gasping for air. In those last, waking moments I saw all the spectres that are never allowed the light of day: failure, anger, remorse, competition . . . God, what a nightmare. I needed . . . caffeine . . . sugar . . . no, wrong order . . . a match to light the candle to find the contact lenses to see the latch to open the window to let some air into this room which smelt like . . . smelt like . . . a laundry-bag of old gymshoes.

I had to pull a heap of sticky cycle clothing from the window-sill before I could open the shutter. The scraping of wood on stone drowned for a moment the ebb and flow of snores, tongue rattles and nose-whistles coming from the ranks of sleeping bags. Fresh air flooded in; freezing air. It was still dark outside. I collected an armful of clothes and trod boot-less out into the courtyard. The courtyard was sloping with patches of straw on the ground. The door to the outside world was still barred. By the time I had successfully put on layers of salopettes, thermal jumpers, gloves, scarf, socks and then loosely laced my boots, dawn had spilled into the courtyard.

First: check the puncture. I pumped up the tyre on my bicycle; if it didn't deflate in the next 20 minutes, I'd leave it. I also checked all the gears and tightened the headset; the continuous hammering of the front wheel on rocks had loosened the steering bearings. Next: the maps. On the flat roof by the embers of the previous night's fire I spread the five 1:100,000 Carte du Maroc sheets. The fact that these detailed sheets were now part of the game gave cause for some reassurance; at Zaouia Ahansal, we had pedalled onto the map.

I ran my finger along the remainder of the route. We still had a huge distance to cover before reaching the Atlantic; at a rough estimate, we had covered about 450 kilometres. We had another 750 to go, and had used up just over one-third of our allotted 20 days. But the figures were distorted by the big distances which we had covered on the first three days of tarmac-riding; if we continued at the daily average which we had managed since leaving Imilchil, it would take us another 23 days to reach the coast. Somehow we had to double the distance we covered each day.

"Nick! Good morning! I expect you'd like a *chai*!" It was Jeremy, wearing his Peruvian blanket and carrying a huge, dented kettle. "Got to get this fire going. That'll warm things up. Mind if I have a gander at the map?"

Nobody else appeared to be up. With a mug of muesli holding down the windward corner of the map, I showed Jeremy what lay ahead. I broke the remainder of the journey into manageable chunks: from Zaouia Ahansal to the valley of Bou Guemez we appeared to have a jeep track of some 70 kilometres; from there westwards we had 130 kilometres of mule tracks over some big mountains until we touched a road again at Telouet. This section was, however on 'safe' tracks since Matt had used them 18 months earlier during his footsteps-of-Thesiger trek and he was sure that most of it was rideable. After Telouet, we had a difficult, partly-untracked section of mountains to cross to reach Mount Toubkal, which we planned to climb in order to reach the highest point of the Atlas range. From Toubkal to the coast we would use mule tracks if we had time, or roads if we did not.

If we could reach Bou Guemez in one day, then I reckoned we would still have a chance of completing a genuine high-level traverse of the High Atlas in the time available. It all depended on Chris.

As I was poring over the maps people began to emerge from the courtyard; making their way to the fireside; fetching bits of gear from the Land Rovers parked on the far side of the stream; fighting their way into knotted clothing. There was a hint of frost on the ground. Alan walked over to the maps: "How's it look?"

I described the remaining journey and explained the shortage of time. "It all depends . . ."

Alan seemed unperturbed: "Well, Chris is getting changed into his cycling gear now. He says he's going to see how the knee feels. Anyway, I'd like to go up on that hill (he pointed to a conical peak a kilometre away) and film some sequences that explain how you got lost on the plateau. It'll only take an hour. The crew are setting off now to climb the peak; you can come with the bikes as soon as you've finished here."

Chris came by, hobbling stiffly. Logic pointed towards Chris pulling out: on any trip of this kind, two people can move faster than three. There was another problem: Chris was not a natural madman. Matt had proved himself to be manically dedicated to the concept of a bike-walk-or-bust traverse of the entire mountain range; but for Chris the absurdity of carrying mountainbikes had for the last few days progressively undermined his enthusiasm for a high-level mule-track traverse. I suspected that he hankered after the bikable surfaces of the jeep-tracks lower down. But Chris was the one who would have to make the decision, and until he did so, the expedition would hang in the balance.

Mccadam carried the breakfast out to the fire. There was sweet tea, hot bread, scrolls of slightly cheesy butter and a pot of runny honey. I had just dipped my first piece of bread in the honey when Alan reappeared, hands jammed in pockets, clipboard under arm: "Gentlemen! I think that we should rock on. The crew are up on the hill."

"Give me a finger, Nick."

Chris was standing with his trousers round his ankles and a huge, white bandage covering the middle portion of his left leg. I held the end of the bandage while he fixed it tight with a safety pin. He straightened and took a tentative step.

"What's that feel like?"

He tried another step. His leg swung like a plank. Managing a simultaneous wince and grin he said: "Too tight."

Matt came past: "Looks terrific Chris; Alan'll love it!"

Chris was still fitting his pannier as Matt and I pedalled off towards the foot of the hill. We could see the occasional glint of reflected glass up on the peak. The crew would be getting hot, up there in the sun.

"What do you think about this? This business of re-creating incidents for Alan?" I fretted.

Matt was reassuring: "Don't worry. At least we haven't started making anything up yet."

At the foot of the hill, we climbed off the bikes and lifted them onto our shoulders. Matt continued: "You know this couldn't be better for Alan."

"What couldn't? Making us miss breakfast?"

"No. Chris' accident. Alan'll be hoping that Chris is going to drop out this morning; then he can film a heroic stand-down; Chris sacrificing his dream for the benefit of the team."

"How d'you think Chris is this morning?"

"Seems OK."

The peak took twenty minutes to climb. The top was no bigger than a tennis court and was scattered with waist-high bushes. On the crest of the peak overhanging Zaouia Ahansal there were the remains of an old wall. It was a superb defensive site commanding the end of the valley, with views across to the retaining walls of the gorge. Above those walls, but out of sight, was the plateau across which we had travelled from Imilchil; a secret, untouched world whose dramas were already being overshadowed by those we sensed were about to unfold. The crew – and Alan – were waiting for us: "Right chaps, we'd like you to come up through the bushes and step through this gap in the wall. Make it look as if you've just climbed onto a plateau."

Matt and I stood chatting quietly in the warming sun. Down below, we could see the slowly-moving figure of Chris bowed beneath a bicycle as he made his way up the rocks and scrub towards us.

"Action!"

We walked through the wall.

"Once again chaps please. Then we'll get Chris too."

We walked through the wall again. The second shot was a close up of one-quarter of each of the three bicycles' front wheels rolling into frame using the mountains and sky as a backdrop. For the shot to work, the wheels had to come to a halt in staggered formation, at two-second intervals. We tried it four times before the director called "Sod it. Cut!"

The third shot required us to position ourselves one above the other in a narrow cleft on the cliff beneath the prow of the peak and then pass the bicycles down the human chain. This would be the 'descending-the-gorge' shot. Above a not inconsiderable drop we straddled ourselves across the cliff and, with much (authentic) grunting, and screeching of metal on rock we wrestled the bicycles down, from hand to hand, till they reached the scree below.

"Lovely. Lovely!" came Alan's appreciative voice.

A dislodged rock bounced down the cliff and crashed through a bush beside the camera crew.

"Missed!"

"Now chasps. There's a rather nice ledge just round the corner . . ."

We climbed with the bicycles three-quarters of the way back up the cliff to join a narrow shelf where we were filmed walking through the foreground and then round the cliff and out of sight.

"You know, this is a real shame. Nothing up here is going to equal what *actually* happened yesterday."

Alan must have overheard me, for after the third 'take' of the ledge-shot he called me over to the camera: "Have a look through here."

Graham stood aside. I bent over the leather-cupped eyepiece of the heavy Aaton. The comfortable landscape which we had lived in all morning, with its valley and village, road, occasional mule track, and our diminutive hill with its man-made wall, were instantly cropped to the narrow, contained view seen by the camera. The small rectangle of the viewfinder was occupied by the black silhouette of a cliff, with a pair of cyclists attached. In the background were some gigantic painted mountains which I had never – on the other side of the lens – noticed before. The viewfinder made our games on the 10-metre mini-cliff look like a bicycle ascent of the North Wall of the Eiger.

The next shot required us to lie face-down on a part of the ledge where an overhang reduced its height to a metre, and then pass the bicycles to one another. The sun continued to climb and we pulled off layer after layer of clothing.

"Right. Good. If you could climb back up to the top, the crew and I'll go down to the bottom of the hill and take a long shot. When you see me waving, move forward to the prow and stop with the three front wheels hanging over the edge. OK chaps? It's a 'where-the-hell-are-we?' shot. You know the kind of thing: you've come to the edge of the plateau and you're looking for a way down the gorge."

Afterwards, on the way down the little peak, we met the film crew climbing back up: "One more shot chaps: we'd like you riding down this track towards us."

We slid from the saddles, lifted the bikes onto our shoulders, and walked back up the track. And waited.

"Action!"

We hadn't rolled more than five metres when the distressed voice of Alan wafted uphill from his hiding place behind a bush, out of view of the camera: "OK Cut! Cut! Too close together! Can you come down further apart, same speed?"

We turned round again.

At the bottom of the hill, Alan noticed a gully containing a few patches of ice and some foraging goats. "I say chasps. It would be nice if you could just . . ."

It was noon by the time we bounced down the flank of the peak and returned to Chief Mccadam's house for a final glass of tea. We now had to squeeze a day's cycling into one afternoon.

"Let's go."

But Alan had one more shot in mind: The River Crossing. One kilometre away, separating Zaouia Ahansal's *souk* from the old, main part of the village was the log-bridge spanning the river. We cycled over the bridge four times and eventually pedalled away at 12.30. We had not had time to visit the village.

Zaouia Ahansal lies at the end of the road. Southwards the way is blocked by the central spine of the High Atlas. The main route in is from the north, but there is also a dirt road heading westwards over the passes to the Bou Guemez valley. This road leaves from a sharp bend several minutes north west of Zaouia Ahansal. After the filming, I'd spent a few moments stripping off and packing away clothing ready for what the map promised would be a very long, steep, hot climb. Matt and Chris pedalled gently along the track. Five minutes later, I followed. The Land Rovers were waiting at the junction. I looked inside Mohammed's diesel, and the $2\frac{1}{4}$.

"Where's Chris?" I'd expected to see him inside the Land Rover, bike on the roof; he couldn't – surely – be pedalling today? Andy poked his head out of the driver's window. He's already gone! Came round the corner like the clappers and went straight up the hill."

The summit of the Tizi-n-Ilissi is 753 metres above Zaouia Ahansal. For 20 kilometres the road wriggles upwards, in and out of side valleys. The bends are the steepest part. I caught up with Matt after 10 kilometres. He was going very slowly. The Land Rovers came past: three filthy beasts covering us with exhaust fumes. The filthiest by far was the diesel: "Ought to be abolished," muttered Matt between coughs.

I left Matt.

What was Chris up to? I kept looking up, peering along the serpentine coils of the road as it unwound towards the pass, but never once caught the tell-tale glint of sun on steel. Maybe he had given up and got into one of the vehicles.

By crossing the Tizi-n-Ilissi we would leave the tributaries of the Asif Melloul and the whole system of gorges and valleys which drained into the Melloul and the huge, dammed reservoir south of Beni-Mellal; a system we'd lived with since Imilchil. Crossing watersheds often brings a new type of geography and it can change a journey.

It took two hours to reach the top of the pass. The 2¼ Land Rover was parked on the bank. A new, raw wind whipped in from the west. The mountains here were well-covered with snow; most of them were over 3,000 metres. At 2,603 metres, the Tizi-n-Ilissi was the highest road we'd cycled over. I pulled on my jacket as Andy walked over holding a slab of bread. "Chris came by 20 minutes ago. He didn't even stop. Just raced by. Muttered something about nobody accusing him of holding back the schedule. Alan's chasing him in the V8 so they can film him!"

I took the piece of bread; it would do for lunch. As I rolled away I called back to Andy: "Tell Matt I'll wait for him down the road where it's warmer."

There was no need to pedal: gravity tugged the bike forward and faster till I was bucking from bump to bump with aching fingers hooked over the brakes. The road cut along the north side of a steep ridge. In a rare patch of sunlight I stopped and ate half a 'Snicker' bar, and left the other half balanced in its bright red wrapper on a stone in the middle of the track, for Matt. I dawdled; it was less freezing to freewheel slowly. Matt caught me just above the tree-line, and we twisted together down a muddy corkscrew lined by a grim, shaded forest.

It was irritating: we had dropped 300 metres from the Tizi-n-Ilissi, and now had to regain that 300, plus some, to reach the top of the next pass – the Tizi-n-Tsalli-n-Imenain; a name with a sound like a train derailing; we called it "That Snowy One."

The road up the second *tizi* was wedged into the bottom of a claustrophobic trench running along the foot of the cold, northern face of Jbel Azourki. Snow, crystallised on the sunless side of the mountain, coated Azourki's long flank and reached the road, which was little more than a pair of muddy ruts. In the mud we caught the occasional imprint of a mountainbike tyre. Matt and I had the entire valley to ourselves. There was no wind. The rhythm of our labour was almost restful. Matt talked about his wife Fiona; their first foreign holiday together had been to the

Sahara Desert. Matt had bought an ancient Land Rover and the two of them had driven down through Europe and then out into the sands of Algeria where the chassis had broken in half. They were a three-day walk from the nearest oasis, and had drunk all the radiator water by the time a French desert team had stumbled across them. There had been other adventures in the meantime, but this bicycle journey through the Atlas was the realisation of an old dream.

For Matt, the journey was about to become safer and infinitely more predictable: at Tabant, we would join the route he had used during his Thesiger trek, all the way to Telouet. He had survived the hard part of the route; the plateau crossing from Imilchil to Zaouia Ahansal where Chris – the bike-handling expert – had fallen.

"Y'know, I never expected to get this far. Really thought I wouldn't be able to keep up with you and Chris when we got into the mountains."

"Well, neither of us can keep up with Chris today."

Matt appeared not to hear: "Bou Guemez is a beautiful valley and there's this *incredible* inn. Run by a Frenchman . . . Bernard . . . Monsieur Bernard. It's famous among the climbers who come here in the summer. It's in a place called Tabant I think. I tried to stay there on my trek, but it was locked up. Be great if we could reach it tonight."

"How far is it from the bottom of the pass?"

"Not quite sure . . ."

He paused while we slipped into single file to avoid an iced rut. Matt now had the Tabant to Telouet section of the ride in the bag. All he had to cope with was Telouet to the foot of Toubkal, for he had climbed Toubkal six or seven times, and none of us were going to worry about the final dash from Toubkal to the sea.

"Nick, d'you think your attitude to the expedition's going to change when Annabel joins us at Telouet?"

"Don't see why it should . . ."

Travelling on the same road as the support crew and film crew complicated things considerably; access to the vehicles with their spare parts and food boxes, conversation, and concern, took away the risk and the obligation to think Moroccan. Today, on these forgotten *tizis*, there seemed to be more worries than miles: why hadn't Jeremy managed to organise more than a slice of bread for us all day? Why was Chris pedalling like the mountain-leader in the Tour de France when he only had one good leg? Was the morning's re-creative filming faking or necessary? What were we doing setting off to cross three massive passes as late in the day as 12.30pm. If we didn't reach the Bou Guemez valley tonight, would Alan use the journey along the rest of the valley tomorrow as an excuse to hold us up with hours of filming? Life on the plateau with the Berbers had been much simpler. I wasn't enjoying 'today' at all.

We reached the top of the pass at 4.30pm. The temperature was below freezing, and we stopped for the time it took to haul from our packs every stitch of clothing we had – Goretex jackets, mittens, overtrousers – before climbing on the bikes and setting off for the third pass of the day.

Actually, the third pass, a tiddler at 2,629 metres, was not separated from the 'Snowy One' by a valley, so all we had to do was roll along on near-level ground for 10 kilometres. Long stretches of the road were covered with snow, and the mud that had been soft earlier in the day was now freezing into slippery ribs. We cycled round the blank face of Tamelmelt, a vast slab of snow-plastered mountain scratched with the fine black lines of hundreds of layers of horizontal strata. The road used one of the lines to balance upon. Somewhere up here we ran into the film crew. They were looking cold and miserable. Earlier they had filmed Chris on the long lens: a sliding dot set against the vast white screen of Tamelmelt.

"How long ago?"

"Ages."

"Don't wait," Matt said to Alan, "We'll see you in the valley."

"Where d'you want to sleep tonight?" asked Alan.

"Not up here! We'll get as low as we can before dark."

The Land Rover went. Matt and I pedalled on in companionable silence. Before the Tizi-n-Tirghist there was a road junction. We had become sufficiently suspicious of our maps not to believe that we were at the junction suggested by the Carte du Maroc and for several minutes we walked carefully about trying to isolate tyre marks which belonged to our Land Rovers or to Chris. There were Land Rover, and mountainbike, treads going in both directions.

"Either there's a hell of a lot of people up here with Land Rovers and mountainbikes, or these're all from our lot, who went the wrong way, then had to come back to the junction and go the other way."

"Question is, which is the right way?"

It was getting a little late and cold for these kinds of tests. The road to the left descended more steeply. We took it, and twenty minutes later passed through the notch marking the Tizi-n-Tirghist.

The dirt road scissored down the southern side of the pass and into a valley which seemed to be squeezing the last golden drops of the day from a sun gripped by the encircling peaks of the glorious valley of Bou Guemez.

We fell downwards into the warm, darkening valley; racing the failing light, racing Chris, racing time. At 60kph down the stones, red dust and ruts of the last pass, the bicycles were best left to their own devices; all we had to do was keep them pointing downwards, and relax. The three Land Rovers were drawn up in the dust of Ifrane, the village at the foot of the pass. We burst into the village with streaming eyes and with fingers that had cramped around the brake levers. Chris was standing in front of the Land Rovers. He was pulling a newspaper from under the front of his jersey, and looked grey, haggard and mildly bored. I was relieved to see him:

"You were flying today!"

"Just got a rhythm," he replied laconically.

Matt's feet had hardly touched the ground before he said, "Are we off then?" Chris and he set off at a tremendous pace. The dirt road twisted along the valley, curving round spurs and bumping across stream beds. At breakneck speed and in gathering darkness I tried to follow, wanting to enjoy the same madness that had gripped Matt and Chris. A sharp corner reared from the darkness, I had a glimpse of a black space beyond the road edge, touched the front brake and went down.

By the time I had pulled the bike upright, and checked that the pedals were not bent, I was alone and very tired. In the gap between sunset and moonrise, Bou Guemez was utterly dark. Ahead, thin lances of light from the Land Rovers waved crazily to and fro across the valley and swept the mountainsides.

We re-grouped on the edge of one of the villages and rode on using the headlights of the Land Rovers, caught like moths in the glare, till we reached a village where a man knew of M. Bernard.

The *auberge* stood several hundred metres back from the road, and was surrounded by high, blank walls. A man from the village told us that M. Bernard was away, but that as caretaker, he would open up the building and let us stay for the night. It had taken seven hours to cross the mountains from Zaouia Ahansal. Eleven pairs of hands fell into a smooth routine, ferrying the 27 aluminium film boxes and the personal rucksacks and sleeping bags into the *auberge*. Jeremy and Abedelilah disappeared into a small kitchen and began assembling a meal. The *auberge* seemed a maze of thin, tiled passages and narrow stone staircases, off which ran a multiplicity of small, square rooms fitted with one or two beds. It was monastically still, and clean, and for the thirty minutes it took to inhabit the building the walls shimmered with moving shadows projected from the lighted candles placed in alcoves and on windowsills. Downstairs there was a large, rectangular room, the corner of which was occupied by a fireplace.

Up on the first floor, I fell onto a bed. We still had to tackle the day's biggest problem. I was dreading the confrontation which seemed so inevitable. At the far end of the passage, Chris was leaning back on his bed, with his injured leg out straight in front of him.

When I walked in, Matt was sprawled across the second bed, peeling the wrapper off a Mars Bar. The single candle deepened the shadows of eyes and beards; it was cold enough in the room for jackets and scarves. For a few minutes we lay in the semi-darkness, ruminating over the chocolate. How to start?

"Chris, you were flying today . . ."

"I got so far ahead on the passes; couldn't wait up there, too cold, so I just pressed on. Kept pedalling. When I got to that junction between the passes I had no idea which way to go. So I just guessed. Then I got a puncture coming down the pass into Ifrane. Didn't have anything to repair it with, so had to push the bike into the village. The people gave me tea. I had no idea whether I'd gone the wrong way or not and I'd started making all kinds of plans. I'd arranged to stay with a family in Ifrane, then tomorrow morning I was going to either press on to Agouti and see if you had somehow got there ahead of me by another route, or I was going to hitch back to Marrakesh and wait at the airport till Annabel's plane came in, and bump into the support crew when they came to pick her up. But after another 45 minutes, you turned up."

"How's the knee?" It looked a lot more swollen than it had in Zaouia Ahansal.

"Not too good," he replied. "It's OK when I'm sitting down and pedalling in low gear, but I can't get out of the saddle when it's steep."

"Well, we need to decide how we're going to play the rest of the ride."

Chris had been thinking about this: "I don't see why our route should stick to the high level tracks, where we're going to end up carrying the bikes most of the time." Despite our problems it still seemed too early to be beaten by the mountains.

"I don't think we can give up the original plan; besides it may get better. It seems to me that there are two options: for you to battle on over the mule tracks to Telouet, or for you to cycle round the mountains on roads, and meet us at Telouet."

Chris did not respond. Matt shifted his weight onto the other elbow and demanded: "So, what are you going to do, Chris?"

"I don't want to give up . . ."

At that moment, Alan Ravenscroft walked into the room: "I hope you're not having an important discussion that we're missing!"

He turned to Matt: "Look, this is the sort of discussion we ought to be filming. Will you stop, and come downstairs?" Then, as an afterthought: "A fire's been lit."

But Matt was determined to extract the decision from Chris: "I think Chris should give his answer first."

Alan was adamant: "No, keep it for later."

As we filed out of the room, Chris looked wretchedly unhappy.

Our journey from the Sahara Desert to the Atlantic Ocean began in the Chebbi Sand Sea. *Above:* Chris Bradley and Matt Dickinson. *Below:* Nick Crane. Initially the sand was too soft for cycling.

Above: Chris Bradley leaves the Chebbi Sand Sea. *Below:* the Atlas Mountains seen from the south (taken on the day before the ridc began from our camp near Ouazazarte).

Above: The village of Sountat, on the dirt road between Rich and Imilchil. The towered building is the old, fortified *kasbah*. *Below:* Chris Bradley (still leading) on the overhanging ledge set into the gorge wall above the village of Oulghazi.

The gorges of the eastern Atlas force the mule-tracks to climb onto the plateaux *(photo: Matt Dickinson/Nick Crane).*

Above: Two minutes after flying over his handlebars, Chris Bradley considers his knee while Matt Dickinson sets up the film equipment. *Below:* The bivouac site on the plateau above Zaouia Ahansal.

The all-but-abandoned route down the gorge-wall above Zaouia Ahansal. *Above:* The Second Unit at work. *Below:* descending.

Above: A man carrying a bicycle meets a man carrying a rock; the Tessaout valley. *Below:* Matt Dickinson fording the river below the village of Toufrine on Day 11. There was a bridge just around the corner.

Above: An 'action delay' shot of the team which scaled the Tizi-n-Fedherat: Nick Crane, Ahmed Mansour, Matt Dickinson, and a mule. *Below:* Our host in the remote village of Ichbakene.

The Glaoua *kasbah* at Telouet. *Above:* Director Alan Ravenscroft (far right) with Graham Smith and Phil Millard. *Below:* Berber dancers and musicians inside the *kasbah (photos: Chris Bradley).*

Above: Alan Ravenscroft directs on a hill outside Telouet. *Below:* Day 14, seconds before disaster; Matt Dickinson's mountainbike hits rocks above the Tizi-n-Tichka *(photos: Annabel Huxley)*.

"Come over here . . . there's some really good blood!" *Above:* Matt Dickinson after falling on the Tichka, then *below* having the wound closed with adhesive 'stitches' *(photos: Annabel Huxley).*

Mount Toubkal, the highest mountain in North Africa.

Right: Phil Millard, Stuart Bruce and the bikers on the summit, *(photo: Annabel Huxley)*.

Right: Matt Dickinson pauses above the final descent to the Neltner Hut *(photo: Annabel Huxley)*.

Matt Dickinson, Annabel Huxley and Nick Crane before finding out that the French had already taken mountainbikes up Toubkal.

Left: Nick Crane on the upper slopes *(photo: Matt Dickinson)*.

Chris Bradley on Day 18: "I'm coming with you . . .!" *(photo: Matt Dickinson).*

Flying down the Tizi-n-Test to the sea. *Above*, Alan Ravenscroft and the First Unit, filming near the top of the pass. *Below:* under the overhangs on the Tizi-n-Test *(photos: Annabel Huxley)*.

Agadir and the Atlantic. The difficulties we had in desalinating the bikes after the final shot of the film far outweighed the fun of pedalling them into the sea *(photos: Annabel Huxley).*

Down in the main room, a circular table had been pushed in front of the fire. The film crew were sitting in the shadows. We sat round the table, facing the glare of a paraffin lamp, and picked at the plates of *cous-cous* and cabbage that Jeremy had made.

The film crew moved out of the shadows. Alan Ravenscroft leant forward and said: "So Nick, what are the options?"

The following conversation was one which each of us had been rehearsing all day, but like all rehearsed speeches, the mind proved more fluent than the mouth:

NICK: "Well, we've only got a certain amount of time to finish the ride off, and we've got three of the hardest sections yet to do. Next we have to do 130 kilometres over the mountains – over a very high pass. And after we've been over it, it'll be quite snowy probably, and it's going to be . . . well Matt . . . you reckon 30 per cent carrying . . . you've been over there before . . ."

MATT: "I reckon a minimum 30 per cent carrying, even if the riding conditions are perfect."

NICK: "The only way we're going to pull this thing off, is safely; we're not with a support group who can get us out of difficulty. We're going to have to rescue ourselves if things go badly wrong . . ."

CHRIS: "I don't think that's a problem. The thing that worries me is the fact that we have a deadline to hit, and I was slowing you up, quite an amount, after my fall, and if it's going to be the same in the future, then . . . I wouldn't want to be the reason that you didn't get to the end, that's the . . . that's the thing. I can do it, but . . ."

MATT: "Oh, we know you can do it . . ."

CHRIS: ". . . But not in the . . . maybe not in the time scale."

MATT: "My own fear is that you do some long-term damage to your knee, which is going to take, you know, years to . . . or months to recover. It's fairly clear that your knee needs a lot of rest. It's already swollen up twice the size that it was two days ago."

NICK: "Well you've already pressed on further than any ordinary normal human being would have done – just to get off that plateau that the accident happened on; you pressed on for two days and half a night to get off the plateau. And that's a pretty magnificent achievement, by any standards. You haven't got anything to prove now, Chris, because you've done it already and . . . we know you can do it. But there's going to be a lot more carrying . . ."

MATT: "And that's the problem. That is the problem."

CHRIS: "Well I'm not sure that my knee could stand up to that. I think that's the basics of it."

MATT: "Or there is always the option of taking a few days' rest; going with the Land Rover south again, down to the tarmac, because the

Land Rover's not going to be with us now for what, four days, while we do that crossing. Minimum. You could go with the support vehicle and then come back up and meet us at Telouet, and if the knee's better, just carry on . . ."

CHRIS: "Oh, I don't know . . . oh why the hell did that wheel disappear . . ."

NICK: "It was bad luck. It was very bad luck, but to make these trips work, everything has just got to be . . . to click at the right moment. There . . . there isn't room for . . . for mishaps."

Chris stroked his knee.

NICK: "It's enormous isn't it . . .?"

CHRIS: "Yeah . . . it's like a football."

NICK: "It's actually a lot more swollen than it was yesterday . . .

CHRIS: "Yeah, it is, yeah . . ."

MATT: "So, what's the decision, Chris, what are you going to do?"

CHRIS: "I'll sleep on it I think."

ALAN: "Cut!"

After the others had left, I sat with the lamp and my notebook. Unless Chris had made up his mind by the morning, the bell would have to be rung on the slugging match between gentility and pragmatism. In the corner, the flames tried in vain to soften the chill of the night.

Well Met at Telouet

Then There Were Two (Day 9) – Falling off Horses – A Meal with Mansour – Riced Out (Day 10) – Over the Snow to Tessaout – Flattened by Ichbakene – Carrying Rocks (Day 11) – A Time Dilemma – Fluffing the Drowning Sequence – Travels With a Mule in the Atlas (Day 12) – Last Take

Day 9 – 12

The alarm snatched me from sleep at seven. I used my headtorch to find the cigarette lighter and lit the candle. I dreamt for ten minutes then threw myself at the shutters. The small, white room ignited with light. It was a dazzling day.

Last night, a single sentence had changed the expedition: after I thought everyone had gone to bed, Matt had returned to the big room and said: "Chris is pulling out." Chris had told him as they had been getting into their sleeping bags. It was a decision that had been long in the making. A few minutes later, after Matt had gone, Chris had come down to tell me himself. There was a look of resignation and disappointment on his face. I said that I hoped I would have had the courage to make the same decision had I been in his situation.

So the dawn of day 9 brought with it a renewed momentum. Two is an ideal number for fast, difficult journeys. On the floor of the room, I tipped out the contents of the small rucksack and pannier which I had carried since the desert, and crammed everything into a single larger rucksack. If we were going to be lifting the bikes on and off our backs as often as we had on the Imilchil to Zaouia Ahansal section of the route, then it would be less hard work if weight on the bike was minimised. I was spooning muesli into my mouth and weighing up whether to take or leave a spare inner tube when Matt walked in. "We're filming on the balcony. Alan wants us all for a tracking shot."

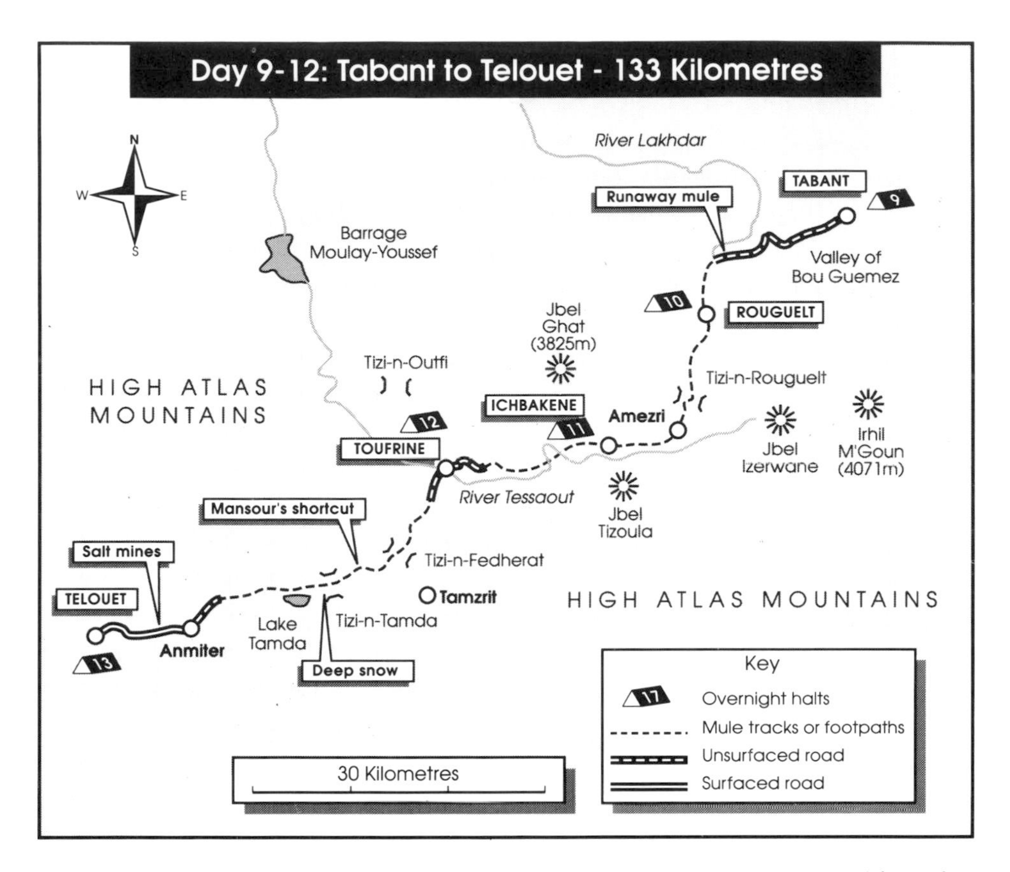

Alan and the camera crew had been up since dawn. Overlooking the courtyard, along the front of Monsieur Bernard's inn, was a balustraded balcony. Beyond the walls of the courtyard, the valley of Bou Guemez waited under a fresh sky. Above the brown walls of the valley rose the white caps of Jbel Waougoulzat. The film crew had already set up their 'dolly': the camera-trolley which runs along a railway track. In front of the railway lines lay a jumble of rucksacks, maps, guide-books, tools, spare tyres, mugs of tea and two partly dismantled bikes. Alan, wrapped in his Arabian scarf and sleeveless down jacket, was organising the chaos: "Nick, we're doing a long, tracking shot. It begins in Chris' bedroom with him lying in the dark on his bed looking at his knee and then moves out into the daylight to Andy, who'll be servicing a bike, to Matt, who can be pumping up tyres, to you, who'll be looking at maps. It's the set-up shot for the next stage of the journey . . ."

On cue, we each sighed, spannered, pumped and measured, while Phil Millard pushed the small trolley loaded with Graham, his tripod and camera, along the railway. We did it four times. After each take, low, whimpering sounds could just be heard coming from Graham; his usual way of reacting to a BAFTA-grade shot.

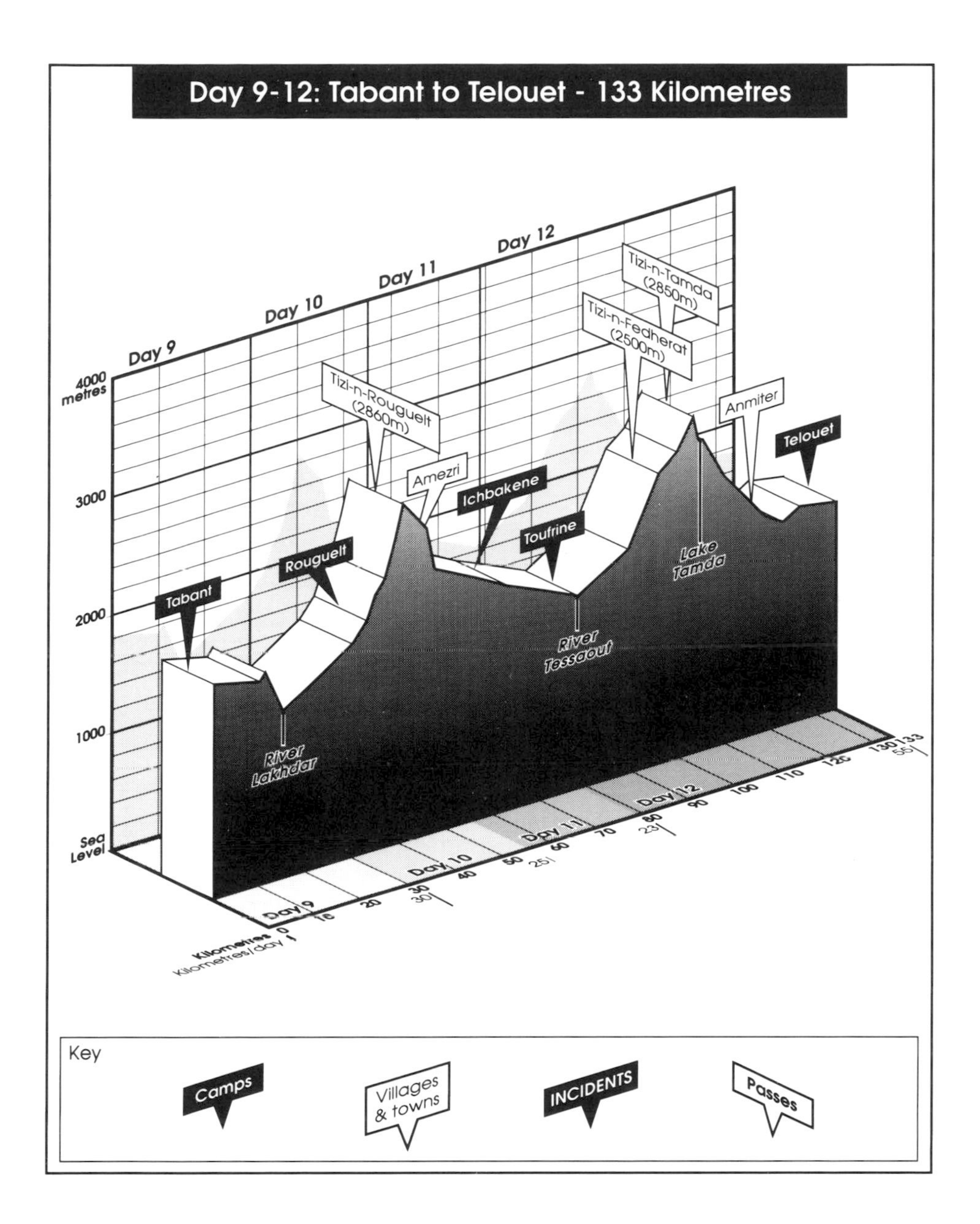

While we were waiting in the sun between takes I had time to run the map-measurer over the next section of the journey: we had about 130 kilometres of High Atlas mule tracks to cross between Tabant and Telouet, where we would next meet a road and the Land Rovers. We had two high passes to cross, the Tizi-n-Rouguelt, and the Tizi-n-Fedherat. They were separated by what looked on the map to be a long, flat-floored valley, the Tessaout. Matt had walked this valley two years earlier, and was convinced that we would be able to fly along in a few hours. There was, said Matt, a third pass we had to cross, which was somehow attached to the Fedherat, but the height difference was not worth worrying about. The plan was clear: on Day 9 we would cross the Tizi-n-Rouguelt; on Day 10, we would ride along the valley of the Tessaout and sleep at the village of Toufrine; and on Day 11 we would cross the Tizi-n-Fedherat and its neighbour, and arrive in Telouet that evening. Making Telouet in three days meant averaging 50 kilometres a day, but it looked possible.

After the balcony sequence, we spent an hour down in the village riding the bicycles up and down the dusty road while Graham filmed us from shaded alleys. The village was waking up and we quickly had a colourful cast of small children, donkeys and the odd horseman to complement the glinting bicycles. Alan's excitement could be gauged by the depth of his frown.

Time slid on towards midday; I was itching to leave; filming with the First Unit always diverted attention from the real journey. A space was opening between the actuality of a bicycle journey through the High Atlas, and the imaginary script in Alan's head. There was one critical shot which had to be filmed before memories faded: the re-creation of Chris' accident. Matt had filmed the immediate aftermath of the accident, but there was obviously no footage of the crash itself. The mountainside behind the *auberge* was surprisingly similar to the rock-slope before Agrrnooweera, where Chris had damaged his knee. Chris changed into the travel-stained jersey that he had used up on the plateau and we carried the bikes up the rocky slope.

Chris lay on the mountain, head downhill, with one leg threaded through the frame of his 'crashed' bicycle. Matt and I waited uphill. The camera crew organised themselves below Chris. Alan picked up a handful of dust ("Got to make it look authentic . . ."); Graham Smith took a light reading, and withdrew to his eyepiece; Phil Millard held the clapper-board in front of the lens; Stuart Bruce settled his head-phones and swung his microphone boom to face the rocks. He put out his cigarette. Graham said "Running"; Alan called "Action!" and threw the dust at Chris; the clapperboard snapped; Matt and I jumped down the mountain; rocks clattered; dust hung in the air. Matt shouted "Pull the bike off him!"; Chris moaned; I pulled the bike; Alan cried "Cut!".

We did it three times. There was still a problem: the shot as it stood looked as if the First Unit camera crew had been waiting on the mountainside below Agrrnooweera and that by miraculous chance Chris had chosen to fall off his bicycle right in front of the lens. Matt – who had been hyper-active all morning – had a blinding inspiration: "Let's make it look as if this was filmed by the Second Unit; pretend that I saw the accident about to happen, and pulled the camera from under my jacket and started filming."

So we played out the fourth 'take'; this time Graham started the camera running with the front of the lens in Matt's armpit. On "Action" he pulled it out, waved it at the sky and surrounding mountains, and then followed Matt's imaginary 'eyeline' down the rocks to Chris' prone body.

Alan frowned. Then smiled and said, "That'll do!"

Back at the *auberge* we made our final preparations for the mountain crossing. Chris kindly repaired a puncture which had mysteriously appeared in my back wheel, while Matt and I divided up the Second Unit film equipment. The Aaton, its lenses, meter, clapperboard and sound gear now had to be carried between two, not three people. "We'll leave the sound gear," announced Matt.

I added "And the clapperboard." On top of our sleeping bags and cold-weather clothing we packed the dismantled Aaton, a 400-foot roll of film and a handful each of chocolate bars. I took two stills cameras and three lenses. The packs were extraordinarily heavy. Andy handed us a piece of bread each.

At 12.30 pm, we pulled away from the *auberge*.

We rode along the track towards the headwaters of Ait Bou Guemez. For a few kilometres, the film crew bumped along behind us in their V8 Land Rover.

Alan pipped the horn of the Land Rover.

"See you in two days?"

"Maybe three. At the outside."

"'Bye."

The engine note of the Land Rover quickly died and we were on our own. Released once again from the complications of travelling with a large group and a film unit, we were back in a natural balance.

We pedalled past a string of hamlets set behind the empty, wire branches of wintry trees, and overtook a large group of women on horseback, wrapped in blue and turquoise with eyes sparkling through face-scarves. At their head was a young man on a white horse. The tails of the horses had been cut just clear of the dust and brushed so that the hairs at the edge fluttered freely like the wind-blown spume at the edge of a waterfall.

At the head of the valley, the track reared steeply to climb the short scarp separating Bou Guemez from the valley of the River Lakhdar. At the top of the climb the track narrowed then switchbacked down through old pine forest to the river, a torrent only just big enough to merit a bridge. The water was as clear as glass and we filled our pint bottles.

From this bridge the Lakhdar makes its way north through the gorges of the Atlas, to join the River Tessaout on the flatlands east of Marrakesh, where the two converged streams run on to pour into a river which already carries the waters of our old friend the Asif Melloul. From there it makes its increasingly sluggish way across the low plateaux of the mountain hinterland to dribble grubbily into the Atlantic Ocean south of the utilitarian concrete acres of Casablanca.

We followed the Lakhdar upstream, riding easily on a hard trail which became increasingly confined by tightening cliffs on each side of the water. The river became narrower, faster, and deeper. At first there were stepping-stones. Then we came to a place where the current slid quickly, uninterrupted by rocks. For the horses and mules used by the locals, this was a ford; for Matt and me, it was the first of many river-problems we were to come across on our passage to Telouet.

We were dithering on the bank, debating whether to take off our trousers and wade, or go prospecting for stepping stones, when two mules arrived. On them were two young men, the taller of whom immediately hopped to the ground and waved cheerily. He had a fine *djellabah* striped in gravy-brown, cream and speckled-thrush with thin, plaited piping across the chest. On his head he wore a blue and white diamond-patterned acrylic ski-hat.

The man insisted that we use his mule to cross the river and led us to a large rock. Clutching my mountainbike in one hand, I climbed carefully across the saddle. I was handed the reins, the man slapped the mule's rump, and we jumped into the water. I thought I heard someone laughing.

At this point I was faced by a dilemma which would have been better resolved on dry land: how to steer the beast. Was it like an English horse, which is steered by pulling on one or other side of the reins? Or was this an American-West mule, which would be steered by 'laying' the reins on one or other side of the neck? Or was it like an Afghan horse, unsteerable by anyone other than its owner? It was a difficult conundrum to resolve from the top of a mule in the middle of a fast flowing river whilst wearing a huge, lopsided rucksack and clutching a bicycle. By midstream the mule had clearly decided to take the initiative. I felt uneasy when it stopped and turned its head, to observe me with a malevolent, gob-stopper eye. I got the message when it began to buck. From the bank behind me, the shouting and laughing cut through the sound of the river. I had just a few seconds to field-test each of the three steering techniques and when none of them worked I abandoned the reins and gave the animal a hefty kick with my heels instead. This had the effect of making the animal leap upstream. I turned to the bank and caught sight of the mule's owner who was indicating with the flat of his hand that I should slap the animal's rump. With some difficulty because of the bicycle, I leaned backwards from the saddle and whacked the mule's haunch as hard as I could. The response was immediate: the mule sprung upwards on all four legs at once, cleared the water and then gave the impression of galloping across the surface of the river. By the time we reached the far bank, the weight of the rucksack and bicycle had pulled me to one side, and I was travelling west with one ankle hooked over the pommel, the other leg squeezing the mule's belly and the bicycle scraping along the ground. The mule was still galloping. Disaster seemed imminent.

I dropped the bike. It crashed onto rock. A sandy patch between river boulders raced towards my face. I unhooked my ankle. I hit the ground rucksack-first. The mule stopped for long enough to stamp on my calf with a steel-shod hoof. Then it took off up the valley.

I was terribly embarrassed. Having accepted the muleteer's generous gesture of a lift across the water, I had in return lost his mule. Dumping the rucksack I ran after the mule. It had stopped around the first bend, and was glaring meanly with that eye. I reached for the reins, and was amazed when the animal did not even flinch. As I turned its head back towards the river, it reared on its hind legs and rocketed forward. Wiser this time, I dropped the reins and threw myself into the scrub.

By the time I'd caught the wretched animal and returned to the river, tranquillity had been restored to the ford, and Matt had appeared, as if by some miracle, on the west side of the river.

"Did you come across on the other mule?"I panted.

"No," he grinned. "There are some stepping stones just downstream."

Soon the track came to a widening in the valley. There was space for fields. A slot appeared in the mountain wall opposite, which Matt reckoned was the way to the Tizi-n-Rouguelt.

Two kilometres before the road ended at the village of Abachkou, we lifted the bikes down the embankment, and carried them round the edge of the fields to the banks of the river. Stepping stones led us across to a wide mule-track heading south towards the foot of the pass. I sat on a rock, staring at the map while Matt crossed the fields to Abachkou to see if he could buy any food to see us through the afternoon. The top of the Tizi-n-Rouguelt stood at 2,860 metres; the village of Rouguelt, at the foot of the pass, lay at 1,850 metres. To climb 1,000 metres, carrying the bikes and the packs, would take a minimum of three hours. And we were still a couple of hours away from Rouguelt village. The sun was already shut out from much of the valley, and the valley air was cold enough to deter any adventurous thoughts of bivouacking part-way up the pass. We would have to scrap plans to cross the pass today, and make an early start tomorrow instead. The morning spent filming had set us back too far.

Matt returned carrying three tins of condensed milk, and two cans of spiced sardines. We ate them perched on the rock, flattened the cans and buried them.

We alternately cycled and carried the bikes along a shoulder-width red-dust trail which clung to the side of Jbel Tifdaniwine and, just before 5pm, came in sight of Rouguelt. The houses seemed stacked on top of each other with their feet in the stream and their roofs reaching towards the sun-touched snow ridges of Jbel Tarkeddidi, which formed an apparently impenetrable wall behind the village.

A small bridge led across the water to the first house. The houses were built on such a steep slope that the only level land was the stone-buttressed ramps leading to the front doors. With the bikes on our shoulders, and a column of children in tow, we climbed up through the village while Matt tried to remember which house he had stayed in eighteen months earlier. We eventually found it, but the owner, Er Mhor Mohammed, was away. Instead, his neighbour, a young man called Mansour, insisted that we stay with him.

Mansour showed us into a long, thin room, with the door at one end, and a tiny, barred window at the other. At the window end there were rugs and blankets. We pulled off our boots and sat, backs to the wall, absorbing the stillness. The roof – as always – was flat, with seven great beams, and above them a lattice of thinner branches. Above them would be the mud. Running around the top of the wall was a patterned band, 20 centimetres deep, of repeating squares in red, blue and green; bold, primary blocks edged by a twined gold border. A large black and white print of Hassan II looked sternly across to a touched-up colour poster of a popular Egyptian singer with voluptuous lips and an avalanche of midnight ringlets.

Against the far wall (we were leaning against the wall with the window) was a rack with three shelves piled high with the family possessions: folded blankets and *djellabahs*, a kettle, a teapot, sundry small wooden boxes, some metal pans and a *tagine* pot. Hanging on the wall beside the Egyptian singer was a pair of bellows, with a half-metre long tapir-snout and a chaotically-painted side plate decorated with shiny studs and a rectangular mirror. The uneven walls had been painted white; the paint had splashed up onto the ends of the roof beams.

Bit by bit, we readjusted to real time. As the light faded, the temperature plummeted. We pulled blankets over our legs. Mansour returned to the room with his wife, wide-mouthed and high-cheekboned. She was wearing a purple dress tightened at the waist with a tassled green cord, at one end of which was tied a key. Round her head was a ruby scarf decorated with golden leaves and star-bursts. She seemed very young to have two children. Her daughter, who must have been about two, was called Fatima; we didn't find out the name of her older brother, whose crop-head and sooty hands periodically peeped around the door-jamb. Mansour was twenty-two years old.

Mansour brought us coffee which tasted of acorns, a plate of dates and some Moroccan biscuits. One hour later, he returned with three bowls of *harira*, the oiled lentil soup which (with *cous-cous*) is the staple diet of people living in the High Atlas. He gave Matt and I spoons, but drank his own soup straight from the bowl. The *harira* steamed in the lamp-light, a cooler version of *dahl* but with the same dead-grass colour. Some time after the soup, Mansour brought into the room a portable hearth which he set on the floor in front of our feet. It was loaded with glowing embers which had been scraped from the cooking fire in the adjacent room. We sat round the hearth, holding our hands to the coals. Mansour slipped away, and returned holding in his *djellabah* a scoop of walnuts. He sat with a stone and chisel, battering at the shells and handing round the soft, sweet, wrinkled hearts. Every hour or so, Mansour's wife brought fresh embers to the hearth.

More people gathered in the room: as well as the two children, who were by now watching quietly from the shadows, there was another woman sitting beside Mansour's wife. Then Er Mhor Mohammed arrived. For several tumultuous moments while Matt and Mohammed recognised each other, there was a frenzy of huggings and *'salaams'*. Mohammed was convinced that Matt was from the Soviet Union, and kept thumping Matt on the back and exclaiming "Russ! Russ!" while laughing so much that his eyes completely disappeared.

The *tagine* we were served that night was a *tagine* to end all *tagines*. As Mansour began to lift the lid, the first spurts of steam billowed out and enveloped us. When the room cleared, we could see a whole chicken, surrounded by potatoes, eggs and olive oil. To soak up the juices running round the base of the pot there was a disc of flat-bread, hot and soft from the oven. Mansour lifted the chicken clear, and the four men positioned themselves around the pot, picking up pieces of potato, or egg, with folds of the bread. Afterwards, Mansour pulled apart the chicken with his fingers. He gave Matt and me a leg each. When we had finished, the lid was replaced on the pot, and it was carried out of the room. It was not until later that evening that we realised the mauled contents of the pot were probably dinner for Mansour's wife and children.

We were woken by a baby crying. Mansour brought tea and then some bread into the room, which we nibbled while stuffing away sleeping bags and pulling on clothing. We had just pulled on our boots, and were preparing to find and thank Mansour for his kindnesses, when his wife strode into the centre of the room bearing at arm's length a tin platter trailing steam. She put the platter on the floor before silently leaving again. We blinked. In front of us was a mountain of white rice surrounded by a moat of warm oil. I had only seen this dish a couple of times before, in the Hindu Kush range of Afghanistan, where it is currently regarded as an extravagant treat.

Mansour appeared and joined us for breakfast. We picked up our spoons and began to quarry the great, shivering mound, dipping each excavation of rice into the smooth lubricant which ebbed and flowed round the base of the plate.

"Takes a bit of getting used to," I said encouragingly.

"Most specialities do," replied Matt, digging deeper.

The oil around the base seemed to move with self-induced currents, maintaining its tide-mark on the flanks of the scree. Mansour urged us on. Three spoons working for five minutes did not noticeably diminish the size of the task ahead of us. As a spoonful of rice was removed, the small indentation was immediately filled by a landslip of grains from above, the trace of every endeavour being instantly concealed. Was this slippery slope some kind of bizarre, cosmic, oleaginous mirror of our increasingly futile attempt to ride mountainbikes through the High Atlas? No: it was just an oily heap of rice. Mansour told me to eat more. I scooped on.

With this progress came an increasing inability to swallow. I had to move from sitting cross-legged, to kneeling, so that my stomach could be allowed full stretch. I began to have to employ my tongue as a plunger to assist each freshly-received bolus in its passage to the back of my mouth.

"Matt?. . ."

Distended by the latest arrival of rice, Matt's cheeks pulsed weakly like the gills of a dying goldfish. His eyes bulged.

". . . I don't feel very well."

Matt's head gave the impression of a nod; I watched the breaking of beads of sweat on his temple, as he contemplated, then completed, the act of swallowing, then said: "You can have my share too, if you like."

As Mansour's wife lifted away the platter, the sun now streaming through the small window caught two indistinct dents in the cone, and, on the far side, a single excavation reaching from the summit to base and extending for nearly one third of the circumference of the exhausted lagoon. Mansour smiled, pointed at the departing plate, and said: "*Du riz*! Good for the legs!"

As I looked towards where my legs should have been, I sensed what it must be like to be pregnant.

After coffee, we groped through the passage to the open air and, reluctantly, said our goodbyes. Before we left, Mansour and his family lined up against the wall of their house for a photograph.

It took four hours to carry the bicycles up the 1,000 metres from Rouguelt to the top of the pass. For the first three hours we were in a defile, which in one place narrowed to the width of a bus, a vehicle which would have been only slightly less suited to the terrain than the ones we had. In this thin place, water reached from wall-to-wall of the defile, and we had to teeter upstream, bikes round necks, balancing with the balls of our feet on the few slippery stones which still protruded from the flow. The slot of sky above our heads was cold and heavy with imminent snow. It was miserably inhospitable; a dramatic place for filming.

Using three shots, Matt created a 'carrying-the-bike-up-a-water-filled-gorge' sequence: the first shot was a long view which panned down from the cliffs above the stream and then zoomed gently in on a pink-coated man hopping unhappily from rock to rock in what looked from above like the entrance to a cave; the second shot was a close-up of the man's glum face; the third shot followed one stride behind a pair of boot-heels, which on the third take, skidded from a rock and disappeared under water.

"Lucky we haven't got any sound," grinned Matt after the splash. "It would've been a hassle dubbing out the swearing."

I wrung out my socks while Matt disassembled the camera.

A little further on, the defile forked. "Could be awkward," I mused. "If we take the wrong one, it's bound to lead us to a cliff. The right route's got to be the one with the biggest stream, because the biggest stream will cut lowest into the col."

Matt thought about this. "Both streams are the same size."

We looked at the two streams from all angles. It was impossible to say which was the bigger.

One stream headed slightly east of south, the other slightly south of west. According to our map, the route over the Tizi-n-Rouguelt headed south, then south-southwest, then south-southeast, then west, then south, then south-west and finally west.

"Well . . . this is a bit of a prob . . ."

Matt, staring at the ground a few metres away, interrupted: "Hold it, we're OK, here's a mule turd." We took the left fork.

The defile finally opened into a bowl-shaped hollow, walled by cliffs and floored by frozen grass. The cliffs were split at intervals by streams which met on the grass and filtered down to the defile from which we had just emerged. In the face of one of the cliffs was a vast cave-mouth, partly closed by a man-made wall of balanced rocks. "Perfect place for a bivouac," I called to Matt.

"Wonderful!" he replied. The first snow-flakes began to fall.

We emerged onto the exposed shoulder of Jbel Wagraraz. Through the snow-laden wind we could see the matching shoulder of Jbel Tarkeddidi. We stopped to film again, Matt framing two shots of me wading up through knee-deep snow towards the col. It was so windy on the col that the snow had been blown clear. Ahead, the ground fell away to the deep cleft of the Tessaout valley, and beyond the valley we could see the rims of various *jbels*, among them, Izerwane and Tizoula. This was the highest pass we would cross during the Atlas traverse, and it was only 1,300 metres below the summit of Toubkal itself.

In front of us, a dirt path curved away through the snow-dust. The wind hammered on our anorak hoods.

"Film. Must film this," bawled Matt. "We'll set it up on this rock. Then we can both be in the shot."

With freezing fingers, Matt brought together all the parts of the camera. Using small stones as wedges, he set the Aaton on the top of the chest-high boulder, took a light reading, adjusted the aperture, locked the trigger and sprinted for his bike shouting: "We're running."

We pedalled past the unmanned camera and freewheeled down the dirt path and around the corner, where Matt leapt out of his saddle and sprinted the 100 metres back to the camera to turn it off before precious film was wasted.

"Great!" he enthused as we packed the camera, magazine and battery away. "That looks absolutely amazing. That's the first high-altitude footage we've got. I'll go berserk if that shot's not used in the film." (It was.)

The descent to the Tessaout was depressing: to spend four hours shouldering a mountainbike up a pass, and then find that the far side is an unrideable rubble heap, is upsetting. As I skated from the saddle on yet another unmanageable twist of the track, I described my feelings to Matt, using every short word I could think of.

"It's not quite what I remember," he admitted.

Despite this, it took us less than an hour to descend to the valley and an abandoned hamlet marked on the map as 'Tasgaiwalt'. No road has ever forced a passage through to the upper Tessaout; maybe these mountainbikes would be the first wheeled vehicles to have rolled down the valley? Two kilometres beyond the hamlet we pedalled into the highest village in the Tessaout: Amezri.

The houses had bolted themselves to a flattish shelf above the river on the south-facing slope of Jbel Wagraraz. There were no wires here, no wheels or metal. Just a scattering of earthen cubes separated by spilt straw and foot-patted mud. As we passed the first house, a shriek rent the air. Children burst from unseen corners, calling to each other, pulling more from doorways until they formed a chorus of drumming feet around the bicycles. Their faces were filthy, and their feet bare, their upper-lips shiny with rivulets of mucus. Shirts and jackets so ripped, soiled and frayed that their original colour and cut had long been obscured, flapped round hands that were caked with years of mud and animal and body-grime. Matt and I fled from the houses as if we were trying to shake off a swarm of bees. About ten of the children chased us to the next bend in the river. And then there were four. They stayed with us for an hour, cutting us off on the bends by nipping over ridges or sprinting along the rocks of the riverbed. We last saw them screaming and waving from a mound of earth above the track.

Much of the track was unridable. Rock-steps and detours down to the riverbed meant that it was less laborious to carry the bikes than to try to ride them. Bcside a rock, we lowered the bikes to the ground. I pulled out the map.

"We're not going to reach Toufrine tonight."

I looked at the sky; it was grey, beginning to dull. Matt sniffed, then coughed, expressively: "Timecheck?"he asked.

"Four-twenty."

"Mmm."

"Maybe an hour and a half."

"I reckon we can make Ichbakene. It's where I stayed last year."

I bent over the map: "Ichbakene's meant to be one kilometre downstream from Amezri. We should have passed it an hour ago."

"The map's absolutely crazy. It's got this end of the valley totally wrong. I remember last year being confused: Ichbakene's miles down the valley. But we should be able to find it before dark."

We carried on carrying. It was 6pm when we rounded a corner and the tall houses of Ichbakene came in view. The village knelt beneath the massive cliffs of what had for the time being turned into a gorge. Each house seemed indivisible from the next, so tightly were they packed. Like a giant staircase the flat roofs descended from the sheer rock to the valley bed with just a field width separating the lowest house from the river bank. Round the metal-grilled windows and the doors, the inhabitants had painted white borders, so that the village looked like a crowd of totemic faces staring wide-eyed at the toppling mountain opposite.

Unlike Amezri, we entered the village without being spotted, and it was not until we had walked casually through the stripped trees leading to the first tier of houses that a couple of curious children tagged along behind.

"Can't exactly remember which house I stayed in last time," pondered Matt, as we started up the slope to the second tier of houses. Ichbakene was tidier than Amezri, but its roofs were roughly made, with tufts of branches and straw sticking from under the mud. In the half-light we were intercepted by a man wrapped up to the eye-balls in *djellabahs* and scarves. He pulled the butterscotch-striped turban off his mouth and asked if we wanted somewhere to stay. We said that we did. He crooked his arm and rubbed his thumb and middle finger together.

"Waha, waha!" we replied. Yes, we'd pay money. The man told us to follow him, and as he led us to his house other villagers appeared, shouting angrily. Our host shouted back, and we dipped beneath a wooden beam into a narrow gully between high walls. At the end he led us into a tiny courtyard which was just big enough for the five sheep, half a dozen chickens and small calf to turn around without treading on each others' feet. We left the bikes against the courtyard wall, and crouched through a doorway. Steps led up to a room with an open front which looked across the gorge. We were led into the store room, a blanket was spread on the floor, and we both sank down and lay flat on our backs in the darkness.

Matt came round first.

"We've arrived."

"Somewhere."

"I wonder where Ichbakene is."

"Maybe halfway to Toufrine."

"Maybe."

"I could kill a tea."

"This valley's incredibly poor compared to the eastern Atlas."

"It was almost as if they were arguing to see who would have us to stay. Visitors mean money."

"Can't be many visitors to Ichbakene. Maybe a trekker or two in the summer. If they can find the place."

By the light of a three-quarters moon we walked down to a field, and then along the top of a wall to the river bank to wash. Snow lay in patches, bright in the moonlight.

Later, as we sat round the small brazier of coals with tea, hot bread and fresh butter, we tried to explain to our host where we were going. Whenever we said 'Telouet', he shook his head.

It was very cold in the room, and we were each given a thick *djellabah* to wear over our own clothes. By the light of a gas lamp, our host's wife peeled potatoes and onions. A man came to the room with a plucked chicken, which he wedged into the *tagine* pot together with the vegetables and a dose of oil. Two hours later, we ate, and later still we were led across the balcony to a room full of sacks and bits of wood, to sleep.

I was woken at 6.30 by very loud panting from just outside the door. In socks, I peered outside to see our host's wife squatting, her back against the wall, huffing a pair of long-snouted bellows at the small portable brazier. The battered kettle sat on top, smoking optimistically. It took a long while for the water to boil, and by the time we sat down in a foursome round the brazier to eat the hot bread and cheesy butter, an iron grey light had spread across the valley.

We left at 8.10, carrying the bikes up a zig-zag path to the top of the village, across the diamond ripples of a spring and onto the mountain beyond. Matt was in high spirits, and as we stamped along the track his voice carried across the gorge:

"Postman Pat,
Postman Pat,
Postman Pat and his black and white cat.
Early in the morning, just as day is dawning,
He picks up all his postbags in his van . . ."

"Matt! What's that horrendous tune?"

"It's . . . Postman Pat, Postman Pat, Postman . . ." And so it went on. And on. And on.

"It's Alistair's good-mood marching song," explained Matt.

Almost immediately, we found ourselves 100 metres above the valley floor, and unable to get down. The path we had started on, had run out. Matt stopped singing 'Postman Pat'. The peace and quiet was almost worth getting lost for.

We picked our way across a series of abandoned terraces which had been built on the tilt at staggered levels so that as we climbed down the terrace walls thinking that we were walking towards the valley, the downward gradient of the valley itself worked with the upward tilt of the terraces, to carry further from the river.

We were saved by a tall boy in a threadbare *djellabah* who beckoned for us to follow him. He set off at a cracking pace across the scree slopes, finally turning left to slide down the mountain. At the bottom, the boy paused for a moment among the rocks littering the river edge, chose one the size of a small cushion, and hefted it onto his shoulder. We continued down the valley: a boy carrying a large rock on one shoulder, leading two men carrying bicycles.

"Matt . . . d'you think he's carrying the rock to humour us? Maybe he feels guilty not carrying anything."

"It's shampoo. They grind the rock and use it for washing their hair."

There was no answer to that. We walked with the boy for an hour, scrambling along the river bank, sometimes following the remnants of the track, at other times picking tortuous routes across the river's bed. Frequently a meander in the river would force us up onto the wall of the gorge itself, and here we would tread warily round crumbling goat tracks above leg-breaking drops. The boy left us to set off up the wall of the gorge on a tiny goat track; he was still carrying the rock.

The valley went on and on. We were hemmed in by claustrophobic walls. It was arguable whether it was worse to push the bicycles or to carry them. Pushing usually led to ankles being gouged by the rock-sharpened pedals. Or the bike would jam between two rocks. Carrying allowed a predictable pace, but the 30-plus kilograms of bike and pack dragging at our shoulders became increasingly unendurable. Morale began to sink. We knew we would have to carry the bikes over the Tizi-n-Rouguelt and over the Tizi-n-Fedherat, but between the two we had expected to race west on smooth mule tracks. Now that we were walking along the Tessaout too, it looked as if we would be spending three continuous days carrying the bicycles. The expedition was getting a little more ludicrous than intended. I blamed Matt. When he had walked along the Tessaout with his mules the previous year, he had been convinced that he had been travelling over the velocipedal version of the M1.

I rounded on him accusingly: "Carrying the bikes is becoming very boring."

"I do concede," he replied equably, "that mountainbikes are not quicker than walking over some of these mule tracks."

A village appeared, like Ichbakene, built into the lower face of the cliff, its houses seemingly glued to the rock wall. Matt was encouraged: "This'll be Ait Hamza. Toufrine's just round the corner."

I stopped and pulled out the map. The village was just as likely to be Ait 'Ali-n-Ito. As we walked between the houses, not a soul appeared. I wanted to stop to buy food. Matt was adamant that it wasn't worth it, since we would be in Toufrine any moment and would therefore be able to eat in the *souk*.

We came to a place where the river bounced off a vertical cliff. Either we had to ford the water, as the mules using the route did, or we had to climb the cliff. Neither of us wanted to get our feet wet. We lay on a small patch of grass and stared at the sky.

"Timecheck?"

"One."

We rested for five minutes, then I climbed out onto the foot of the cliff and we relayed the bicycles between each other, dragging them thoughtlessly through the water. At the far side, I threw mine to the ground with disgust. Matt kept on walking. When I caught him up, he was humming:

"You know Matt, my father had this system when he took us climbing in Scotland in mid-winter. He called it 'the train'. When we had to walk three hours through deep snow to get to the foot of a mountain, or when we were tramping down the valley by moonlight after a climb, he would get everyone to walk in the footsteps of the man in front, in a long line. It was easy: you could switch off; go onto auto-pilot. It was actually quite relaxing, even if you were totally done-in."

I watched the back of Matt's ripped trousers plod through the rocks.

"Sounds a good one. I like singing myself . . ." and in time with the thump of his boot-soles he began to put words to his earlier hum:

"Dan is the man,
The man in the van,
The van at the back of the train.
The man at the front,
Thinks Dan is a . . ."

Rooftops crept round the bend. Matt accelerated: "Maybe this is Toufrine . . ."

It wasn't. We sank back into our marching mantras.

We had been walking for six hours since leaving Ichbakene when, inexplicably, the appalling mule track metamorphosed into a full-width jeep-track. Scarcely able to believe our eyes, we dumped the bikes on the ground and climbed onto the saddles. Matt's bicycle had a puncture.

"How can a bike get a puncture when it's not being ridden?" he asked incredulously.

We stuffed the spare inner tube into his rear tyre and 15 minutes later rolled down the final slope towards the houses of Toufrine. As we got closer to the village, it became clear that Toufrine lay on the west side of the river, and that the jeep-track followed the eastern bank. From our vantage point thirty metres above the water, we could see the river curl out of sight round Toufrine's defensive bluff. The river was wide and deep, unruffled by any rocks breaking its fast, metallic surface.

"There's no bridge."

"Doesn't appear to be."

At the bottom of the bank, we took off our boots and socks, lifted the bikes onto our shoulders, and waded into the river. The water level was just high enough to reach my thighs and the bottom of my rolled-up salopettes, which then wicked the freezing moisture upwards to my underpants.

"This is thoroughly unpleasant," I complained. Behind me Matt was skidding on the slimy boulders, a pair of boots swinging from his handlebars and clouting him in the face with every westward lurch. He'd stopped singing. On the far side, we dried our feet on the tops of our socks, and walked up towards the houses.

"I know a really great guy here," said Matt. "Hope he's in. Not gone down to the pub or anything."

Ahmed Mansour's house was the highest in Toufrine. Ahmed had acted as Matt's guide between Toufrine and Tabant the previous year and he seemed pleased to see Matt again. Within a few minutes of our arriving, he produced a steaming *tagine* stuffed with carrots, potatoes and onions.

Ahmed was about twenty-five, dressed in flared trousers of slate and white stripes and a coffee-striped suit jacket several sizes too big. The cuffs and hem were frayed but his moustache was as sharp as a new brush. He had had a busy year, working as a guide for trekkers who drove in to Toufrine over the narrow dirt road which came from the north and over the Tizi-n-Outfi. Years ago this road used to press on south from Toufrine to Tamzrit, then over the Tizi-n-Fedherat to Ouzazarte on the desert fringe. The southern portion has now been abandoned to the landslides and wash-outs, but it is still possible to reach Toufrine by car from the north.

"If we'd known it was going to take us this long to reach Toufrine, we could have made a rendezvous here with the Land Rovers." I said it, knowing how pleased I felt that the Land Rovers were not there.

"I know, I know." Matt was slumped against the wall. "It's always the same: here we are in a real Berber village, in daylight, and the First Unit isn't here to film."

"I think we should rest an hour, then set off up the Fedherat."

"Sounds mad!"

"We've got another three hours of light left. We can't afford to waste it now."

Matt looked at the guide: "Ahmed? Would you be prepared to take us over the pass to Telouet?"

Ahmed said that he would take us as far as Tamda and carry our luggage by mule.

"How late is it now?"

"Three."

It was essential that we reached Telouet by the following day, however outrageous the obstacles between might seem. I looked at the map. The horizontal distance between Toufrine and Telouet was about 100 kilometres, and there was first the Tizi-n-Fedherat to cross, then the Tizi-n-Timililt. The higher of the two, Timililt, stood at 2,588 metres, a full thousand metres above Toufrine. Measured against all our previous days of mule-track mountainbiking, the odds were impossible, but there were two causes for optimism. The first was that we were getting desperate; if we lost another day now, we would surely have to call off the high-level traverse of the Atlas, and destroy the point of the challenge by resorting to lower roads. The second was that Ahmed assured us that the climb up to the Tizi-n-Fedherat was smooth and fast, and we knew from the map that there was a road for the last ten kilometres into Telouet. It was only the middle 80 kilometres that would be rough. Maybe it was just possible to do it in one day.

We were now in a dilemma: we could leave Toufrine at 4pm with Ahmed and a mule, and arrive at Tamzrit at the foot of the Tizi-n-Fedherat by 8 or 9pm, two hours after dark. This would leave us well-placed to climb the pass first thing the next morning. Ahmed was not keen on this option, pointing out that in daylight we need not go to Tamzrit at all since a high route took a short cut across the mountains above the village. Detouring to Tamzrit would be a waste of effort.

The second option was to leave Toufrine at 4pm without Ahmed, and bivouac as far up the track as we could get. Ahmed thought this was insane.

The third option was to spend the remainder of the day resting at Ahmed's house, then leave at the crack of dawn with Ahmed, who would show us the short-cut over the mountains to Lake Tamda. With the rucksacks carried by the mule, we would be able to cycle over tracks which we would otherwise have to walk over. Ahmed was angling for this option.

"Seems obvious to me . . ."concluded Matt.

Matt left with Ahmed to look for food in Toufrine's *souk*. I spread out and looked around. Ahmed had a grand house. Not only did it occupy the highest site in the village, but it was also two-storeyed and built of stone. From the dirt terrace in front of the building a green-painted 'keyhole' door opened onto a staircase leading up through a 90-degree bend to a broad landing, off which led several doors. The main room was 10 metres long by 3 metres wide, with a bench seat hugging the walls. The seats were covered with thick, woollen blankets and at the end where I was sitting, there was a small round table for the tea-pot and glasses. Five metres above the floor, the ceiling was beamed and planked in clean, white wood. Behind my back were stacked four pillars of folded blankets, rugs and sheepskins. I explored the windowsills: there was a gas lamp, a wooden box of beaten-up cassette tapes, a pile of French-language tourist brochures of Morocco, a stack of postcards sent to Ahmed by his foreign clients (mostly French), there were several dud batteries, a huge, plastic radio-cassette, and four small, stamped posters from Mecca.

Matt and Ahmed returned carrying eight cans of condensed milk and some hats and gloves Matt had bought for Ahmed's family. Matt had some news: "You won't believe this Nick, but the *souk* is on the far side of the river."

"How come your legs are dry?"

"There's a bridge. Just round the bend. If we'd gone another hundred metres down the road we'd have seen it."

"Amazing."

"Thing is . . . there's still some light left, and it would be good to film a river-crossing sequence. Go down to the water and wade across the river carrying the bikes."

"Bikes?"

"Well, *bike,*" answered Matt. "*I'll* have to do the filming."

On the bench seats the camera was assembled. We were about to leave the house when Matt stopped in his tracks.

"Wait a minute. This is the only time we've arrived at a Berber house in daylight. We'll film ourselves arriving here and being greeted by Ahmed. Do the river afterwards."

The scene was the terrace outside Ahmed's home. The main characters were one tired cyclist, and one Moroccan wearing a new maroon bobble hat. I would push my bike up to Ahmed; he would greet me and lead me through the green door of his home. With Ahmed would be his family of sundry children. By the time Matt had chosen his filming position, Ahmed's family had swelled to eight, and by the time the light reading had been taken there were sixteen. The first shot went without a hitch: I walked up to Ahmed, he greeted me warmly, and we bent through the low door followed by the stream of children. For the second shot, Matt wanted to film from the inside of the building, so that he had a silhouette of first me, then Ahmed, then the children, coming through the 'keyhole'. We all waited outside for the call. On "Action" I headed for the door, but before I could duck through, I was overtaken by a tidal wave of children fighting to reach the camera first. From outside, I could hear Matt trying to sort out the scrum:

"OK try again. This time, see if you can get through before the children. We can't have the outside shot showing you arriving at the door first, then the inside shot showing the children first. Doesn't make sense. Looks like we're faking it."

We tried again. This time there were more children, and they were more excited. They hit the 'keyhole' all at once; the door frame shook, arms waved and legs got wedged as every child tried simultaneously to squeeze through the tight opening.

Matt struggled outside with the camera: "Mayhem, total mayhem. Let's do the river."

The water was very cold. The route across the river which we had used earlier was the widest and least deep.

"I think it'll be better down there," said Matt, pointing to a small cataract. "The waves make it look more exciting!"

I waded out. The current was much stronger in the deeper water, and the boulders on the bottom bigger and more difficult to balance on. In the centre of the river, with the pack on my back and the bike lifted above the water, I was struggling for balance. Twenty metres away, Matt was crouched over the viewfinder. He shouted: "Now walk backwards, upstream!"

Feeling my way against the current with my skidding heels, I made several metres of progress, until my right foot caught in a slimy cleft and I lurched sideways. For a few appalling moments I swayed lopsidedly on one leg with waves battering at my backside and a bicycle slowly pulling me off balance. I could feel my bare foot sliding with the current. A desperate shrug shifted the weight of the bike across to the opposite shoulder and I staggered to the bank. As I wrung out my trousers on the bank Matt nodded glumly and said: "A drowning sequence would have helped the pace of the story."

A woman on the shingle was boiling a kettle on a fire of twigs. She called me over, and in the gathering darkness I squatted on my haunches in front of the flames, steaming contentedly.

There was one other guest in Ahmed's house that evening, a Frenchman called Christophe who was on a reconnaissance for a trekking company. The company was considering 'opening up' Toufrine and its surrounding valleys to organised adventure holidays. Christophe had stomach problems.

Before we ate, Ahmed brought in a small three-legged brazier of coals. In the quiet hours before bed, we reviewed the rest of the journey. We were now at the end of Day 11 and were roughly halfway between our start in the Sahara, and the finish in the sea. Our original premise that it was possible to use mountainbikes on mule tracks had proved untenable. If we were going to make the Atlantic by the middle of Day 20 – the absolute deadline – then we might have to face the alternative of using lower-level jeep tracks to complete our Atlas traverse. Working back from the sea, we knew that the final dash from Toubkal through the last hills could be done on roads if we ran right out of time. But between Telouet and Toubkal we had another chunk of the High Atlas. Matt thought that there was a mule track from the summit of the Tizi-n-Tichka, above Telouet, to the mountain village of Setti-Fatma, and from Setti-Fatma our maps showed some kind of track – with a break in the 'dashes' for an ominous pass – heading all the way to Tacheddirt and then Imlil, where the climb of Toubkal would begin. The mountain crossing from the top of the Tizi-n-Tichka to Imlil was at least 70 kilometres, with very real possibilities of protracted bike-carrying. We'd just have to go up onto the Tizi-n-Tichka and see what the view looked like.

But for the moment, it was Telouet, our next target, which occupied our minds. Since the days when Atlas Biker was little more than a line on a map in London, Telouet had assumed a significance far beyond its physical scale. On the map it was just a sprinkling of dots, but here we would be reaching a landmark not just in our journey, but in Moroccan history. At Telouet we would bounce off our mule tracks and onto tarmac—albeit for a short distance; here we would have passed our half-way mark between the Sahara and the sea; here we would cross over the main highway that straddles the High Atlas; and here we would meet again with the support crew. But Telouet's most powerful image was of the great ruins described by Gavin Maxwell in his book *Lords of the Atlas*—the ruins of the great Glaoua *kasbah.*

Of the three dominant Lords of the Atlas, the Glaoua clan were the most powerful and based themselves for three generations in an isolated valley on the old trade route that crosses the Atlas spine between Marrakesh and Ouazazarte. The Glaoua found real power at the start of this century, and they peaked with the coming of the French in 1912. They were cunning and ruthless, and at their height were reputed to control over one million men. For this reason, they were courted by Europe's major powers; they had been hosts to Lloyd George and to Churchill, and T'Hami, the most notorious of the Glaoua chiefs, was knighted at the coronation of Edward VII.

One of the many popular legends surrounding the family has it that, in the years before it was clear which of the European nations would finally win control of the Berber lands, four of the brothers decided to back each horse. In order that the family retain control, whatever the outcome, one brother allied himself to the Spanish, one to the British, one to the Germans and one to the French. T'Hami chose the French. The Glaoua *kasbah* at Telouet reflected the aspirations of its owners. It had over 1,000 Negro slaves, a harem, a network of dungeons, a fleet of limousines . . . and a cinema. When the writer Rom Landau visited Marrakesh in the late forties, the Caid Brahim (T'Hami's son) provided him with a beige Studebaker so that he could make an excursion to Telouet. Landau found two *kasbahs*, side by side, one crumbling to ruin, the other new and immaculately white. Inside, he found marble floors and columns, and walls covered with mosaics. A negro served him mint tea from a silver tray. He was treated to a series of dances by a beautiful troupe of Berber women, which he compared to a swarm of butterflies. Ten years later, all this had disappeared. Within a year of Morocco gaining independence from the French, in 1956, the Glaoua were in exile, imprisoned or dead. By allying themselves to the colonial French, and by perpetrating the Moorish feudal wars, they had won the arms of Europe but had lost the hearts of their own people.

Matt and I hoped to reach Telouet, this place of ghosts, in one day's time.

At 6am I wriggled far enough out of my sleeping bag to reach the lamp. With my left hand I turned the knurled plastic knob anti-clockwise until I could hear the faint hiss of escaping gas. With my other hand I fired the cigarette lighter at the fragile mantle behind the glass. The gas ignited with a pop and a flare which quickly subsided into a steady, yellow glow. I looked across the room. Ahmed had already got up; his blankets lay crumpled on the bench. Against the far wall, a carrot-top of hair stuck from the top of the Frenchman Christophe's sleeping bag. Opposite me, the familiar blue woollen cap of my companion was all that protruded from the six-foot silver slug of goose-down.

"Matt! It's six."

A muffled voice said: "Terrific!"

I was pulling on my gloves when Ahmed came into the room with a tray. He laid it on the three-legged table, and we gathered round the coffee and hot bread, tearing off strips and dunking them in the small bowl of warmed oil.

"Shall we take some bread with us?"

"No. Not worth it. We'll be over the passes by midday and the map says there are villages on the far side. Not having any food'll give us an incentive to move faster. If we don't get to Telouet today, we'll have to forget Toubkal."

We said goodbye to Christophe and carried our packs down the stairs, collecting our bikes on the way through the porch. Stars still speckled the sky. A mule was standing against the wall of the alley, muzzle deep in a nose-bag of hay. Slung over the back of the mule were two gaping panniers. Ahmed took our packs and tipped one into each of the panniers, then lashed them tight with a rope. A tent-like *djellabah* perched on a pile of rocks beside the firewood, the only indication of habitation being a pair of hands which poked out of the front trying to tune Ahmed's radio-cassette player. Ahmed pulled away the nose-bag and said "*Ça va*?" We nodded, and he led the mule down the slope of the alley. We carried the bikes until we joined a wide, smooth track. We told Ahmed that we would ride the bikes, and wait for him further up the track.

The bicycles seemed to glide up the gentle gradient. With no packs on our backs, and the remnants of the old French road to Ouazazarte under our tyres, we seemed to move upwards with no effort.

"This is what it was meant to be like!" I called to Matt.

"Can't hear!" In the semi-darkness, Matt's black outline looked like a hole in the night. A tyre split an iced puddle.

"If it's like this all the way up the pass, we'll be over by midday."

Between the early-morning exhalations, I caught snatches of a tune: ". . . black and white cat . . . just as day is dawning . . . postbags in his van . . ."

"Mustn't get too far in front of Ahmed . . ." Matt breathlessly replied from the far side of the track.

"Speak up Brown, you're through."

Daylight percolated into the valley without our noticing. Being able to ride the bicycles had filled us with new optimism and vigour; instead of being a burden, here they were spiriting us effortlessly over a high pass: "Can't believe it!" marvelled Matt pointing at his wheels. "I'd been wondering what these round things were for."

Suddenly the track fell over a cliff into the river. Floods had caused the water to ricochet off the bank holding the old road, which had been undermined then carried away. A narrow shelf edged along the face of the cliff. It was carrying time again. At the far side the track resumed, leading us towards a mountain face whose snow-covered flank reflected the unseen, horizontal sun.

"Pass must be to the right of the mountain."

As we crept towards the Tizi-n-Fedherat the valley narrowed and steepened, and the track curled in and out of bluffs. In places, icicles three-metres long hung down to touch the frozen soil of the old road. When at last we climbed into the sun, we dropped the bikes and sat on a hump of grit. Ahmed and his mule were only fifteen minutes behind us. We reached the top of the pass at 9.20 am, and paused only long enough for Ahmed to point out the distant village of Tamzrit. The cork-coloured houses looked lost amid the sea of white-capped ridges rolling eastwards.

Instead of descending the far side of the pass, Ahmed led us off the track, cutting across a stony shoulder which had been blown clear of snow, and which showed no sign of hoof or foot. Our short column – a mule, a Moroccan in a maroon bobble-hat, and two men pushing bicycles – turned in and out of rocks and snow-patches, then climbed the side of a mountain on a snowy ramp. Only once did Ahmed seem unsure of the way; he halted for a moment beneath some crags then turned to the left to climb on upwards beneath the rocks. From the top of the ridge we dropped down over tussocks of grass then scrambled down to cross a gully. About an hour after we had left the Tizi-n-Fedherat, we joined a disused dirt road. Was this another section of the abandoned trans-Atlas highway to Ouazazarte? It couldn't be; we were now heading west and the old road was meant to be going south. Our course seemed to bear little relation to the map, and yet Ahmed had clearly cut off a huge bend in the route.

Immediately ahead of us was the Tizi-n-Timililt. So convoluted was the dirt track up the pass that Ahmed took us in a straight line to save time. It was agonizingly steep, and we became spread over a kilometre of rocks and snow. As we closed on the top we had to kick through knee-deep *névé*. The dirt road disappeared.

Ahmed only waited long enough for us to catch him up, then tugged his mule up the next slope. We were climbing beneath a cliff. Ahead, and above, we could see the sky. Maybe this meant the top; the final 'top'. Would we be able to peer over an edge, straight down into the blue waters of Lake Tamda, beside which would run the smooth track down to Telouet?

It was when the snow in front of us had been nearly – but not quite – replaced by sky, that I realised that Ahmed was not about to introduce us to the descent that we longed for. Just before the crest of the pass, we turned to the side and began to climb towards a high ridge. The closer we came to the sky, the colder became the wind. In the lee of a band of rocks 20 metres short of the top, Ahmed halted his mule and released the rope round the panniers. He asked us to lift our packs out of the panniers. There was a moment's confusion while the truth dawned on us: "*Ahmed, pourquoi restez ici?*" "It's cold here. Shouldn't we carry on?" we asked in our halting French.

Ahmed shook his head: "*Maintenant je retourne à Tamzrit.*" He tapped his watch. "*Tamzrit est à deux heures d'ici. Je retourne à Toufrine demain.*"

So, Ahmed was not going to come any further. I pulled out the map and spread it on my knee while Matt held down the flapping corners. We must be on the sharp ridge just below Jbel-n-Anghomar, at a height of around 2,800 metres. It was the highest we had been yet. It is not every day that you carry a bicycle to an altitude equivalent to the highest peak in Bulgaria. Ahmed pulled out a slice of bread and tore off two pieces, handing one each to Matt and me: "*Tamda, là!*" he said, pointing up towards the ridge. Following Ahmed's outstretched arm, I scrambled up the snow and peered over the crest of the ridge.

What greeted me was a sight of such Arctic desolation that I thought at first that Ahmed was playing a practical joke. Ahead, there was nothing but a vacuum of icy space: we were poised on the lip of an enormous snow-bowl which marked the head of an empty, utterly white, valley. There was no sign of the lake. The head of the valley was ringed by peaks. I withdrew to the shelter of the rock and looked at Ahmed.

"Tamda?" I asked, pointing. He nodded vigorously then stood up, took the halter off his mule, and left us.

We started the descent into the bowl by dropping the bikes off the ridge into a snow drift, then followed them down a rock step. The snow was thigh deep and the angle of the slope steep enough to allow gravity to do most of the work. We pushed the bikes along the surface of the snow, on their sides, following them on our backsides. Thirty metres down the slope I began to feel uneasy. The time was about 1pm, and the sun would have been warming the snow for at least two hours. I stopped. A wide slurry of heavy powder continued to slither past me. Matt, moving much faster, was already twenty metres lower.

"Matt! It might avalanche. We're better to keep to the side, under the rocks."

Matt looked around. He was right in the middle of the slope, where the built-up snow would be deepest and least stable. Thirty metres to his side, a row of dark spots marked the crest of a buried ridge of rocks which appeared to run down the side of the bowl to the valley floor below.

"Go to the right. Onto that rock band." I watched Matt slide to a halt, then begin a laborious traverse to the rocks. I turned round, and began to tow my bike horizontally across the slope to the shadow of the cliff which cut diagonally down the slope. It was an incredibly stupid situation to get into: even a small avalanche would carry us right to the bottom; if one of us broke bones it would mean a bivouac of at least one night – probably two – while the other went for help. Or it would mean a piggy-back to Telouet. Sweating and cursing I reached the safety of the rock, and began a much more cautious descent.

At the bottom, we fell into a tearing wind which had stripped the loose snow from the valley floor, exposing a fragile crust of ice which gave way with every step, so that our legs plunged through to the knee. We stopped and ripped at packs with frozen fingers; dragged out windproof jackets and hoods. Matt bawled through the wind: "Film! Got to film this!" There were still a few feet of unexposed film left in the Aaton's magazine. In a gale which was strong enough to blow the bikes around as though they were made of cardboard, he filmed me walking down the valley for ten steps.

"Finished! That's it: no more film!" There was nothing we could do now except concentrate on getting to Telouet as quickly as possible.

Matt set off and was soon a pin-figure in the hollow of the 'U' of the valley. I tried to keep up with him, using his deep footsteps for my own. I could see Matt pushing his bike, but when *I* tried it, the wind kept snatching the machine so that the wheels skidded sideways on the snow-glaze and I had to haul the thing back to my side. Finally I lifted the bike onto my shoulders; it was physically harder; psychologically easier.

It was an interminable descent. We were too concerned about the possibility of not reaching Telouet that day to relax. The lower we got, the more frequently we could ride the bicycles. From ice we moved on to rock and grit, then tufted grass. At about 4pm we came to a wide junction with another valley, and took the descending, left fork. Now there were some high pastures; we joined a well-trodden track and suddenly the bikes were flying downwards on a roller-coaster of smooth-earthed dips and bumps. It lasted for twenty minutes, then the valley narrowed to a gorge and the cord of red dust began to jump up and down rock-steps and squeeze through shoulder-high boulders. Tiny terraced fields had been carved into the far bank of the valley. We could hear the echo of water, and of children calling.

The map said that we would reach a place called Anmiter. Matt was sure that a jeep track led from the village to Telouet. Because of this, we knew that the Land Rovers would have come to Anmiter to meet us. They would have collected Annabel off the plane in Marrakesh by now. With the vehicles would be tea and food, and the First Unit could film our reunion in the daylight.

We came to a village. It wasn't Anmiter, but a maze of mule-width alleys led us by right-angles to a widening in the track. Suddenly we were flying down on hard mud marked by the imprint of recent vehicle tyres. The valley began to open: clusters of mud walls peeped through groves of trees in the flattening land ahead. At every bend I expected to see the shoebox-nose of a Land Rover. We rode faster and faster, spinning the pedals in top gear; touching the brakes only on the sharpest bends. Ahead, a heavy cloud slumped over the mountains; never mind: we'd be in the tents in twenty minutes.

The sky cracked and sleet began to slash through the darkening valley, as we swept round the final corner to Anmiter.

There was nobody there. We didn't even stop. If they weren't waiting for us at Anmiter, then they had to be at Telouet, which was another 12 kilometres further on. Another shock swiftly followed: the dirt track switched to tarmac; it was the first surfaced road we had been on for ten days. It felt as if the bike was sliding along on a cushion of air.

The novelty of tarmac was quenched within two minutes by the stiffening sleet and the interminable hill out of Anmiter.

At the top of the hill there was a broad valley: was this Telouet at last? I spun down to cross a river, then the wretched road began to switchback up a steep hill. Again the thunder cackled: a laugh in the dark. Against the rent in the sky I could see the black outlines of buildings on the hill-top. It must be Telouet. Near the top I looked down and saw Matt cycling no faster than walking pace. The road was awash with rain, and in the near dark it shone like oil.

It wasn't Telouet. At the top of the hill was a solitary farm. The road turned a wide bend into the driving rain then tapered into the gloom. I waited again, this time using the pause to tighten my cuffs and the drawstring around my neck. I could feel my body-heat fading with each minute of inactivity. It was incredible that we had not met the Land Rovers yet. Where were they? I saw the un-focused form of Matt emerge from the corner. The wind was so strong that he was having to pedal down the hill. When he drew level with me, I pushed off again.

The road descended evenly. All around were the dark stains of the mountains. Somewhere on the road between Anmiter and Telouet, I had stopped rehearsing what I was going to say to the camera; we were playing a different game now.

It was getting so dark that we had to slow our speed. Whether we found the Land Rovers or not, we were going to have to stop at the next building for shelter. It seemed a pity to have tried so hard and yet to have failed in the last minutes of the day. We would find shelter, rest for an hour, then see if we could find anyone who had seen three Land Rovers.

Through slitted eyes I saw the black angles of a large building – or buildings – grow on the hillside about 500 metres from the road. This had to be Telouet. I wondered where the hotel was; the *Rough Guide* spoke of an hotel which was – small and basic. As long as it had a roof, I didn't care whether I slept on a concrete mattress.

Just then, a pair of yellow headlights burnt two holes in the wild night and, just as quickly, they disappeared. I watched the spot, my retinas retaining the image for several seconds. The lights had come from the black walls over to our left.

"Matt!" I shouted. "See that? Maybe it was one of the Land Rovers."

There was no reply. The road twisted round a bend, and a track led off to the left.

"Better go over to the building. See if the lights were ours. This must be the Glaoua *kasbah*."

A narrow lane led us back up the flank of the hill beneath a towering slab of wall. At the end, the lane stopped at an archway which opened onto an empty, glistening courtyard. We had pedalled into the heart of T'Hami's ancient fortress. No sign of light, or life, could be seen. We turned round and fled to the road.

We were turning to freewheel down the hill when a snatch of engine noise grumbled through the percussive rain. We waited, feet on the streaming tarmac. The sound grew closer. Suddenly we were bathed in yellow light as the orbs of two headlights swung round the wall beside us and juddered to a standstill. An electric horn blared above the storm, gears crashed, and as abruptly as the light had arrived, it pulled back around the wall. We kicked at the pedals, chasing the reversing vehicle up a gritty track and across some mud. There were other vehicles: one, two Land Rovers, and people. A flare of white light stabbed down from the roof of one of the Land Rovers. Arms reached for the handlebars. I blinked in the searing light. I saw Graham Smith advancing with his Aaton on his shoulder. Then I saw a red anorak. The bicycle disappeared. The red anorak advanced and gave me a big, nylon hug.

"Hello there!" said a familiar voice from somewhere inside the hood. The hood leant forward: mouths collided, front teeth clashed. Was that a kiss? I hoped it wasn't one of the camera crew playing a prank.

Matt was trying to lift his leg off his bicycle as Alan Ravenscroft's voice demanded from behind the Aaton, "So tell us what you've been going through?"

Matt swung towards the lens: "Oh, we went through the most horrendous four-day bash over the top of the mountains, and I thought of Chris many times and realised he made the right decision. We just climbed and climbed and climbed, carried and carried and carried – this character over here, I'm sure he's a plant, he doesn't need food, he just photosynthesises."

The camera swung towards me: "What have you learnt in the last few days?"

"We've – learnt – zat – amounnainbike – isnverry – goodfor – muletracks – inna – Atlas – mounnains –" I tried to continue but my face had seized up with the cold.

"And are you ready for Toubkal now?" Alan demanded.

"Gizza-halfanhour-forra-cuppa-tea . . ."

We trooped through a wall of wind-blown trees and found Jeremy squatting over a hissing camp-fire beneath an awning fringed with drips.

"Guys! Good to see you!" he bellowed. "You look as if you could use some *chai*!" He thrust two steaming tin mugs into our hands.

Chris came into the light. Simultaneously, Matt and I asked: "How are you?"

"I had the knee X-rayed. It's ligaments or maybe the cartilage – they can't decide without looking inside the knee."

"Did you go to Marrakesh?"

"Yes . . . I was taken there in the back of the Land Rover, with plastic bags of snow packed around my knee. The day after you left, or that afternoon, I just couldn't move. I couldn't even walk up the steps in the *auberge*. I couldn't do anything."

"Good hospital?"

"Good. Jabbed me with hypodermics and sent me away with pain killers."

"Well, you did the right thing, because we had to carry the bikes for two days continuously."

More faces joined the semi-circle of steaming anoraks. Annabel poured more tea. Jeremy's hand extended over the flames bearing a paper bag full of dates. Everybody was talking at once.

"These dates are . . ."

"What were the maps like?"

". . . not as sweet as the ones we ate in Tabant."

"Well, they were really bad, but at least they had contours."

"So along came this Berber troupe, all dressed up . . ."

"The last bit was the hardest . . ."

"Whaddya mean man! I only bought them yesterday. With the chickens!"

"We having the sardines?"

"You're kidding, they've got '1971' written on their bottoms."

"The dates?"

"No, the chickens."

". . . pedalling into a Force Ten gale."

". . . in tribal costumes."

"Jeremy, this *chai*'s rather severe!"

"So we laid the dolly and shot the singers."

"It's the ginger."

One by one lost faces crept under the awning: Abedelilah, Andy, Mohammed, the camera crew, Alan, until we looked like one long, continuous grin. Behind us, the tents glistened in the firelight.

Matt looked up from his third mug of tea and drew his last deep breath of the day. "It's . . ." he announced, then paused for a moment as if he had forgotten what he was going to say, ". . . good to be here."

Friday 13th

Ghosts (Day 13) – Intermission – Dawn on the Tichka (Day 14) – Matt's Accident – Down and Out of the Atlas – Hanging On (Day 15) – Infectious Apprehensions – In the Dark Again – the Siege of Toubkal (Day 16) – A Night Among the Socks

Day 13 – 16

By morning, the mountains which gripped Telouet had tired of their tantrums and the only reminders of the previous evening's ill-temper were a few quickly-drying drops clinging to the leaves and blades of our glade, and a mantle of white which had extended 500 metres further down the brown walls surrounding thc valley.

The sun had climbed too far to film by the time a voting quorum had dragged themselves from their sleeping bags and assembled over mugs of muesli around Jeremy's tucker-box.

"If we can have you around mid-afternoon chasps, we'll go up to the *kasbah* and film you arriving and walking through the door to watch the dancing we filmed yesterday."

"How long's the filming going to take Alan?"

"An hour. Or two. Three . . ."

"Can't we film now, then move on this afternoon?"

"Light's not right. We only get the colour in the early morning and late afternoon. It's already 11 am . . ."

"So we'd better plan to sleep in Telouet tonight and leave for Toubkal first thing tomorrow."

Quietly, people dispersed. I was too tired to argue for an earlier departure, and in any case, if we had wanted to leave Telouet earlier, I should have got up at dawn and pressed for a pre-breakfast filming session.

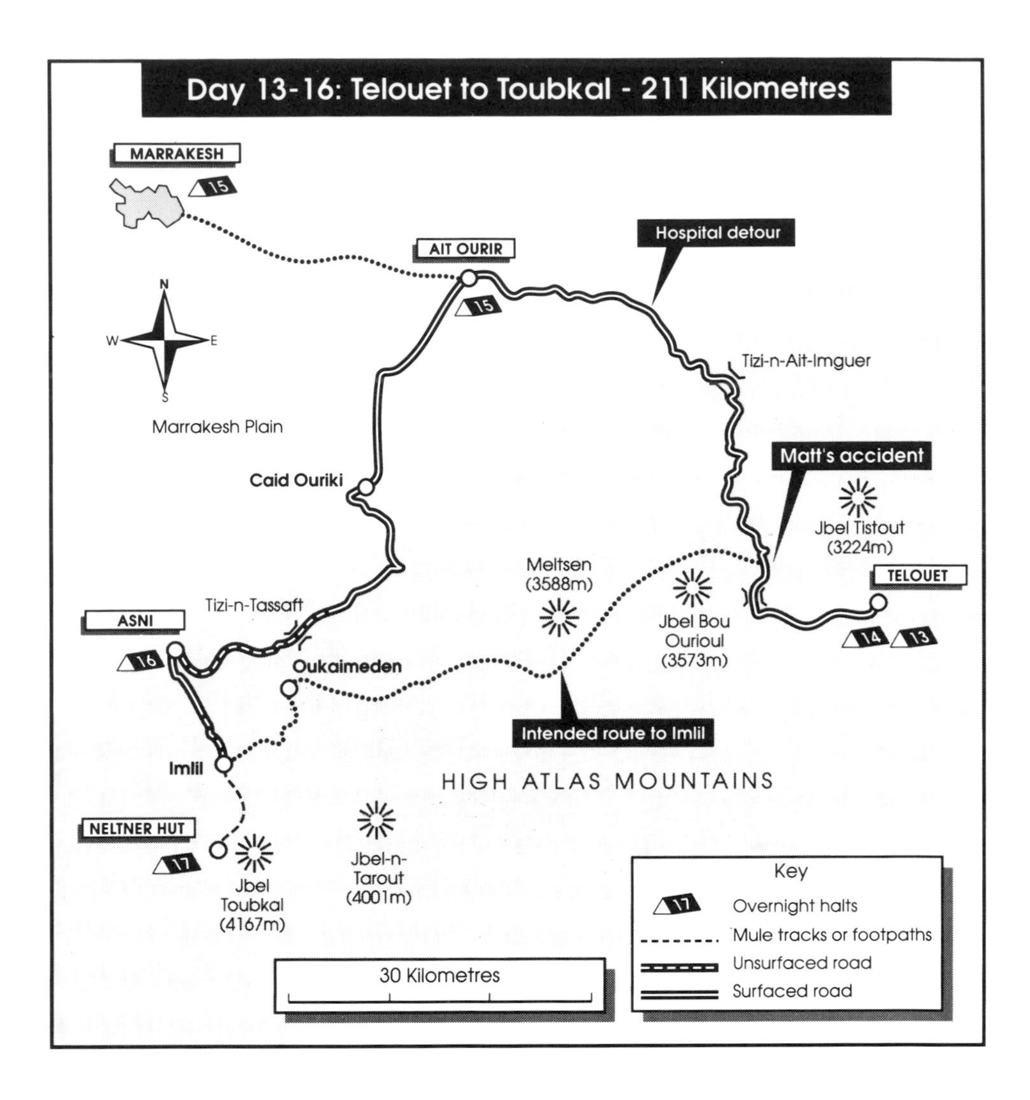

Round the weatherbeaten camp lay the detritus of an expedition which looked as if it couldn't decide whether to dig deeper, or disintegrate. Graham Smith lay in a foetal curl on a Karrimat hugging his stomach; Stuart sat in a collapsible chair staring through his sunglasses at a distant mountain, smoking roll-ups; Phil the Grip continued cleaning lenses; sleeping bags, socks and rancid T-shirts steamed on bushes; Mohammed dozed in the cab of his diesel Land Rover; Alan wandered off to look at filming angles in the *kasbah*; the two bicycles rested against a tree, their once-sharp profiles obscured by encrusted mud; Chris re-bandaged his knee; Abedelilah threw some hand-stands then went with Jeremy to look for food in the *souk*; Andy had disappeared. Annabel (defiantly dressed in red boots, a thick wool skirt, sweatshirt and silk scarf), Matt, and I rounded up a towel each and set off for the river.

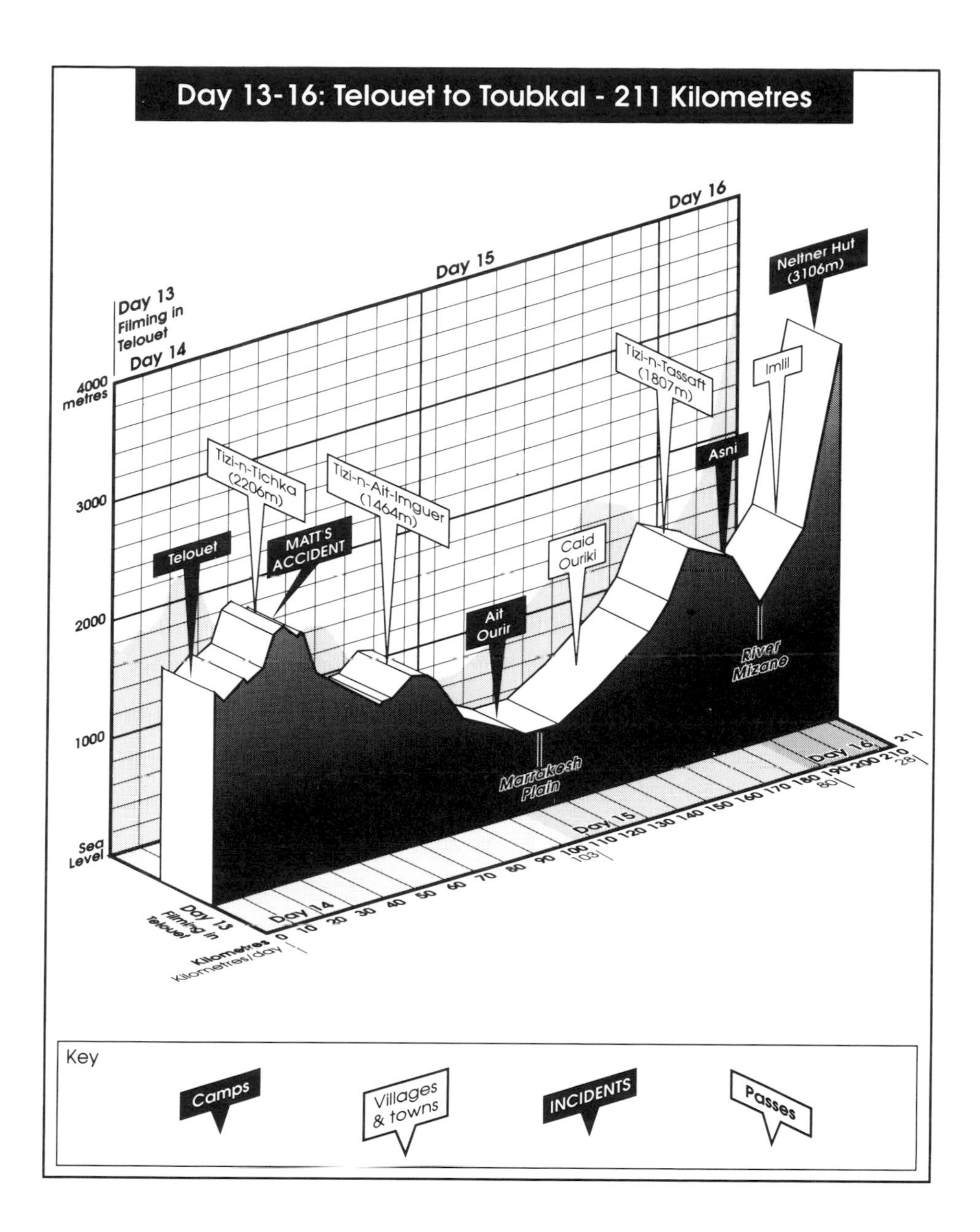

The stones on the river bank were sprinkled with new snow, but the water was relatively warm. From a knee-deep pool we could look towards the crenellations of the old Glaoua *kasbah*. In the foreground, fifty metres upstream, a bearded man stood in the middle of the current, naked except for a pair of green wellington boots. "Don't want to get my feet wet," shouted Matt.

An hour later the whole team gathered over *cous-cous* on the outside table of Telouet's only open café. Alan outlined the sequences he needed to shoot later in the day, and with the maps spread on the table I traced out the remainder of the route.

If we were to reach Agadir in time for Alan to film a finishing sequence during the afternoon of Day 20, we had only 5 days left to ride through the Atlas to the sea. "We can't leave out Toubkal; it's the climax of the journey." Nobody disagreed with Matt, but it was clear that we had run out of time. I was reluctant to abandon the high-level route: "Trouble is, we're back on unknown ground again. From here to the top of the Tizi-n-Tichka is easy; it's all road; but from the top of the pass to Toubkal, we're on mule tracks and at least a couple of sections where the map marks no tracks at all. At its quickest it will take three days to reach Toubkal; if things go wrong again, it might take four. We always have the fallback option of a flat-out night-ride from the top of Toubkal to the sea. It's about 300 kilometres; we could do it in 24 hours if we didn't stop."

There was no enthusiasm for this idea.

"We'll just have to go up to the top of the Tichka early tomorrow, and look west. If we can see a good track we'll take it; if not we'll have to find a lower route round to the north."

There was an hour to spare before the sun sank low enough for Alan to film. Annabel and I wandered through the waist-high grass of the graveyard to the tottering walls of the Glaoua *kasbah.* In the corner of the courtyard, the heavy, studded wooden door was firmly locked. The caretaker appeared. He wore an old Army greatcoat, and carried in his hand the biggest key I had ever seen. We had no time for a full exploration, but Annabel led me to the room which had been filled with dancers the previous day. Here, in the heart of the *kasbah* was a large, vaulted room, patrolled by circular pillars and minutely decorated with millions of glazed chips to form floor-to-ceiling patterns of roundels, octagons, grids and arabesque motifs. The colours; turquoise and ochre, ice-white and midnight blue, and several shades in between, seemed to be those of a Moroccan springtime.

Away from this main room, no attempt appeared to have been made to preserve the *kasbah.* A pair of storks had nested on the top of the minaret; the balcony that Rom Landau had watched the dancing from forty years ago was hanging drunkenly from the wall; the garage that had once housed T'Hami's limousines was collapsing. The reluctance of the Moroccans to allow this symbol of tyranny to become a national monument is causing it to crumble, bit by bit, back into the soil from which it was moulded. We wandered through rooms that had been stripped and their windows broken; the skeletons of their frames were outlined against the harsh, outside light. Only the mosaics remained, glued to the walls like faded snapshots.

From the roof of the *kasbah* it was possible to look west towards our next barrier: between us and the sea lay the highest part of the High Atlas. It was a windless day with a calming sun; at odds with the tension caused by our unrealistic goal. Tomorrow morning, up on the Tizi-n-Tichka, we were going to have to decide between two routes: one was hard but true; the other a safe compromise. An adventure which fails at some point to create this confrontation is not an adventure at all; and a successful adventure is the one which takes the right one of the two roads.

The green-rimmed terraces and empty sky; the clean mountains and dry road all seemed to be smirking at us. It was Day 13: a Friday.

Alan had made such a thorough reconnaissance of the area that the afternoon's filming was as tightly choreographed as if he had been working in a studio packed with props and hands. He needed three sequences to draw us from the mountains into the *kasbah*, where the film would then pick up with the previous day's singing-dancing routine. The first sequence was a long shot of two cyclists stumbling wearily across the river three kilometres outside Telouet. The second sequence recorded our arrival at the walls of the *kasbah* and the third sequence watched us ride across the courtyard, prop our bikes against the wall, then disappear through the huge, studded door. We finished filming at dusk.

By torchlight, Matt and I packed rucksacks ready for the following day. "Nick, we'll have to be away by 6.30 tomorrow; Alan wants to film us in the sunrise at the top of the pass."

"How far's the top from here?"

"About 25 'k'; they say about 40 minutes should do it."

"Apparently the café on top of the pass will be open for breakfast. A quick sprint, then we can decide over a huge fry-up what we're going to do between the Tichka and Toubkal."

My boots were frozen solid and it was still dark. I hoped that the dawn-shot on the Tichka would justify this sub-zero start to the day. The film crew had already taken down their tents and were packing the V8 Land Rover by torchlight. On top of my thermal underwear, salopettes and insulated jersey I pulled on overtrousers, waterproof jacket, gloves, overgloves, down hat, trilby and hood, and I still felt cold. There was not yet enough light to read a watch by as Matt and I pedalled stiffly over iron-hard mud-ruts to the road then turned onto the smooth tarmac and freewheeled down the hill past the *kasbah*.

"Ice. Watch the ice!"

Frost had grown like mould across the hollows in the road. It is particularly horrible to start cycling in the dark, in a sub-zero temperature with no breakfast. Still, we only had to last for forty minutes then we could pile into the steamy warmth of the Tichka café and demolish an omelette. Or three. My stomach rumbled at the thought.

For three kilometres the road followed the valley of the River Telouet. Our tyres snapped through black ice, and clouds of white breath streamed from our mouths. The wind rushing over my unmalleable boots refrigerated my feet, and so the arrival of the first uphill climb came as a chance to warm up. I lost touch with Matt, who seemed to be going slowly.

Near the top of the first uphill, the film crew grumbled past heading for the summit of the Tichka where they would set up the camera and wait for us, and the dawn.

I flicked through a small hamlet. A man wearing two *djellabahs* was standing by the bonnet of his red Bedford truck, poking with a long stick a flaming pyre of twigs he had lit under the sump of his frozen engine. A dog jumped up and down on a bank, barking insanely but reluctant to chase. The sky which had begun to lighten was burning away the stars. Where the road steepened to haul us up the Tizi-n-Tichka I stopped and pulled off some clothes. Deep snow smothered the trunks of the stunted junipers dotted erratically across the slopes on each side of the shiny strip of tar. Despite the long view I had down the valley, Matt was still out of sight.

Twenty minutes later, I pedalled into the sun. I looked at my watch. Someone had miscalculated: I had left camp 1½ hours ago on a journey which we had been told would last only 40 minutes. We were already too late to film in the dawn.

The single-track road up from Telouet joined the Marrakesh – Ouazazarte highway three kilometres short of the top of the pass. Snow had been packed by passing traffic into slippery ruts of ice. Ahead I could see the notch in the skyline marking the high-point. I could almost smell the hot olive oil. I felt sorry that I hadn't waited for Matt so that we could enjoy the ecstasy of entering the warmth of the café together. I had been too cold and too impatient to stop and wait for him.

The crest of the Tizi-n-Tichka occurred on a broad bend etched into the end of the massif of 4,000-metre peaks lorded over by Toubkal. The Tichka is the highest surfaced road in Africa north of the equator. I watched the café approach. It was surrounded by waist-high ridges pushed up by the snow-plough. The Land Rover was parked outside. I seemed to be pedalling through an imaginary barrage of omelettes, mint tea and hot bread. Stuart walked round the back of the Land Rover as I pulled up. He was shivering convulsively, and looking nervous: "You're out of luck I'm afraid."

"What?"

"It's closed. The café's closed."
"Oh no! – You can't be serious!"
"Where's Matt?"
"Coming," I said quietly, leaning my bike on a snow bank.
I waited in the cab of the Land Rover until I got too cold then got back on the bike and freewheeled back down the pass. I met Matt near the junction with the Telouet road. He was moving very slowly, and swearing: "Forty *** minutes, my *** ***! Those *** need their *** heads *** looked at!"
"Matt, I've got some bad news!"
"Bad news? My *** knees are playing up; a forty-minute ride turns out to be two *** hours; it's *** Arctic conditions. How much worse can it get!"
"Well, the café's closed. We can't get breakfast here!"
"***! ***! ***! ***! ***! ***! ***s!"
The atmosphere at the top of the pass was tense. Fortunately, the film crew had found an *auberge* several kilometres down the north side of the pass. This information averted a messy incident. Matt and I were filmed pedalling past the signboard saying 'Tizi-n-Tichka 2260 m'; a transposition of the Tichka's actual figures of 2206. After three takes, we freewheeled downwards for about six kilometres through sunny snow-banks to reach an isolated building at the foot of a tall mountain.
The front of the building was a café. It smelt of damp, and old newspapers. Nailed to the wall of its reeking lavatory were pages torn from pornographic magazines. The cistern was broken. The small omelettes looked as if they had been rinsed in warm grease. The bread was stale. In silence we ate the remainder of Jeremy's dates folded into the dry bread. The morning's miscalculations with time, distance, and the café had put Matt in a bad mood. It had been an unnecessarily tough start to what we already knew would be a long day.
The sky was empty and blue, and everything except the narrow strip of wet road was coated in a thick cloak of new snow. The mountainous country around us reminded me of Switzerland. This was the only opportunity the First Unit would get to film us in deep snow. Ever since we had described our descent down the snowy valley above Lake Tamda, Alan had worried that we had not recorded it sufficiently. Here, on the accessible slopes of the Tizi-n-Tichka, was a chance to film mountainbikes on snow.
In a column led by Alan, the three men of the First Unit camera crew, followed by Jeremy and a hobbling Chris acting as the Second Unit, followed by Matt and me carrying bicycles, tailed by Annabel with the still cameras, set off up the slopes behind the *auberge* to re-create the mountain crossing to Telouet.

Ahead, Alan stopped and turned, staring down an imaginary camera-line. A concrete bunker stuck obtusely from the snow in the valley behind the *auberge*. Alan pursed his lips and said to Phil Millard: "Pop down and move that blockhouse will you dearie!" We started climbing a short but steep spur. Alan looked upwards. I tried to be helpful: "We can come over the skyline on that next-door spur then hurtle down the crest of it to the valley."

"Well, go up to the top and we'll see what it looks like." He turned and spoke to Jeremy and Chris, who peeled off and barged a route through the snow to a spot 50 metres from the foot of the spur. Matt and I climbed to the skyline and waited. Half way between our position, and the valley, the First Unit went into a huddle around the camera. I said to Matt: "Shall I go first?"

An unusually detached, taciturn Matt said "Sure," and sniffed.

"About 5 yards apart," Alan said.

"Sure."

It wasn't cold in the sun, but this filming – later in the morning than planned – was postponing our start on the final leg of the mountain traverse to Toubkal.

I saw Alan lift his arm and wave.

"OK! See you at the bottom . . ."

I pushed off. The bike quickly gathered speed. From above, the snow on the spur had looked as if it had a hard crust, but the sun had softened the surface so that the bike's wheels slashed straight through to the rocks beneath. There was no time to shout a warning to Matt; I was flying downwards on a bike which felt as if it was skating on marbles. I forced my weight back as far as I could, hanging on to the stuttering handlebars, not daring to touch the brakes. My trilby flew away. Any sideways slip and I'd be head over heels. I hit the valley at full tilt and the bike buried itself in snow, catapulting me over the handlebars. I pulled myself upright and turned to watch Matt follow me down.

Matt was lying under his bicycle about half way down the spur. He was not moving. I bellowed upwards.

"All right?"

There was no answer. He was in a half-sitting position, and I thought that perhaps he was taking a breather before continuing down the ridge. Or maybe he was waiting for the film crew to finish what must have been a dramatic shot of his fall. Leaving my bike at the valley, I started climbing back up the spur, to check that Matt was unhurt.

After several steps I heard him shout into the snow: "Come over here . . . There's some really good blood!"

With the camera on one shoulder, Graham Smith was floundering through deep snow from the adjacent ridge, spurred on by the prospect of blood on celluloid.

I reached Matt. He was trying to sit up. Then I saw his forehead. An enormous serrated gash ran parallel with his left eyebrow. The side of his face was already scarlet and his eye-socket was puddled with blood. Inside the gash I could see layers of lard-coloured tissue.

"That's a good one," I said encouragingly. I pulled the bike clear.

"Is it?" asked Matt.

I pulled off my pack and stuffed it under Matt's head. Alan arrived. I looked around for someone to provide warm clothing but the slope seemed full of people fiddling frantically with cameras and microphones. A wide-angle lens the size of a dinner-plate arrived. Using the tiny first-aid kit I carried in the lid of my pack, I cleared away enough blood to see that we were going to need the larger medical kit carried in the Land Rovers.

"And get the man in the *auberge* to boil some water too," I bawled down the slope. Andy ran downhill.

Matt walked back down the slope, got half way back to the *auberge*, and on the first snow-free rock, lay down. Andy arrived with the big medical kit. Six different hands swabbed liquid antiseptic into the wound then scrabbled for the privilege of attaching the sticky 'butterfly stitches' that would drag the gaping split in his head closed. Once the blood flow had stemmed, we plastered a vast white dressing across the side of Matt's head. "D'you think you can walk?"

"Yup." Matt pushed himself into a sitting position, then stood up.

"How do you feel?"

"I feel great, but I've lost my glove," he said through clenched teeth.

"It's in your mouth."

"So it is . . ."

"Matt, we've got to get this looked at by someone sensible. It needs stitching."

"Yup."

There was now no question of setting off across the mountains on the direct route to Toubkal. We needed to get Matt to Marrakesh as soon as possible.

"D'you want to get in the Land Rover?"

"No. I'll ride."

Matt walked slowly to his bike, then changed his mind and crossed to the diesel Land Rover. He climbed inside. A few seconds later he came out again.

"What's the matter?" I asked him.

"Where are my over-trousers?"

"You're wearing them."

Matt climbed onto his bike and rolled out into the road. I rode beside him, unsure as to whether he was likely to pass out or develop delayed shock and pedal straight on at the next corner; we had 2,000 metres of hairpins to descend. After Matt had swerved successfully around the first few bends, I relaxed.

As we rolled past the snow-banks I sifted the options. If Matt was able to cycle down the Tizi-n-Tichka without falling off, it seemed likely that he would be able to manage a modified route to Toubkal. There was not any point in looking further ahead than that. But the only way Matt could contemplate cycling to Toubkal would be if he had his head 'fixed' today. A day spent in a Marrakesh hospital, however, would make it impossible to reach the coast in the 20-day limit.

On the way down the Tizi-n-Tichka, I got a puncture, and then the road tired of sticking with the steeply falling valley of the Ghdat, and climbed over an irritating little pass called the Ait-Imguer. At 2pm, we found the Land Rovers parked outside a café just over the pass. We rested for an hour; another two hours' cycling took us to the plains. We had agreed that the entire caravan – bicycles, support crew and film crew – should rendezvous at the village of Ait Ouriki, a small market town beside the junction of the main road to Marrakesh and the side road which turned west to skirt the mountains. It was at this junction that decisions would have to be made.

"How d'you feel about carrying on?" I asked Matt. The bandage on his head had a roundel stain the size and colour of a Victoria plum.

"Oh, I'm carrying on all right."

"Then we need to dump the bikes here, drive into Marrakesh and get your head fixed, then come back here in time to cycle on to Toubkal tomorrow. How's that sound?"

"Sounds fair enough."

The camera crew's V8 was designated an 'ambulance'. The patients (or victims as we insisted) were one battered cyclist and a cameraman with gut-rot. Alan drove, Abedelilah came to iron out formalities, and I came for the ride. We arrived at the walls of the city at dusk, and drove round to the great gate of Bab er Rob. Grinning, Abedelilah pointed from the window: "*Le cimetière!*" And then, as we came through into the gloomy ducts of the ancient Medina, he pointed again: "*Les tombes! Les tombes Saadiennes!* No problems!" The two victims stared ahead, not appreciating his humour.

The doctor Abedelilah had guided us to in the Medina was not at home. We became lost in the maze of illogical roads running crookedly off the north side of the Square de Foucauld, so Abedelilah asked a boy on a moped to guide us to Gueliz – the ordered grid of the French quarter.

Here, behind the wide metal gate of 92 Boulevard Mohammed Zerktouni we found the clinic of a clean-shaven physician in a tweed jacket. He carefully peeled back the congealed dressing gummed to Matt's forehead while Alan held a stainless steel trough at Matt's cheek to catch any bits which fell off. Dr Gamil was clearly impressed by the efficiency of the butterfly stitches.

"*Les sutures sont bonnes.*" He told us that it wasn't necessary to do any more.

This was a disappointment. Surely a hole as mortal as this demanded real stitches: needles and yards of twine?

"Let's find another doctor," I insisted.

In the excitement of exploring Matt's injury, we had forgotten the other victim.

"Where's Graham?"

Alan left the room, and returned, a few moments later. "Being sick in the street."

Graham was led into the room. Dr Gamil listened to his symptoms, and prescribed four courses of drugs.

"It's OK," we assured Graham, whose skin in the electric light had assumed a malarial pallor, "one of those drugs is bound to be an antibiotic."

Dr Gamil kindly came with us in the Land Rover to show us the way to the Polyclinique du Sud, on the corner of Boulevard Yougoslavie. The doctor explained to the receptionist that we had a patient requiring surgery, then he took his fee, and departed. A few minutes later a small, greying man wearing a trim, grey suit appeared. He introduced himself as Dr Faligant and said that he would take Matt to the operating theatre right away.

The hour and a half that Matt was away seemed interminable. Alan had left with Abedelilah to take Graham to the Smara Hotel, where he could be sick less publicly. When Matt walked slowly back to the reception desk, he was wearing a lobotomy-sized bandage around his head.

"What happened? Was it OK? Did they use new needles? How . . ."

"11 stitches: 4 deep ones and 7 on top. And 3 anaesthetics."

Dr Faligant reappeared, wiping his hands on a snow-white towel: "*Il y a une blessure profonde*," he beamed, and shook us both by the hand.

We were kept in Marrakesh overnight because the chemists which could supply the anti-tetanus serum Dr Faligant insisted we obtain for Matt were all closed. Matt departed before breakfast, calling first at a *pharmacie* and then at the Polyclinique du Sud where he had the serum injected into his backside.

He hobbled back to the Smara clutching a buttock and muttering about the unexpected additional challenge of one-legged mountainbiking. We drove the 30 kilometres back to Ait Ouriki in time to catch the rest of the team engaged in a slow-motion breakfast in the middle of a field. Half-dismantled tents, tea-mugs and last night's pot of spaghetti *ragoût* occupied a square of mown hay belonging to a farmer whose wife had woken the campers with a tray of mint tea.

By 10.30, Matt and I had recovered our rucksacks and bicycles, and pedalled the two kilometres back to the road junction which marked the end of our previous day's ride.

"I'm not going to have anyone say that I missed an inch of this ride," winced Matt.

"How d'you feel?"

"So-so. It's the anaesthetics mainly. They'll wear off."

The road ran like a pencil line across the irrigated panels of green which had once been the giant garden so coveted by the Glaoua tribes of the overlooking mountains. Now, not even the wind ruffled the gently rising air of the fertile pediment separating Marrakesh from the High Atlas. In front of our tyres the pencil line tapered to a vanishing point buried at the foot of an obliquely angled silver wall which was still fifty kilometres away.

Our options had now narrowed to one: all we could do was limp to the foot of Toubkal. Whoever was fit enough could then make the ascent of the mountain, and then sprint for the sea for the midday deadline on Day 20. Unless Matt made a miraculous recovery, mule-tracks would from now on be out of bounds. We had five days left.

For 25 kilometres we pedalled on our own along a seemingly level but imperceptibly rising road which turned only one corner. Twelve kilometres from the Marrakesh road, our single-track byway elbowed left and drew another ruler line into the distance. This time the line pointed straight at the mountains.

Matt rode slower and slower, and we became separated over two or three kilometres. Some boys at an isolated farm took a break from hitting each other with sticks and threw stones at me. I waited out of range for long enough to watch Matt survive the barrage. I arrived at Caid Ouriki on my own. The main street angled up from the bridge over the Ourika, and was lined by cafés whose owners were carrying out onto small tables their lunchtime ranks of seeping *tagine* pots. I chose a café, ordered 11 coffees, and waited.

Matt arrived and slumped into one of the plastic chairs. The coffees came, with cinnamon. It was warm and peaceful in the street. The Land

Rovers had disappeared and unknown to us, were involved in a minor domestic drama. The diesel vehicle, occupied as usual by Jeremy, Mohammed and Abedelilah, had had a puncture. When they tried to mend it they found that they had a jack with which to lift the injured vehicle off the ground, but no wheel brace to remove the wheel. With the encouragement of Jeremy, the threesome decided that their time could most constructively be spent in a Zen routine, lying on their backs in the sun.

The disabled Land Rover and crew were discovered by the $2\frac{1}{4}$, driven by Andy who had returned to find out why the despised diesel was no longer filling his rear-view mirror. Made cross by yet another reminder that, but for him, the entire fleet of vehicles would have fallen by the wayside days ago, Andy dropped a wheel-brace out of the window, and turned around to catch up with the camera crew's V8, driven by Alan who was fuming about the absence of the two support vehicles.

It took an hour for the subdued remnants of the team to arrive at the café in Caid Ouriki. The village was at the foot of the foothills. If we really were going to have a crack at the rest of the Atlas, we needed an infusion of enthusiasm.

The map implied that some sort of track existed from Aghbalou (the next village), over the Tizi-n-Tassaft to Asni, the village lying at the foot of Toubkal. Nearly all of the track was marked with two parallel lines, suggesting a route wide enough for vehicles, but two sections mysteriously thinned to a single, pecked line. These parts of the route would clearly be unsurfaced, but overall, the route promised an immediate return to the mountains over a trail where at least we would be unlikely to become lost. It was certainly a lot more interesting than the sensible route round the bottom of the mountains to Asni, which involved a gentle climb on tarmac which we could have completed in time for afternoon tea.

We left Caid Ouriki early in the afternoon. The road ascended gently beside the silted floor of the River Ourika then swung hard right into the tributary valley of the Tarzaza. I leap-frogged ahead of Matt, wanting to peep around every next corner to see what problems lay ahead. The Land Rovers were waiting for us in the small village of Magast. It was from here that the map showed a pecked-line track leaving the road for the crossing of the Tassaft pass. Nobody in the village knew of the track, but we were told by a man in a taxi that there was a *piste* to Asni leaving the valley ten kilometres further on.

Twenty kilometres later we had found nothing. Matt had dropped far back on the steepening climb and I began to doubt that we would reach Asni that night. So long as we left this valley before dark, I knew that we would be committed to finding the route over the Tizi-n-Tassaft; if we hesitated in the valley of the Tarzaza I knew that the journey would never recover its momentum. Every kilometre, the angle of the climb seemed to steepen; above the forested crags of the Atlas, storm-clouds blocked out the sun.

I passed the film crew squatting behind the camera under the damp rocks of a road-cutting. I heard Alan say: "OK, cut!" and then shout after me: "There's a track just round the corner Nick. It's signed to Asni."

They were all waiting at the junction. Where the main road to Oukaimeden swung round a hairpin, a grit track launched upwards into the trees. On the corner sat a huge yellow earth-mover with Jeremy in its driving seat wearing his Andean poncho and a bobble hat.

Matt arrived twenty minutes later.

"How d'you do it?" I asked encouragingly. "Three anaesthetics in the arms, tetanus in the bum, 11 stitches in your head and a pair of duff knees." He managed a grin and asked for chocolate.

"Looks as if the Land Rovers are going to be able to come with us to Asni after all."

"Good," replied Matt.

The grit track zig-zagged up through the trees and onto a bare shoulder of mountain. It began to rain. Since leaving Caid Ouriki we had climbed about one thousand metres. It was getting cold. At first, the track was flooded and muddy. Then it switched to snow patches. It was just wide enough for the Land Rovers, and deeply rutted. As we gained more height, the rain turned to heavy sleet. The light began to fail. With no mudguards on the bikes, arcs of freezing mud spun from the tyres, splattering us from our foreheads to our navels. Water ran down our legs and filled our boots. The Tizi-n-Tassaft must have been at a T-junction we passed without stopping. With the light fading and no land less than 45 degrees steep, except for the narrow shelf of the road, the urgency to find lower, warmer, drier, flatter ground on which to camp pushed us on. There were two steep little rises – too steep. Willpower was now rationed. We climbed off the bikes and pushed them up the snow-ruts of the long-gone Land Rovers.

While Matt and I were preoccupied with issues such as how to prevent icy water from running down our necks and how to balance a slithering mountainbike on runnels of snow fringed by a rock face on one side, and a precipice on the other, the occupants of the three Land Rovers were preoccupied with their own concerns. In the leading vehicle, the film crew's apprehensions were building fast. Up until this point, they had been spectators; they had been voyeurs and witnesses, but not participants. The ascent of Toubkal was to be the climax of the film, and a moment they needed to record; the one moment the film could not do without was the arrival of a mountainbike on the snowy summit of Toubkal under a clear blue sky. But to record this moment, the First Unit would have to climb Toubkal too. As the vehicle swayed and crashed, Graham Smith held his stomach and repeated: "I'll have to see tomorrow. Phil, you may have to take the camera for me."

One hundred metres back, the occupants of the $2\frac{1}{4}$-litre Land Rover were pensive. Chris was once again pinning his hopes on rejoining the 'active' part of the expedition on the following morning. The swelling in his knee had subsided, and he was planning to limp to the summit of Toubkal, then pick up his bike on his return to the valley, and cycle with Matt and me to the coast. There was no need for Andy to climb Toubkal, but he had promised himself that however horrendous it might turn out to be, it would be a welcome break from mending engines. He had climbed fells in the Lake District. Since Toubkal was more than four times higher than Scafell Pike, its difficulties for Andy could only be imagined. For Annabel, who had been at the base camp of the 1987 British expedition to Shishapangma in the Tibetan Himalayas, the altitude was not a problem. She was going to be the only one on Toubkal who would have time to take still photographs.

One kilometre back down the track, the cab of the diesel Land Rover reverberated to the bellowing chords of Abedelilah, Mohammed and Jeremy, who were singing 'Hey Jude' in Arabic, French, Spanish and English.

With nothing but the dark pines for company, Matt and I were grinding along wordlessly. We camc to a sleet-swept huddle of houses sitting in a notch in the mountains. Graham had somehow found the energy to film again. The soil was very red: the colour of dried blood, and a family were standing in the shelter of their doorway watching the film crew. A sickly bloom of orange light percolated through the clouds as the sun expired over someone else's mountain.

After we had cycled out of 'shot', we stopped. Alan walked across to us. "It's downhill from here chaps." Matt looked up: a pair of red-rimmed eyes staring from a face concealed by two weeks' growth of beard and three hours of mud. "It started going downhill a long time ago!" he muttered.

Alan continued: "We'll leave you two to go at your own speed, and we'll drive on and get some digs sorted out down in Asni."

It was a much longer descent than we had expected. For twenty kilometres the track writhed down the mountain. It became completely dark about one-third of the way down. Andy had waited behind with the $2\frac{1}{4}$ Land Rover, and now drove behind us illuminating the way with his headlights. Under the harsh burn of the electric light every bump, rock and pot-hole on the track stood out in exaggerated relief so that it looked as if we were trying to cycle down a riverbed. My fingers ached so badly from gripping the brakes that I had to ride one-handed, shaking the circulation back into the relieved hand. I could only guess at Matt's discomfort. Far, far below, we could occasionally see the pinpricks of the other two vehicles' lights. I prayed that those lights would not stop moving. Just a small avalanche or mud-slide would stop us getting through.

An hour after nightfall we reached the first houses. The track suddenly levelled, then turned across the shingle of the River Rhirhaia. In the dark, the water swooshed by as smooth and black as ink.

We waited until Andy caught us up, then climbed onto the bumper of the Land Rover and, clutching the bikes to our chests with one hand, clung to the wing mirrors with the other as the car bumped and slithered through the current. Alan was waiting on the far shore. He had driven back to the river to meet us. As we cycled up to his window, he said: "Welcome to Asni chaps. Dinner's waiting."

The morning of Day 16 was one of those mornings which gives rise to unbounded optimism because it starts so badly that life can only improve. By the point of no return (breakfast), I was asking for the chance to re-wind to dawn, or fast-forward to the afternoon. It started at 6.30, with one of the staff of the 'Grand Hôtel du Toubkal' hammering on seven bedroom doors. This was quickly followed by a reminder that I had inherited Graham's stomach problem. Breakfast in the dining room consisted of toast and marmalade, which seemed insufficient fuel for climbing a 4,000-metre mountain in winter. At the cost of a twenty-minute delay, the kitchen staff produced some omelettes. Graham Smith hadn't been seen since our arrival the previous evening. Matt came down late, said little and ate little, and looked depressed. He had missed the previous evening's meal, had been sick, then suffered half an hour of feverish shakes. He didn't know if he would make it to Toubkal. Having sacrificed his breakfast to pack the Land Rovers, Andy came into the dining room as everybody was leaving and said, "Mohammed has just driven over someone's rucksack."

"Never mind," I said charitably, "he didn't do it on purpose." When I got outside I found that it was my rucksack he had driven over.

Mohammed was now the only one in the group who remained above the undercurrent of tension and expectation which had invaded the group. He was consistently cheerful. Wordlessly the film crew carried their big silver boxes from their rooms.

Climbing Toubkal would take us a minimum of two days: first we had to pedal up to Imlil, at the end of the road, and then climb the narrow valley of the Mizane on mule tracks, to the Neltner climbing hut. After a night in the hut, we would launch our bid for the summit of the mountain.

I quickly checked over the two mud-caked bicycles and peered south-westwards through the dead light. It was impossible to separate Toubkal from the cluster of peaks that crammed together on the Atlas spine. Toubkal is an elusive mountain; all but invisible from below and reached by a dog-leg climb up a valley which has a habit of sending the unwary the wrong way. One of Budgett Meakin's many Victorian adventures in Morocco was an attempt to locate and climb the highest peak in the Atlas. At the time, it was thought that this was a mountain called 'Miltsin' (probably a confusion with Meltsen, a 3,588-metre peak 40 kilometres east of Asni), and Budgett Meakin determined on an assault. Well, he did not find Miltsin, but ironically he did attempt to climb Toubkal. In Aremd he hired three guides, and, promising them a dollar apiece if they could get him to the summit, they set off up the valley. After being apprehended by a band of armed men, Budgett Meakin climbed some way up the mountain above the shrine of Sidi Chamharouch before being beaten by lack of light. On his descent, the armed men were waiting. Blows were exchanged, and Budgett Meakin was obliged to part company with an undisclosed sum of money before he "rode back disgusted" towards Marrakesh.

It was still not properly light when Matt and I climbed onto our bikes at 7.40 and began the 16-kilometre climb up the side valley irrigated by the black waters of the Mizane. I had been along this valley before, on a sunny morning a year before when the water had been splashing against the small meadows. Now all colour and life had been frozen out of the valley. After 8 kilometres, the tarmac ended and we bumped back into the familiar purgatory of grit and rock. My rear tyre punctured. "Carry on, I'll catch you up," I shouted to Matt. I mended the puncture, and resumed the climb. Ten minutes later, the tyre was flat again. Rather than go through the whole tyre-lever, look-for-the-hole, clean-the-innertube, apply-the-cement, wait-for-it-to-dry, affix-the-patch, stuff-in-the-tube, replace-the-tyre, pump-it-up, pull-on-the-rucksack, remember-the-pump, take-off-the-rucksack rigmarole I decided to pump up the tyre then ride as fast as I could. I reckoned that if I could make two kilometres between deflations, I would only have to stop and pump up the tyre three times before reaching Imlil. It was not a day for logic.

The dust-patch in front of Imlil's few houses contained a circus of mules and people attempting improbable balancing acts with bits of bicycle, film cameras, mountaineering equipment and personal luggage known to include at least one bottle of brandy, two Sony Walkmen and several paperbacks. Circling the entertainers were an appreciative audience of Moroccans drawn from Imlil's shifting population of mountain guides, shop-keepers, bar-owners, porters and the driver of the Asni-Imlil taxi, a Peugeot pick-up, who had assumed (correctly) that not all the foreigners who had so boldly set off from Asni to climb Toubkal would get beyond the end of the road.

In the epicentre of all the juggling and animal tricks I saw Abedelilah trying to organise a squad of porters, and Chris trying to insert half a mountainbike into the pannier of a mule.

"What's that for?" I asked.

"Spare!" said Chris. "In case one of your bikes wears out while you're carrying it!"

With some glee, the camera crew, directed by Alan, were recording this metamorphosis; they had had lots of opportunities to film the bikes being carried by human beings, but this was the first time they had been able to work mules and bikes into the same scene. "Can we have the front wheel down a bit chaps, so we can see the reins?" intoned Alan above the bobbing *djellabah* hoods and balaclavas. "No, on second thoughts, let's put those six spare tyres in the other pannier; it's a better balance!"

I coiled two 50-metre lengths of 9 mm climbing rope and wedged them into my rucksack. Matt walked by carrying an armful of ice-axes rented from Imlil's store of climbing cast-offs. We were an unlikely mountaineering team: none of the four-man film crew had climbed a mountain before, although both Alan and Stuart had filmed in the Antarctic, so at least they would know about cold, and snow. Both Matt and Chris looked as if they would be partially incapacitated by their cycling injuries, though both were experienced in mountains. Matt had climbed Toubkal several times during his short career as a guide in the Atlas. Andy and Annabel would be solid, though relatively inexperienced, and Jeremy had already expressed doubts about coming any further than the Neltner Hut. Abedelilah appeared to be potentially the strongest in the party, and had recently revised the number of times he had climbed Toubkal from 100 to 150. Mohammed had wisely elected to remain at Imlil and keep an eye on the Land Rovers and equipment. The team had no accepted leader, but I was keenly aware that should we have to resort to an emergency bivouac or snow-hole, I was the one who had probably had most experience.

As we assembled for departure, there were two changes of personnel: Graham Smith decided that his stomach would never make the climb, and reluctantly abdicated his post of Cameraman to Phil the Grip. Phil had never worked as First Unit Cameraman before and was now going to be responsible for capturing some of the most crucial footage in the film. The other change was the late addition to the team of Brahim, a professional mountain guide living in Imlil, whom Abedelilah unexpectedly hired. At the time it seemed unnecessary, but 24 hours later we were to be grateful for Brahim's company.

Forty minutes after we arrived in Imlil, a column of 19 people and 9 mules, led by Jeremy in full Andean costume, walked slowly through the cobbled alleys and out onto the mountainside. Bringing up the rear were the two cyclists.

Not for the first time, Matt and I had imagined – wrongly – that we would be able to ride the mountainbikes. Beyond the next – and last – village of Aremd there were several parallel tracks along the boulder-strewn floor of the upper Mizane. At the southern end of this vast rock-field, all the tracks were forced into a single trail which clambered up the first hundred metres of the mountainside then climbed continually through the snow-line.

A snow-plastered huddle of single-storey huts called Sidi Chamharouch marked the halfway point in the journey from Imlil to the Neltner Hut. The shrine which gave rise to the huts lay on the far side of the iced stream, out of bounds to non-Muslims. There are legends attached to the mountain spirit of Sidi Chamharouch: a botanist in the 1840s who found himself caught in one of Toubkal's storms after ignoring local advice watched astounded as one of his guides cut the throat of a cockerel (which he had carried up the mountain under his arm), in an attempt to appease the djinn. Sixty years later, one of Budgett Meakin's armed antagonists insisted that the Englishman pay for a sheep to be sacrificed before continuing up Toubkal. On Matt's first, and only winter attempt to climb Toubkal he had been caught by a storm in the southern couloir above the Neltner Hut. For two days he and his companions were trapped in a small tent. When the food and fuel had run out, they were forced to beat a retreat back to the valley.

Nowadays, the twin row of houses at Sidi Chamharouch provide a summer service to wilting trekkers. This being winter, only one of the huts was open, the swaddled owner selling sweet tea and biscuits at understandably inflated prices.

While the team re-hydrated, the muleteers unloaded their animals. They had decided that the track was too deep in snow for the mules to continue further. With Brahim directing the operation, the pile of rucksacks and film gear was picked up by the team of porters. Extra rates were demanded for the heavier bags. It began to snow.

Between Sidi Chamharouch and the Neltner Hut, the track gained 900 metres in altitude. The climb took the rest of the day, and it was one which would be remembered particularly by a stoic Alan, who brought up the rear through thigh-deep snow whilst being encouraged by the injured Matt.

The snow was falling hard, and it was dusk by the time Alan, Matt and I plodded up the final snow-slope to the hut. Phil was kneeling with the camera and Stuart was leaning into the wind holding his 'woolly dog' as Jeremy came out of the hut door to greet us: "*Chai*'s on chaps," he said, as he lifted the bike from my shoulders. A plaque bolted to the outside of the hut announced that the altitude was 3,207 metres.

The squalor of the interior of the Neltner Hut beats all previous records for high-altitude mountaineering shelters. The porters stacked our equipment inside the door, and left immediately, setting off at a jog for Imlil. Inside the hut a gas burner spurted a thin ring of blue heat at a blackened kettle. A table ran the length of the room, with benches down each side. The hut smelled of old animal fat and socks. From the corner of the room, a narrow iron ladder reached up to a hole in the ceiling, above which were two sleeping platforms: room enough to squeeze about 20 sleeping bags. The condensation inside the hut made everything damp. With snow piling up against the porch and windows, there was little hope of increasing the warmth.

For once, there was agreement on how long it would take to achieve the following day's journey. "*Cinq heures!*" said Brahim, to an accord of grunts. Five hours to the summit. Of the eight people making the climb, four of us had been to the summit before. There was really no excuse for anything to go wrong.

In the course of the evening, the damp and cold permeated successive layers of clothing. Hour by hour, the summit team shrank in size: Alan decided that if the climb above the Neltner Hut was going to be any harder than the climb to it, he would not make it. Chris had found the twisting action of climbing over snow-covered rocks hideously painful, and knew that even returning to Imlil would be a trial. Jeremy opted to keep the two of them company. That left eight of us to make the ascent: Abedelilah and Brahim to cut the trail, Phil and Stuart to shoot the film, Matt and me to carry bicycles, Annabel to take photographs, and Andy to act as a stalwart long-stop.

"And I'll make a huge stew for you, ready for when you return!" added Alan.

Round the faltering light of three candles, the plan was laid. We would rise at 6.30, and if the sky was clear, eat a fast, large breakfast. Five hours to the top would take us until 1am, an hour on the summit for filming and three hours to return would mean that we returned to the hut by 5pm. We would pause for long enough to eat Alan's meal, then press on down to Imlil, covering the last, easier, kilometres in the dark. We would then be well placed to make the final dash over the Tizi-n-Test pass to Agadir. It was a plan entirely dependent on the weather; heavy snow or cloud would make it impossible to film, and therefore start the climb.

Jeremy produced a huge pot containing vegetables. Stuart unloaded a mugful onto 12 plates (including one for the warden of the hut) and handed the first plate to his neighbour: "Here ye are Abedelilah! Get your laughing gear round *that*!"

"Away wi' yay Jimmay!" replied Abedelilah with a throaty Arabic accent.

Before climbing the iron ladder, I pushed my way through the porch full of freezing clothing, and looked into the night. A mask of cloud hid the moon, and feather-light flakes of snow fell softly onto the saddles of the parked bikes. If it did not stop snowing, we would have to postpone the ascent.

Cut and Run

Summit Shoot (Day 17) – Cycle Slalom – Recovery (Day 18) – The Goundafa Kasbahs – Death on the Test – A Hill Too Far – Zaps and Zooms (Day 19) – The Road to Taroudant – An Unexpected Upset (Day 20) – On the Beach

Day 17 - 20

Using a head-torch to pick a route across the sleeping bags, I made my way to the end of the loft and lowered myself through the hole in the ceiling. The limp skins of yesterday's socks hung from nails and brackets and brushed my face as I trod down the cold rungs of the ladder and felt for my boots. The warden of the hut lay asleep on a bench in the corner beneath a mountain of blankets. I pulled open the door of the hut. Snow fell into the porch. Twelve hours of spiralling temperatures had pinched the air so that it tasted brittle; metallic. Snow squeaked under my boots. I looked up to see saw-tooth peaks glinting in the light of hundreds of phosphorescent stars. I plunged back into the smelly hut and fought my way past the socks until my head protruded into the loft:

"Hey! Wake up! The weather's perfect!"

I waited long enough to hear Matt's voice. "Oh good," he said.

We ate muesli from tin mugs by candle light, then topped the mugs up with Jeremy's *chai*. We left the hut at 7.45. Everyone carried a pack containing their personal clothing but some had extra loads such as a film, camera or a bicycle.

Abedelilah led the way round the corner of the hut and into the snow-filled gully beneath the windows. Unaware of the difficulties involved in scaling such an obstacle while wearing a bicycle around one's neck, Abedelilah took a direct line from the thigh-deep snow of the gully bottom up the 10-metre overhang of the gully wall. Two minutes later, seven of us were floundering up to our necks in white powder as Abedelilah stormed the cornice which capped the gully, detonating armfuls of snow over our heads. The eighth member of the group, Brahim, had foreseen this indignity and was waiting in the gully bottom to lead the rest of the team round by an easier route.

New snow had obliterated any footsteps left from previous ascents. With Brahim in front cutting steps, we zig-zagged up the steep face which rose above the gully. Soon we were looking down on the postage-stamp sized roof of the climbing hut. At one side of the hut we could see three tiny dots. To Alan, Jeremy and Chris, we would appear to be moving unaccountably slowly. As we traversed across and above two outcrops of rock, I made a mental note to steer clear of them on the way down. From above, the rocks were invisible, but each had a vertical face of 10 metres.

We rose into a hanging valley. Progress was slow and laborious, and with every hundred metres climbed, the air thinned and breathing became harder. For the people at the rear of the column, it was hardest of all: the neat steps cut, then enlarged by the leading pair in the line had, by the time a further five tired boots kicked past, been partly demolished. Footholds gave way, and it took several seconds of panting and slashing with an ice axe to carve out a new step.

Brahim led us along the right side of the valley and up a steep back wall which opened into the top couloir of Toubkal's west face. We could see the ridge leading to the summit. Two and a half hours above the hut, we moved into the sun.

We lay on the snow, nibbling carefully-rationed bars of Spanish chocolate. The air in the couloir was still and warm. So far, not a cloud untidied the sky and the clean air seemed to cut through distance so that the summit ridge of Toubkal appeared an arm's length away. With the exception of the two bicycles, we looked like a team of professional mountaineers.

"We're nearly there," I mused to nobody in particular.

"Thank God for that," said Stuart without looking up.

The climb up the back wall of the couloir to the summit ridge was led by Brahim. We were drawing level with the dark spines of Tizi Melloul, the mountain ridge to the west. Banks of cloud were already lifting ominously over the far ridges. The sudden rise in altitude from the plains of Marrakesh the day before was marking itself with respiratory overload. Andy was suffering the worst, and he was having to pay for each step with painful breathing.

The ridge steepened. The group was spread over 100 metres of mountain. Behind Brahim was Annabel, and in Annabel's steps was the hunched form of Matt. He had taken the saddle off his bicycle

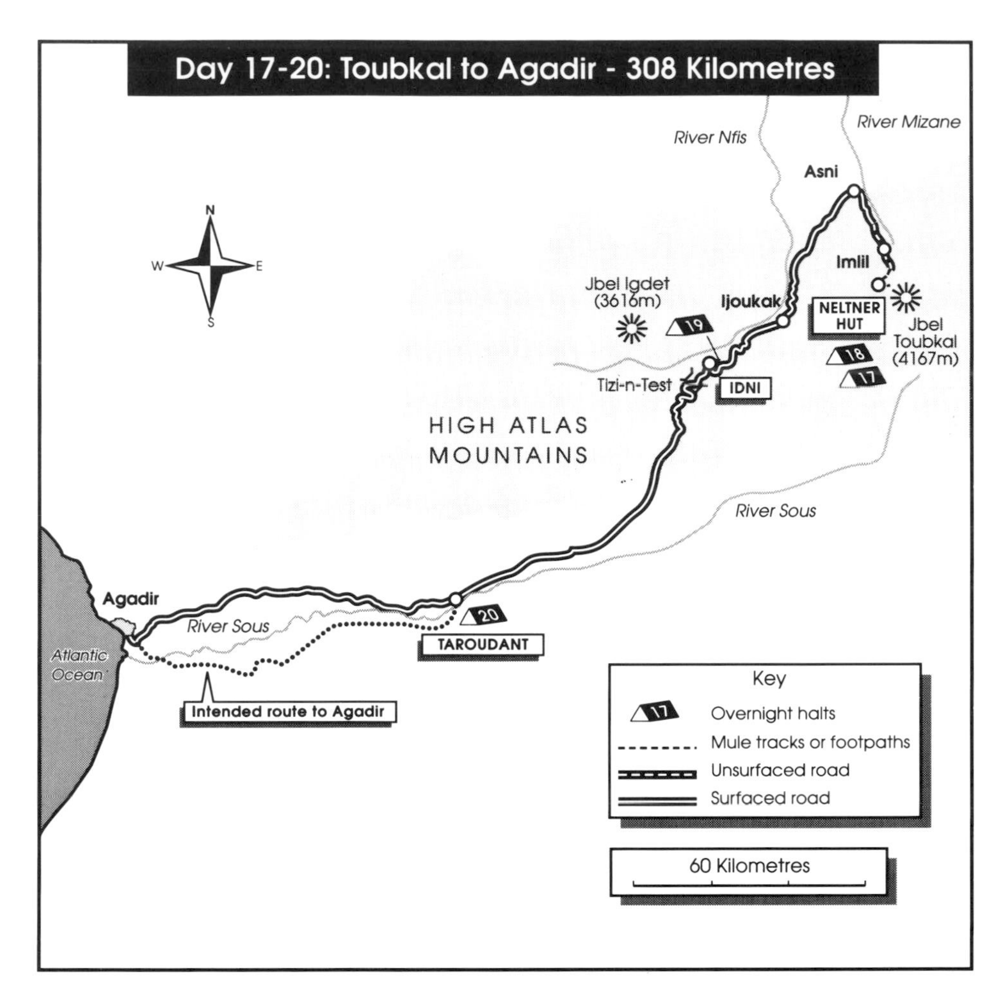

and was carrying it in his rucksack. "It's only another thing to get in the way," he had explained. "And anyway, I'm not planning to sit on it today."

Brahim waited while the rest of us caught up, then he struck off to traverse a series of steep slides of frozen snow immediately below the ridge. It was nearly steep enough to justify stopping and tying everybody onto a rope, but the time it would have taken would have created problems of its own. Below the fragile toe-holds kicked in the snow, the ridge fell away in a smooth curve of sun-polished snow. It was too far to fall safely.

"Brahim!" Our guide stopped and turned. I pointed up to the ridge above our heads and suggested that instead of skating along such an exposed traverse we could climb up to the ridge above our heads, where the occasional hints of a flattened profile suggested that we could move in greater security. Brahim looked unhappy, but changed direction, and

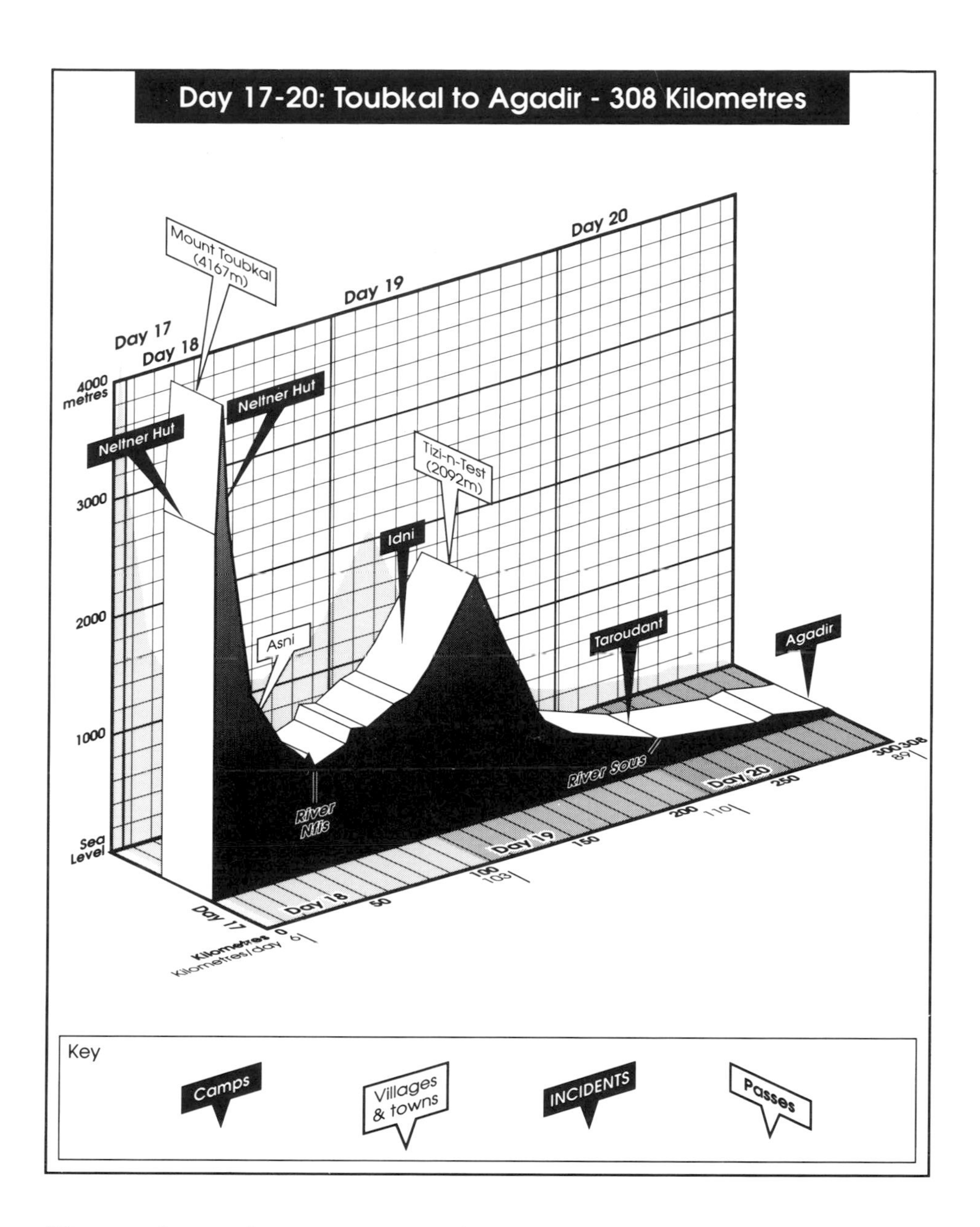

fifteen minutes later we teetered over the skyline to find ourselves clinging to an horrendous knife-edge surrounded by an eternity of space. I caught a told-you-so glance from Brahim, and we began a delicate fingers-and-toes totter along the crest of the gently-rising ridge.

I caught up with Stuart. He was not enjoying himself. "How's it going?" I asked.

"This is **** stupid," came his indignant reply. Phil too was having problems. The treads on his boots had been designed to grip escalators and accelerators. "Can't seem to grip . . ." he commented as one foot shot out sideways.

We saw the summit of Toubkal twenty minutes before we reached it. The highest point of North Africa's tallest mountain is formed by a snow-crusted protuberance jutting eastwards off the main ridge. The knife edge mellowed into a wide, rising ramp, and, one by one, we ploughed through the knee-deep trough towards the extraordinary sculpture which marks the high point. As if the mountain had not already got a well-defined summit, someone has constructed a three-metre high quadrifoliate pyramid of welded steel angle.

This rusting monolith was daubed with the graffiti of previous summiteers. We leant our two bicycles against the pyramid. It was already 1.15pm. At the most, we could afford one hour before beginning the descent. The clouds that had been building all morning now filled in the gaps between the serrated ridges surrounding Toubkal. The mountain felt like an island isolated by a sea of frozen surf. If the clouds came any closer we would have difficulty following our footsteps back to the hut. Matt joined Phil as he unpacked the camera.

"There are three shots we have to have: the long one of us coming up the ridge, then the summit shot of bikes being waved in the air. And there's the panorama. Let's get those in the can."

Having forced themselves to reach the top of the mountain, Phil and Stuart now settled into a routine in which they felt comfortable and secure. Within ten minutes Phil had assembled his Aaton and was crouching in the snow of the summit. Close to his shoulder, Stuart was checking the sound-level on his microphone, a pair of earphones wrapped round his hat.

"OK. Only enough film for one take of each shot." Matt led the way back from the summit, and on Phil's call, we started forward towards the lens, panting authentically and looking expectantly towards the elusive summit. When we reached the pyramid we hoisted the bicycles above our heads and attempted a British cheer. The sound that came out resembled a breathless welling of gargles and chokes, but it was identifiably triumphant.

"Done it!" we said.

"Cut!"

"Let's bugger off!"

I knew that we had left it too late. It was 2.15 by the time we strapped on our packs, picked up our bicycles and began to retrace our steps along a ridge which was now threatened by frozen pillows of cloud. Where the ridge narrowed we met four French skiers. They had left their skis when the ridge had become precipitous, and were continuing to the summit on foot. As they squirmed past us on the narrow footholds, one of them turned to me and tapped my suspended bicycle with a gloved hand. I nearly fell off the ridge. He said: "*La bicyclette? Ici? Et c'est une bicyclette spéciale? Pour la montagne?*"

"Oui. C'est un mountainbike. Le A.T.B. All Terrain Bike. Atlas Traverse Bike."

Beyond the Frenchman, Matt was engaged in a manoeuvre which involved gripping a snow-pocket with the pick of his ice axe whilst straddling a V-shaped cleft in the rock and lowering his bicycle between his legs. The Frenchman watched for a moment, then said definitively, "*Je préfère les skis.*"

To reverse the traverse of the ridge we had not only to contend with the falling afternoon temperature and consequent icing of the footholds, but also with the dangers of being tired. By the time we reached the end of the steepest section of the ridge, the four French skiers had been all the way to the summit and had caught us up again on their return. On the snow shelf where they had impaled their skis, the two groups congregated while ski-bindings were tightened and saddles lowered.

"This is an issue of national pride. We can't be seen to carry these things all the way up here, then carry them down. They'll think we're completely mad." Matt agreed. "But being gentlemen, we'll let them go first. That way they won't see us fall off."

The four French skiers *schussed* away from the shelf to execute a series of whiplash turns down the back wall of the couloir, before easing into endless 'S' bends as they reached the shallower angles of the couloir floor. In a few minutes all four lost about 300 metres in height and had shrunk to insects weaving a plait of vapour trails down towards the teapot in the Neltner Hut.

"Well," concluded Matt in the sudden quiet, "skiing may be fast, efficient and fun, but it's hardly original!"

The two of us launched ourselves from the shelf on a trajectory intended to mimic the skiers. The bikes seemed to accelerate as if they had been dropped into thin air. In less time than it took the skiers to reach the same point I was flying with the wind through my hair and snow-powder spraying my face. My bicycle was still buried to the hubs in the snow below the shelf, but I was flying; end-over-end; round-and-round; upside down; filling my sleeves and trouser-legs with wads of snow which would soon melt then dribble coldly into the most excruciating corners of my thermal underwear. When I stopped moving, I scraped the snow from my face, checked that the French skiers had not been observing my mountainbike descent, then lay back to watch Matt, who had also fallen off, probing for his buried bicycle at the foot of a rude gouge in the mountainside. When he struck metal, he dragged his machine upright, then lifted it level with his chest and hurled it into the air in front of him; it landed soundlessly five metres below his feet. He walked down to the bicycle, picked it up, and threw it down the mountain again.

When we reached the bottom of the couloir it was possible to ride the bicycles for nearly ten metres.

"Marvellous!" said Matt. "Makes it all worth it!"

Now the clouds broke at our feet, completely filling the valley of the Mizane. We dallied for as long as we dared in that hanging valley, watching the shadows slide down the surrounding peaks to quench the prickles of refracted light from the carpet of snow which now crunched beneath our boots. We swapped a ceiling painted with a moving spectrum of fading azures for one of wall-to-wall cloud through which the remaining rays of the sun were diffused with barely enough energy to separate footprints from the slippery crust of the ramp which plunged into the relative safety of the upper Mizane.

Brahim was still in front, kicking in with his heels to make steps for those following. Annabel followed him. It was late enough for accidents. We came over the last lip in the hanging valley in time to catch sight of the roof of the hut before it, and the rocks around it, were smothered by dusk. It was impossible to see where the two rock outcrops were that sat across our route; trip-pits for the unwary. Brahim, of course, knew them, and kept us high, losing height by cutting obliquely across the ramp. At the back of our extended column, Andy was moving increasingly slowly. With him was Phil, who had hung back to film the day's closing antics. I was near them, and was watching the diminutive figures of Matt and two others passing by the second rock outcrop when one of them detached themselves from the others and skidded backwards down the remaining twenty metres of mountain. I stopped for long enough to see the figure stand up, collect his bicycle, and make a no-nonsense dart towards the sanctuary of the hut.

When Andy reached the place where Matt had slipped, he too lost his footing and shot down to the valley. It had been a finely-played day. The last gamble of the journey had paid off with minutes to spare. We had topped off the High Atlas traverse, and nothing could now stop us reaching the Atlantic Ocean by Day 20.

I was glad to be the last one to make the tiresome wallow through the snow-filled ravine beneath the hut. It was good to have this moment to myself. As I stood on the stained snow outside the hut, chipping the ice from my boots and gaiters with an ice-axe, the door opened.

Matt came out: "There's been a disaster!" he said. "Alan and Chris have gone!"

"What d'you mean they've 'gone'?" I asked querulously. I could feel my strength slipping away as I thought of the avalanches, crevasses, exploding cookers or poisonous *cous-cous* which might have claimed them.

Matt wailed on: "Gone! Departed! Are no more of this hut! Scarpered!" He paused for breath. He was still wearing an anorak and hat, but in his haste to leave the hut his feet had been jammed in a pair of unlaced boots. He was wearing no trousers.

"And they've . . . they've taken the brandy!" This was a crisis.

"Jeremy's still here. He says they went this afternoon. Chris was worried that he would hold us up if he waited till we arrived. Alan went with him. Stuart is speechless about the brandy – in some kind of a trance."

There was still enough light to see by; if Alan and Chris had already left, then the rest of us too could leave tonight. We had head-torches, and below Sidi Chamharouch the track would be mostly clear of snow, and we would be unlikely to get benighted if the weather turned.

"Well, why don't we go straight on now! We can walk down to Imlil in four hours, say by 10pm, then ride the last twenty 'k' to Asni by midnight. Then we're all set for a blast over the final pass tomorrow." It seemed an exciting plan.

"Phil and Andy won't make it."

By staying an extra night in the hut, we allowed ourselves the privilege of basking in a whole evening of self-congratulation. A ring of lined faces sat around the candle-lit table. Matt, bearded, red-eyed and bandaged, sat with a knife in his fist and a pot of marmalade in front of him, eating his way systematically through a loaf of stale bread. Phil and Stuart disappeared into the loft and spent two hours carefully removing film and tape from their machines, labelling spools and cursing the condensation. Annabel and Andy wore small smiles of success, as they leafed through the hut's visitors' book.

Suppressed ecstasy hung in the air along with the steam and old socks. I mused on our unique achievement: "D'you realise? This is the first time that bicycles have been carried all the way up Toubkal, and all the way down! That's really something to be p . . ."

Andy interrupted: "Um, not *quite* the first." He passed over the visitors' book. On a page opaque with smeared margarine an entry read: "*La première descente à mountainbike de Toubkal. 19 Octobre 1987.*"

I was incredulous. The entry then provided a list:

"Louis Vergeon
Jean-Pierre Pacome,
Nicole Chappuis,
Christine Melan,

Michele Merlino."

And concluded smugly: "(*ascente de 3 heures*)."

"Ah well. I suppose it was a pretty obvious thing to do. We'll have to settle for an entry on the lines of 'First Winter Descent of Toubkal by Mountainbike'."

"Or 'First Descent of Toubkal by Mountainbike in January in the Company of a Film Crew. One of whom is called Phil'."

I penned our entry into the book, and we each signed our names.

We were awake before dawn, and less than an hour later, Matt and I plodded from the porch, our frames thickened by gloves, anoraks and overtrousers. The tyres of the bikes had frozen to the ground. It was not yet properly light, but as we left the hut behind us, we passed Phil Millard kneeling in a snowdrift pointing the Aaton at our backs. By getting a head-start on the others we were hoping to reach Asni in time for a quick lunch, then launch ourselves over our last pass in the afternoon. The journey was over: it was inconceivable that anything else could go wrong now. Matt was still suffering, but all he had to do was keep going steadily, and he would surely reach the coast.

It was too cold to walk slowly, too cold to stop. It took an hour's fast walking to reach the corner touched by the first rays of the day's sun. I waited for Matt by a large rock, and when he came in sight, rushed on down past Sidi Chamharouch, over the ravine and on to the smoother section of track where it was possible to climb onto the bicycle. With every hundred metres drop in altitude, the air became more oxygenated; lungs and legs pumped with richer fuel and the downward gradient pulled the metal bicycle as though drawn by an invisible magnet in the valley. At last, we had an unstoppable momentum.

I bounced down the boulder field leading to Aremd, watching the front wheel skip over rocks which had stopped me dead two days earlier. Where the mule-track met the sudden widening of the road over the gorge from Asni, I came to an alien form which had been temporarily forgotten: it was the film-crew's Land Rover. Attached to the back of the 300-millimetre proboscis of his Aaton was Graham; beside him was Alan, looking a little sheepish.

"Stuart and Phil felt a bit abandoned. Thought you'd be waiting for them in the hut," I said to him.

Alan winced, but asked: "How did the filming go on the mountain?"

"They got everything. They carried the gear right to the top and got everything: bikes being carried up the snowy ridge, panoramas, bikes above heads on the summit, a descent sequence; the conditions were perfect."

"Oh, good, good." He looked relieved, then explained: "Chris thought his knee would slow you up if he stayed in the hut another night so we decided to take our time and come down yesterday. Chris is down in Asni. He's a bit done in. Did the last bit on the back of a mule. He's a bit low about missing the mountain. He couldn't have done it on his own."

Graham leant against the wing of the Land Rover. He looked drawn. He asked about Phil:

"He didn't complain once: he's chuffed to bits," I reassured him.

Just then Matt arrived: "Phil and Stuart," he panted. "They deserve a medal!"

It was painful to watch Graham's face: it had been his ingenuity, and his determination to film in difficult situations which had turned Alan's creative abstractions into reality. He was bitterly disappointed to have missed the filming climax of the journey.

"How's the stomach, now?"

"Settled down. I didn't eat for two days. Now I just want to get on with it. We've got some ideas for this last pass."

It was time for Matt and me to move on.

"The others will be down in an hour or two. See you in Asni."

Matt and I used the new road over the gorge to reach Imlil, and tore down the uneven hairpins to the village in a welter of spraying snowmelt and laughter. Mohammed was standing next to his diesel in the square. He saw us approach and his face lit up with an ear-to-ear smile. Through the handshaking and embraces he greeted us: "*Labas*! . . . *bonjour*! . . . no problems! . . . *el hamdu lilla*!" We laughed and clapped each other on the back and Mohammed asked if the bicycles went to the top of Toubkal, and we said yes. Which prompted another round of hysterics.

Five minutes later, we were on the saddles again, flicking up the gears as the bicycles jumped the ruts beside the white tops of the River Mizane. Half way to Asni, the beaten gravel ended with a sharp jolt as the bikes kicked over a lip and landed on tarmac. The chains skipped down one cog, then another. The air warmed as we fell through 1,400 . . . 1,300 . . . 1,200-metre contours, into trees, through hamlets, people waiting for a pick-up truck, children shouting, telegraph poles, a kilometre post, and then, in what seemed like minutes since leaving Imlil, we swooped down the blacktop slide into Asni.

Chris was reclining in a plastic chair on the terrace of the Grand Hotel du Toubkal.

"Hi there!" he grinned, as we stalked stiff-legged through the French doors. "Been having fun?"

Nothing lay between the terrace and the backdrop of silver peaks. A stork pottered beside the empty swimming-pool. Chris pushed two chairs towards us: "I've been staring myself cross-eyed through Graham's long lens, trying to work out which of those peaks is Toubkal. Wondering how you were getting on. It's good to see you."

In our absence, Chris' beard seemed to have gained in inches and grooming. He looked clean and rested, and was dressed in the rainbow-splashed cycling shirt he had been wearing when he had his accident two weeks earlier. Apart from the bandage occupying the larger part of his leg between shorts and shin, he looked well.

"I was just about to order a chicken *tagine* and chips," he smiled. "But you two'll be in too much of a hurry to join me."

Matt was demolishing his fourth double-pudding of chocolate cake and fruit salad when the rest of the team poured onto the terrace. It seemed a long time since all eleven of us had sat together. It did not last long.

"We'll be off," I said. "It'll be good if we can get over the Tizi-n-Test before dark. It's about a hundred from here."

Alan looked up from the menu and said: "So we'll catch up with you later, chaps."

Matt and I left the terrace. Chris came out with us to the front of the building. We picked up our two bicycles. "Well, Chris, it's good to see you mending . . . I guess we'll see you on the road to the Tizi-n-Test."

Chris walked behind one of the Land Rovers and reappeared on a mountainbike: "Yes, you will," he grinned. "I'm coming with you!"

The road over the Tizi-n-Test has first to climb over the watershed which separates the valley of the Mizane from that of the Nfis. It was here, on each side of the Atlas spine, that two of the three great clans who lorded over the Atlas at the end of the last century drew their strength.

The M'tougga clan had controlled the pass itself, whilst the Goundafa clan had occupied the Nfis valley.

The twentieth century had seen them both battling for tribal power and for the favour of the Sultan and of the French. The chief of the Nfis, Caid Tayeb El Goundafi succeeded in living until he was 65. He died in his Nfis *kasbah* in 1928, the same year that the French completed one of their most spectacular feats of engineering in Morocco: the road over the Tizi-n-Test.

So steep and complex are the spurs of the Atlas spine that the road writhes round 122 kilometres of bends between Asni and the valley of the Sous, to cover the straight line distance of 65 kilometres; a 'wiggle factor' of two-to-one. This increases to three-to-one for the top 60 kilometres of the pass, which manage to cover only 20 kilometres as-the-crow-flies between the village of Moulddirt on the north side of the pass, and the 600 metre contour on the south side.

At the top of the climb out of the Mizane valley I dropped my elbows onto the handlebars and drifted for a few moments, drinking in the pine and resin-scented air, as my eyes roamed along the grey ridges that leaned over the forest tops. The bike picked its own speed as the road tilted downwards to swerve left-then-right-then-left on perfect cambers through slingshot bends before firing me into the trench cut by the River Nfis.

The village of Ouirgane flashed by and the road began to rise beside the Nfis. My two partners were not in sight, but it did not seem to matter much that afternoon. The journey felt uninterruptible. I pedalled another twenty kilometres along the nibbled lips of the Nfis, and then the spell began to dissolve.

Where were Matt and Chris? I hadn't seen them for two hours. At Ijoukak, one of the tea-shops was open. It was 5.10pm, too early for eating; too late for a long lunch. The tables were empty. I drank coffee and distracted myself from watching the road by drawing a sketch of the day's route into my notebook.

I had been there for twenty minutes when the Land Rovers crawled into sight at the foot of Ijoukak's main street. By the time they drew to a halt outside the café, the bartender had brought another 11 coffees to the table. Alan was first to the table: "They're coming. They'll be here in a minute. Chris is finding it harder than he thought."

Annabel and Jeremy passed by their coffees and opened negotiations with the meat-seller. Stuart opened his tobacco pouch; Andy opened a Land Rover bonnet. Two cyclists came into sight.

"Aren't there any *flat* mountains in Morocco?" muttered Chris. The pedals on Chris' bike were still spinning as he drained his first coffee. Matt pushed back in his chair and rubbed his eyes. The bandage across his forehead was acquiring tree-rings of grime. I was eager to press on; I wanted to get over the Tizi-n-Test before nightfall. Dusk was already deepening the shadows. Chris looked tired; Matt, I could never tell. Alan asked: "How far do you want to go on tonight?"

I looked at the other two. "Twenty-ish?"

"At the most," Chris added.

Alan stood back; not once since the ride started had he directly dictated our travelling plans. He said: "Well, we'd like to film on the summit first thing tomorrow. So we don't want to start downhill tonight."

"Why don't you go on ahead and find a place for the tents," I suggested, "and we'll cycle on at our own speed."

Ten minutes after they had arrived, the Land Rovers were ready to leave. For the last time that day, the three of us pushed our bicycles out into the road. We had no way of knowing that, an hour later, only two bicycles would roll to a halt beside the camp on the Tizi-n-Test.

Shortly after Ijoukak the road momentarily lost its tarmac surface while it twisted down a water-course. Dust from the Land Rovers lingered in the still air. The sun skewered itself on the western peaks then bled a spreading stain over the Atlas. Only ten minutes had passed since leaving the café table, but Matt and Chris had already dropped from view. I decided to yo-yo between the advance party and the rear-guard, thinking that I could keep in touch with both.

Moulddirt had closed its doors for the night by the time I pedalled past its unwelcoming walls. A solitary dog howled at me. Since Ijoukak, the road had changed temperament. With the fading of the light had come a steepening of the gradient as the road tilted upwards for its final assault on the pass.

Presently the dark of the tarmac merged with the dark of the night, and the only way that I could see where to point the front wheel was by catching with the corners of my eyes the pale margin of dust running along each road-edge. Now and again I felt the tyres shiver, and heard the crackle of gravel as I wandered too far to one side. The drop on the right-hand side of the road was deepening with every kilometre. On the other side of that drop, peering down on the road, was Jbel Igdet, the highest mountain west of the Test, and the only one to top 3,600 metres. I could see a lonely constellation of village-lights moored in the blackness below me. Ahead, I thought I caught the sweep of headlights. I wondered how Matt and Chris would be faring in the dark. They had no lights either.

Carrying lights would have been yet another acknowledgement of the support role of the Land Rovers. My bike, and the contents of my pack, had remained (virtually) unchanged since leaving the desert three weeks earlier. The illusion of self-sufficiency was necessary for the integrity of the adventure. For the journey to look authentic on film, its travellers needed to believe in their self-dependence. We had started out from the Sahara Desert as writers of our own script, but now it felt as if we were merely players in someone else's plot. Had Alan, after all, been pulling the strings? On the Tizi-n-Test, our last pass, I found myself longing for some unexpected turn of events so catastrophic that we would be prevented from reaching the Atlantic. Some disaster; some sub-plot of such sudden complication that I too would have a challenge. In spite of the accidents, which had happened to other people, it had all been a bit too neat.

The hamlet of Idni slipped by. Idni has about four buildings, and has always been the tea-halt for bus and truck drivers tackling the pass. I had stayed there with Annabel, when we had travelled down to the Sahara the previous month, looking for sand-dunes. We had come to Idni because we had read in the guide-book of a place called the Hôtel Alpina which was run by an elderly Frenchwoman named Madame Gipolou. Huge dinners were provided, we had been told, cooked using produce from the farm below, and although the hotel had baths, basins and bidets, there was no running water, or electricity; Madame always provided a handful of candles. You paid whatever Madame thought you could afford. Annabel and I had arrived after dark, but were greeted by a derelict building. As we walked through the French doors, glass scraped underfoot. One of the window shutters hung askew. Rocks thrown by passers-by littered the floor. On the other side of the road, in the cold, empty, Café Igdet, the proprietor told us that Madame Gipolou had died in 1985.

I knew that I was near the top of the Tizi-n-Test when I lost the smell of woodsmoke and started breathing snow-cooled air. Headlights blazed around a bend ahead and the thudding roar of a diesel motor straining against the gradient filled the slit between the tree-tops and rock-wall. Blinded, I fell off the bike and shuffled sideways until my feet scraped on gravel, pressing myself as far away from the tarmac as I dare while the truck juddered by. I was still standing there, blinking, and waiting for night-vision to return, when I heard the familiar burble of Land Rovers. I waited. Lights swept the tree-tops. They saw me. There were two Land Rovers, and they were both heading down the pass. Alan leant out of a window; I heard the music of the 'Traveling Wilburys'; smelled the warm fug of duck-down and electric heater, chocolate and cigarettes.

"Hi there! We've been all the way to the top of the pass. It's too steep to camp. It's a knife-edge all the way."

"Oh. That's a shame."

"Where are Matt and Chris?"

"Back down the road."

"What d'you want to do?"

What I really wanted to do was press on to the summit. Somewhere up there there would be space for tents. There always is. The problem was Matt and Chris. If they were having trouble on the pass, the last thing they would want would be another 20 kilometres of climbing in the dark followed by a bivouac on a rock ledge.

"Best that we go back down to that last hamlet. It's called Idni. There's an abandoned hotel with space in front of it for tents."

The Land Rovers slid away. I turned my bicycle around, let go of the brakes, and whistled down following the twin red dots of the tail-lights. It only took ten minutes.

There was no moon. In the gritty car-park of the Hôtel Alpina, the two Land Rovers were already disgorging gear. Jeremy was lifting out his tucker-box; Annabel was connecting tubes to the gas-cooker. Stuart passed by carrying his tent. With Alan, I walked a few yards down the pass. We stared into the night.

"Hope nothing's happened," I mused.

"So do I," replied Alan. "We weren't there to film it!"

After what felt like half an hour, but was probably only ten minutes, the headlights of a Land Rover flickered into view. The lights were moving very slowly. Alan passed me his binoculars. I stared into the lights. I could clearly see the silhouette of a cyclist swaying from side to side.

"Alan."

"Yes?"

"There's only one cyclist."

I wasn't able to tell who it was on the bicycle until the figure was almost upon us. He was pedalling with a slow, long-distance rhythm, shoulders rounded over the handlebars. Alan said: "Hi there, you can stop now."

I asked, "Where's Chris?"

Matt pulled himself off the saddle and nodded towards the vehicle behind him: "Inside."

Chris was spread across the rear seat, his bandaged leg straightened before him. "The old knee just wouldn't do it. Wouldn't do it," he said. "I was going all right until it got steep, but I just can't push. The painkillers don't seem to work."

The car park of the desolate Hôtel Alpina was the least pleasant of our overnight stops. The grit was so compacted that tent pegs had to be bashed with a mallet and a tribe of dogs prowled the perimeter of our enclosure, yowling at the cooker. Across the road, in the Café Igdet, the proprietor kept us supplied with trays of mint tea while Annabel painstakingly pared away the fat from the slab of beef which she and Jeremy had bought in Ijoukak. When the time came – much later – to dine off brown rice and beef stew, the scraping of spoons on plastic plates was accompanied by gratitude for a plate of old-fashioned carnivorous protein. "At last! Some building material!" concluded Matt, as he examined his plate minutely for any remaining morsels. Pudding was hot chocolate made from Mars Bars melted in milk.

Propped on the bonnet of the V8 was the clipboard. It listed the shots which Alan wanted to snatch before we left the Atlas: "Slo-mo, zap, long-shot, tracking, humour, talking heads . . .".

Presiding over a large tin mug labelled with a filthy sticking plaster on which had been etched in biro the letters ALAN, the director of the film concluded Day 18 with a polite request for an early start the following day: "We'd like to catch the dawn on top of the pass please chasps. If you wouldn't mind, up at sparrow's fart!"

It would be our last waking in the Atlas, and to mark this final blinking of the dawn we sat down to – or, more precisely, stood around to – a huge, cooked breakfast of scrambled egg and fried potato, before dividing into start-of-day tasks which ranged from reading dipsticks to choosing film stock. After three weeks, everyone knew what had to be done in order to get the circus on the road quickly: the packing and carrying was achieved with the efficiency of a programmed – if creaky – machine. The film crew were away first. After looking at the map and noting that we had maybe another two hours' climbing to the top of the pass, Chris decided not to strain his creaking knee any further. Matt and I were excused our tent responsibilities, and allowed to climb straight onto the bikes.

The incomprehensible blackness which we had travelled through the previous night was now a magical mountainscape of fingery ridges and silver peaks under an azure sky. Alternately, the road probed gloomy gullies then burst onto sunlit headlands as it spiralled upwards towards the pass. Looking down, we could see the rectangular roofs of mud houses amid the rubble of decaying slopes. A bus lay twisted in the 'V' of a gully, its seats and internal organs salvaged and piled on a terrace 20 metres above the wreckage. The paint was still on the bus; a recent accident.

For an hour, Matt and I were left to relax in the single-minded pursuit of pedalling a bicycle slowly up a hill, but then we rounded a corner to find a man wearing a baseball cap, standing in a bush with one arm in the air. We did not look at him (he preferred it that way), and as we passed him, the arm fell, and somewhere further up the mountain a trigger was squeezed. When we reached the camera, we stopped. The baseball cap arrived:

"Like to do that again please chaps. It's the slow-motion shot: we need to have you tight in to each other, one behind the other. On this side of the road. OK? I'll wave!" We turned round and rolled back down the pass. We cycled through the shot twice more. Each time we reached Graham, glued to his eyepiece, we could hear him whimpering and cooing. He was excited. It was a good shot.

"OK chasps? On to the top now!"

The true summit of the Tizi-n-Test is a wooded notch whose views are obscured by the immediate foreground of encircling ridges, so the Mo roccans have chosen to mark the pass with a slightly lower, false summit, two kilometres further south. There is a small café selling polished gemstones, crystals and atrocious coffee, and there is a tall concrete plinth on which is painted in blue: 'TIZI N TEST, ALTITUDE 2093, ROUTE CONSTRUITE PAR LE SERVICE DES TRAVAUX PUBLICS DU MAROC 1926-1932.'

"That's it then!" I said to Matt as we slid off the saddles and onto plastic chairs.

"The last pass."

A familiar figure appeared.

The next shot required some props: a table, two glasses of coffee, two sardine sandwiches and Jeremy West. The table was set out on the roadside. On it were the two glasses of coffee. With Graham and his tripod squatting at the verge, Matt and I had to ride our bicycles up to the table, and without slowing down, snatch a glass of coffee each and ride out of shot. The second shot required Jeremy to stand at the roadside holding the sardine sandwiches in outstretched arms. Matt and I had to ride past him, each of us snatching a sandwich as he called "Bye guys!".

"Hysterical!" agreed Matt afterwards. "It's what the film needs. Now there's absolutely no risk of anybody taking it seriously!"

We were still laughing when Chris appeared. He was wearing a clean bandage, and pushing his bicycle. He grinned: "I'm not missing *this*!"

"I can feel a happy ending coming on!" said Matt.

We left the summit and swerved down a few hairpins to the best view on the Tizi-n-Test. It is an outside bend in the road which hangs over a shimmering abyss of warm air rising from the desert 2,000 metres below. The viewpoint is celebrated by another café, and a seller of gemstones. From here we could see the road unravelling down a stack of interlocking spurs to disappear eventually into the hot fog of the Sous valley. This had to be the best descent in the Atlas: a flying, spine-tingling hurtle from the snow-line to the shore.

But Alan had seen another shot. It required Graham to be tied onto the bonnet of the Land Rover with climbing ropes so that he could film the backs of three cyclists freewheeling down the mountain pass. We spiralled down for five kilometres, and were halted by a pipping on the car horn. Alan stuck his head from the driver's window. "We'd like you behind the car now chasps, so we can see your faces."

Graham was roped onto the back of the vehicle, camera balanced on his shoulder. Alan's voice floated back: "OK chasps, I'd like this quite fast. Need the sensation of *speed*!"

Graham added: "You'll need to be close to the camera, or you'll drift out of shot."

In what was the most dangerous trick of the entire journey, the three of us flew shoulder to shoulder down the Tizi-n-Test with our front wheels an arm's length from the back of the Land Rover. The road was unfenced, and just wide enough for one vehicle. Grit and dust spat past our faces. It was impossible to see past the Land Rover to the road ahead, and so we could not anticipate pot-holes, or bends. I felt as if I was playing the sort of racing-car video game which always ends in spectacular electronic 'crumps' and a screenful of fireballs.

We stopped when Alan spotted a signpost depicting an avalanche. With the camera on the verge he filmed us hurtling past the sign. A few metres down the road, he filmed the glittering spokes of six wheels flashing past a kilometre post showing the distance to Taroudant as '134'.

"There's just one more shot chaps. We still haven't got a really good long shot of you on a mule track. There's a place a bit further down the pass which might do!"

The place which Alan had noted from the summit of the pass was a promontory of rock topped by a conical hill which jutted out into a massive valley, along the back-wall of which could be seen a precarious mule track. With the camera on the side of the conical hill, Alan could look across 500 metres of clean air to the opposite cliff, which was bisected by the track.

"If you could just pop over to that track . . ." It took half an hour to pick a route round the head of the valley. The day was heating up, and the only way of reaching the track was by linking together rough trails used by goats. The three of us arrived at ten minute intervals, dusty, and soaked with exertion. On the far side of the valley, the film crew were too small to be visible, but we could see the tiny cube of the Land Rover. We waited until the headlights winked, then set off down the track. At the half-way point we paused, as agreed, to give the camera crew time to pack their gear into their vehicle and drive to a new location which would give them an even longer shot. The headlights winked again. We managed to pedal most of the track, which hung in a spectacular manner over a gorge. At the end of the track, Matt said: "They'll *have* to use that shot. If they don't, I'll eat my bicycle." (They didn't; he didn't.)

There was now a short debate concerning the quickest route back to the road. We had come so far off our real route that it was arguably quicker to continue down the mule-track and assume that it would rejoin the road further down the pass. I took the view that it would be quicker to return the way we had come, even if it meant climbing back up some of the pass. We parted, Chris and Matt to freewheel downhill, me to carry my bike upwards. I knew that I was wrong before we even parted, but there comes a point when it is easier on the mind to stick to your own decision rather than to accord with others. It was forty minutes before we re-united at a café half-way down the pass. Matt and Chris were reclining in chairs each side of a table loaded with omelette, fresh bread and coffee. I was soaked in dust and sweat. The camera crew were nowhere to be seen.

At last we won our uninterrupted descent, and for the last half hour of our Atlas traverse we spun down warm tarmac without turning our legs. For the first time, the Land Rovers could not keep up with us. The mountains were over. Ahead lay Taroudant, and the sea.

A bearded figure jumped out in front of us: "I say, chasps . . ."

The last shot that day was of three cyclists riding towards the camera, the Atlas to their backs.

The road angled gently into the bed of the Sous valley. A line of telegraph poles marched beside us through the low scrub of the semi-desert. At a junction marked by a 'Stop' sign and a police jeep, we turned right onto the main road. A kilometre post told us that it was 44 kilometres to Taroudant.

The face of Andy came past my left shoulder, then the windows piled high with a sordid jumble of muddy sleeping mats, boots, a water-bottle, a jerrycan, two rucksacks and the rumpled skin of an anorak, or trousers. Behind the vehicle, being sucked along by its slipstream, grinned Matt and Chris. I swerved in between them. Three hours later, we were sitting beside the swimming pool of the Hôtel Palais Salaam staring at 'Caprice' cocktails.

Taroudant's importance has declined since the silting up of the River Sous and since the sacking in 1913 of the town after a three-day siege by the combined forces of the once-rival High Atlas clans of the Glaoua and Goundafa. Attached to the town's immense walls, there are reported to be old mooring rings – relics from the days when ships could sail up from the Atlantic to trade gold, sugar, saltpetre and cotton. The ramparts still stand, mile upon mile, moated by groves of orange and olive and grapefruit. The *souk* is reputed to be one of the most enjoyable in Morocco, with corners for Berber jewellery, for leatherwork, carvings and clothing. It was agonising to wake in such a place and not to see it; there would be no time to explore Taroudant.

Shortly after first light, the camera crew, led by Alan, set off in search of the *souk* and 'local footage'. They returned thirty minutes later: "It's Friday," said Alan morosely as they all trooped back into the hotel, "*Souk*'s closed on Fridays."

It was 9am by the time the entire team had congregated for an inadequate breakfast of bread and marmalade. It was hard to believe that 24 hours earlier we had been breakfasting heartily on egg and fried potato in front of the tents just below the snow-line on the Tizi-n-Test.

In front of Hôtel Palais Salaam, horse drawn carriages were lined up, waiting for tourists. We glanced over the bikes for a last time. I stuffed a camera and jacket into my rucksack. The distance between Taroudant and Agadir was only 89 kilometres, and it was all gently down hill, on tarmac. I felt quietly proud that, after 20 days, 1,200 kilometres and a spectrum of incidents, we were going to arrive at our final goal exactly on time. Alan had said that we needed to be at Agadir by 1pm, in order to shoot the final sequence of the film during the afternoon. As we left the hotel, at 9.40, I said: "Let's bike through the town first, and join the Agadir road on the far side." At the time it had been an innocent whim, but it had unexpected consequences.

The three of us threaded our way though the horse-drawn carriages and bicycles and pedestrians, breathing in the smells of hot bread and olive oil, of basket-work and spices. We looped round the Place Tamoklate then pedalled idly down the main street to Place Assarag and glanced covetously at the café tables waiting in the warm sun.

"How do we get out?"

"Don't really know."

"Westwards!"

With the sun full on our backs we cut down a side-street. It finished at a T-junction. We turned right, and found ourselves in a narrow street occupied by men in singlets hammering big bits of metal.

"Agadir?" we asked, "*Là? Ou là?*" I pointed in two different directions. The men nodded. The road ended, but an alley led round a corner and brought us back onto a thin street heading roughly west. Ten minutes later we passed through the town walls.

Immediately we were picked up by a following wind which pushed us at frantic speed away from Taroudant. We had covered perhaps ten kilometres when a growing apprehension in each of us finally found voice. Matt said:

"This isn't the right road!"

It was not the right road, but there was no chance that we could turn round and retrace our way back to Taroudant. Firstly the wind was stronger than anything I'd ever experienced before. Secondly, retracing is so depressing. "But it's going west. Roughly. Or a bit north of west," I shouted encouragingly.

Matt was unconvinced: "It's too small. We've only seen one vehicle since leaving town. The main road to Agadir is a huge highway."

I was still quite confident that the road would lead us to the coast near Agadir: "It's fine. It's fine. As long as it doesn't turn any further north we're OK. And if we see a good-sized turn on the left we can take it because it'll lead back to the main road." Which prompted another torrent of expletives from Matt.

I didn't reply, but it did occur to me that Matt was exercising considerable restraint in not including my name in the outburst. It was, after all, my idea to detour through Taroudant, and therefore my fault that with three hours to go until the 1pm deadline we were on the wrong road.

Forty kilometres away, the crew of the V8 Land Rover were perplexed. They had set off from Taroudant just before 10am and had expected to overtake the three of us within half-an hour. After an hour's driving, and no sight of the cyclists, it was clear that something had gone wrong. Annabel was sitting next to Alan in the front of the Land Rover:

"They have either surprised us and gone with the wind and are indeed still in front of us. Or they've had an accident and have returned to Taroudant," she mused.

There was a moment's pause while Alan considered this: "An accident! . . . Damn, I wish I had the crew with me!" They turned the Land Rover round and drove back to Taroudant.

Meanwhile, on a road which was getting thinner with every kilometre, the three of us were being blasted west by the gale and eating up kilometres at a ferocious rate. If it hadn't been for the fact that we had no idea where we were, it would have been very exhilarating. At a cross-roads there was a petrol station. I dived inside. A man with a two-day beard looked up from trying to tune a plastic transistor radio.

"Agadir?" I asked.

"*Oui,*" he said, "*la route direct pour Agadir.*"

I rushed out into the sun as Chris and Matt drew up at the pumps.

"It's OK! We're fine!" I called, and resumed pedalling. Ten minutes later we flashed by a signpost saying "Agadir 42".

Our road met with the main highway from Marrakesh to Agadir at a quiet junction in the foothills. We turned left, and for the remaining kilometres the road rose and fell in smooth waves over ripples of the fading Atlas.

Agadir was destroyed in 1960 by an earthquake which buried half of its 35,000 inhabitants. It has since been rebuilt on a grid of wide boulevards and is now Morocco's premier tourist resort, a package holiday destination capable of digesting planeloads of sun- and sand-seekers every day. The airport is a ten-minute bus ride from town. As we passed the airport and the industrial suburb of Inezgane, roads from Marrakesh, Taroudant and Goulimine converged and concentrated the traffic for the final 13 kilometres into Agadir.

The helpful wind which had pushed us along the Sous was now cancelled by the continual backwash of heavy trucks, buses and motor-cars which swished past our elbows every few seconds. The air stank. We passed a hillside of dead brush, the thorns of which had caught thousands of plastic bags blown there from the adjacent rubbish dump. We came to the 'Agadir' sign which told us that we were passing into the town, and took a photograph. Then we turned down the hill, past the colonnades of palms and swept sidewalks and onto Boulevard

Hassan II, where we chose a conspicuous café from which we could be spotted. Chris picked up the menu; Matt folded his sunglasses; I looked at my watch. The time was 12.20pm.

Chris complained: "We're forty minutes early!"

It was Mohammed who found us. He led us north to the junction with Avenue Prince Sidi Mohammed, onto Boulevard Mohammed V and then down the S-bend to the Rue de la Plage and a terraced café which looked across the road to an extravagant expanse of sea-washed sand. A familiar baseball cap swivelled on the terrace: "Ah! We were getting a little concerned about you chaps. You're too late for lunch. What happened?"

Alan, the film crew, Andy, Jeremy, Annabel and Abedelilah were sitting round the remains of several plates of kalamari.

"We took a wrong turn . . ."

"Is that all!"

Relieved that he was – by the skin of his teeth – in the right place, at the right time, with the right people, Alan launched straight into plans for the film's finale.

"Look chaps, well done. I know you'll be dying to go down to the sea water and finish the journey properly, but would you mind terribly if you waited till the sun's lower and the light's right for filming. I want you to arrive at the sea as if you've only just seen it after 20 days of trying. So if you could save your enthusiasms for later . . . and in the meantime we can film the arriving-at-Agadir sequence."

After we had been filmed weaving through the traffic and swinging exultantly down to the Rue de la Plage, we filled in the thirty minutes until the light was right by cruising aimlessly on the bikes past the camper-vans and sun-bathers parked along the esplanade. What would Said Amgoul, farmer and father of Oudeddi, maker of mint tea and *tagine*, have had to say about Agadir? A lady in indigo-rimmed sunglasses and a black bathing costume which looked as if it was concealing a stack of lorry inner-tubes, hung over the edges of an aluminium chair and licked ice-cream with a tongue which had turned peppermint green. At a collapsible table in front of the chrome fenders of a Winnebago 'Windcruiser', as long as a bus and protected by yellow stickers printed with the word 'Dobermann!', an elderly, leathery, German couple shouted at their dog barking inside. A girl sauntered along the pavement trailing by an unseen leash two local boys with melon-slice smiles.

At four, the director called together his cast and stage-crew for the final scene: "What we think would look good would be if you could ride off the sea-front, down this flight of concrete steps, then pedal down the beach and straight into the sea. With exuberance. A bit of passion chasps."

We made an arrangement with the owner of the café to borrow his freshwater hosepipe to wash the salt from the three bikes immediately after filming.

Shot 1 – the descent of the concrete steps – was achieved without serious injury, although three 'takes' were required before Graham was satisfied with the distance between the bikes. "Just a question of the perspective, really," he muttered to his Aaton.

Shot 2 required us to speed over the sand with the wind in our hair and the salt on our faces. On "Action" we leapt forward. The wheels span, calves twanged, voices shrieked and all three bicycles fell over. We tried again, this time on a patch of wetter sand. The same thing happened, except that two of the bikes collided right in front of the camera. A crowd had gathered.

"Alan! It's no good. Mountainbikes just don't work on sand. This is even worse than the Sahara!"

"Try it once more and we'll use what we can."

On the third attempt, we wobbled manfully with straining legs and sinking wheels for a full ten metres before sagging, winded, over the handlebars.

For the third shot; for the final, ultimate 'take' of the film, we were to ride down the shining sand of the foreshore, throwing off our rucksacks as we went, and pedal straight into the Atlantic.

I looked at my two companions, thin, travel-stained, gloriously bandaged, and felt disappointed that it was all over; a little sad that the comradeship that had bound the eleven of us together for 20 action-packed days was about to be washed away.

In a welter of diamond spray we splashed into the Atlantic and dived over the handlebars. I floated to the surface, soggy Trilby in one hand and an excruciating pain in the other. I had dived onto a sea-urchin.

As we clapped each other on the back, and laughed and howled and fished for the sunken bikes, a distant, insistent voice wafted over the waves. It came from a short, bearded man with his trousers rolled to the knees and a baseball cap shielding his eyes:

"Chasps . . . chaps . . . I say . . . chaps . . . if you wouldn't mind . . . one more time . . .!"

Soho

Deliverance – The First Picture Show – Review – Cast Off

Twenty-four days after arriving at Agadir, eight of the team assembled in the first-floor viewing room of Document Films in Soho's Broadwick Street. In the intervening period, Jeremy, Andy and Chris had driven the two Land Rovers back to Abedelilah's home in Casablanca, then continued across Europe to London. The precious cans of shot film had been flown back to the UK with the camera crew and were then rushed straight to the laboratories for processing.

For a full day we sat through 45 reels of film. The darkness of the room was periodically interrupted by sighs of relief, or murmurs of congratulation at the end of each of the critical sequences: dune-riding in the Sahara; the zap-gun on the road to Rich; omelette-and-map session at Imilchil; aftermath of Chris' accident; the arrival at Zaouia Ahansal; Mansour's family in the Berber village of Toufrine; tribal dancing at Telouet; the horrific head-over-wheels tumble of Matt on the snow-slopes of the Tizi-n-Tichka; Phil's single-handed summit footage on Toubkal; the hair-raising helter-skelter descent of the Tizi-n-Test; and the ludicrous sight of three cyclists pedalling full-tilt into the Atlantic Ocean.

There were some specially proud moments for the two camera teams: on several of the shots taken during our morning's filming on the dusty street through Tabant, Graham had caught the uninhibited curiosity of Berber children who had been watching us cycle past from the shelter of their doorways; for Matt and Chris working as the Second Unit, there was the shot of a mountainbike riding towards camera on a gorge ledge high above Zaouia Ahansal – a shot which had been snatched on the last few feet of the roll and filmed by Chris after staggering for two days with a damaged knee. There were moments of hilarity too: on the

Tizi-n-Rouguelt, after Chris had dropped out, Matt had set up the remote-controlled shot which would record the two of us cycling over the summit of the pass into a snow-storm. The raw footage showed a man running like a lunatic away from the camera, jumping on a bicycle and pedalling with his companion around the brow of the mountain. A second later he reappeared without the bicycle, sprinting with an out-stretched arm towards the camera in a desperate effort to reach the off-switch before precious film was wasted.

At this stage, Alan was the only person who had a clear mental picture of the finished film; for him, the 'rushes' were the chance to make an inventory of the 7 hours of raw material which would eventually have to be cut down to a mere 25 minutes.

The cutting of the film started immediately. The 'Voyager' series was due to begin transmission on 6 June, and after viewing the 'rushes' Alan and Matt felt confident that 'Atlas Biker' had a very good chance of being selected for the prestigious lead programme in the series. Working with the film editor John Hackney in a small room near Carnaby Street, Alan had produced a 'rough cut' of the film by 7 April. He had edited the 'rushes' down to a coherent 35-minute film, and some of Stuart's sound had been dubbed over the images. By 17 April, the film was down to 25 minutes, and I began working with Alan on writing the script which would be added to Stuart's sound-track. On 19 April, John Gau (head of the film's production company), Colin Luke (the Series Editor for 'Voyager'), Alan, Matt, John Hackney and myself gathered in the cutting room to watch the film while the commentary was spoken 'live'.

"I don't mean to be rude," concluded John Gau at the end of the screening, "but it looks too much like a bunch of yobbos barging through someone else's countryside."

"It's a real dilemma," said Alan later. "Atlas Biker's going out at the same time as East Enders on the BBC, so it's got to have *some* crash-bang-wallop. It's a question of finding a balance between the action and interest."

The following day, some of the mountainbiking sequences were substituted for more tasteful shots of Berber villages. There was intense debate about the title of the film. It needed a poky headline.

"High Atlas Bikers . . . Sand, Snow and Sun . . . Sky High in the Atlas – Sky High Mountainbikes in the Sun, Sand and Snow of the High Atlas . . ." The final choice was 'Blazing Pedals'.

On 5 May, in a studio off Richmond Mews, the commentary was recorded. During the next week, this was cut up by John Hackney and spliced onto the film to fit in with the sound-track and music. At the end of the week, the presenter of the 'Voyager' series, Julian Pettifer, came to the studio and recorded his 'top' and 'tail' to the film.

The press launch for the 'Voyager' series took place on 24 May in the screening room of Central TV's offices off Portman Square. 'Blazing Pedals' was chosen as the film to be viewed in full, and short excerpts from the other 12 films in the series were also seen. In the press release the series was described as spotlighting 'latter-day Livingstones' in a series of 'true-life adventure stories'.

One month later, at 7.30pm on 6 June, the film was broadcast. It was several days before the viewing figures were returned to the John Gau offices. 'Blazing Pedals' was watched by 6.04 million people (the highest rating among the 'Voyager' films), and for the week during which it was screened it was ranked 59th out of the top 100 programmes; level-pegging with 'Wildlife On One'.

In the USA, 'Blazing Pedals' was broadcast on National Geographic's own cable TV channel on 9 July.

The reviews were varied: the *Western Daily Press* described it as 'a lunatic journey', then went on to say: 'a lot of shots were too-obviously staged for the benefit of a camera crew and I suspect one of the accidents was carefully mocked up after the rider had sustained injuries.'

The *Kent Evening Post* began its 'Did You See' column with: 'Every now and again, you see some of the nuts responsible for perpetuating our reputation as a nation of eccentrics.' The review continued: 'Riding a bicycle across the Atlas Mountains of Morocco is the sort of hare-brained jaunt which only Britons (or possibly Californians) could contemplate with any seriousness.'

Peter Waymark in *The Times* wrote: 'But with only half an hour to tell the story there is inevitably much compression and the effect is rather like a one-day cricket match – a flurry of activity, a guaranteed result but not enough time to savour the finer points.'

On the Welsh borders, 'Blazing Pedals' was lauded by 'G.C.' in the *Wrexham Evening Leader*: 'Unusually for such a documentary, there was some tight, slick editing which turned an already excellent film into something rather special . . . It was magical stuff, well put together, which – almost – made you want to wheel the Raleigh out of the garage and ask a passing policeman: "Which way to Morocco?"

Thomas Sutcliffe in *The Independent* described the production as 'a film which strained for the heroic but found itself repeatedly bogged down in cliché.' He concluded warmly: 'There was, though, a scientific purpose to the exhibition; the adventurers were able experimentally to confirm the hypothesis that a bicycle is a positive hindrance when climbing snow-covered mountains. Next week – by pogo-stick across the Gobi Desert.'

Actually, that's not such a bad idea; I've already ridden a bicycle across the Gobi, so I guess that it makes sense to try it next time on something a little less obvious, like a pogo-stick . . .

But seriously, Sutcliffe (and one of the other reviewers I've quoted here) have identified a particular problem which arises from making films of journeys: that the director is obliged to condense a score of incidents, atmospheres and emotions, which occurred over several weeks, into a programme lasting (in this case) less than 30 minutes. In the process of compression it is impossible not to distort time, and therefore reality. My lasting (and favourite) memories of the journey – the languid evenings in remote Berber villages – are not seen in the film. It was impractical to operate our camera in darkened, smoke-filled houses and even if we had managed a successful shot of one of these evenings, it would not have compared as visual entertainment to the hundreds of sun-filled shots of castles, mountains, markets, gorges and so on. Reality is mundane and enduring; television is entertaining and ephemeral. The point of the 'box' as an escape from reality would be lost if programmes were absolutely true to life. The documentary film-maker has the added problem that he or she must entertain *and* present the facts in a truthful, representational light; a difficult tight-rope to tread. Alan Ravenscroft's film of the 'Atlas Biker' journey recorded events as they happened, and in the few instances where cameras were unavailable to record key incidents, these were re-created. This was essential if the complete story of the journey was going to be seen on the screen.

Putting the camera on the backs of the travellers themselves will in the long run produce more honest travel films. Light-weight, highly mobile film units like Zanzibar can record events in the wild, as they happen. Such self-contained film-travel units have to bear the burden of heavy, bulky equipment, and often interminable periods setting up shots in frequently inconvient locations – but in return the gap between reality and conventional TV can be narrowed without sacrificing truth or entertainment. The quest for a 'real' travel documentary will continue.

Was the film clichéd? For some people maybe; one person's cliché is another's ripping yarn. Incidents which befell us during the journey happened to create a will-they-won't-they sense of suspense. The two accidents and our mapless wanderings on the eastern plateaux injected drama, but they were not deliberate. Chris is still bitterly disappointed that he had to pull out of the ride; Matt still bears the scar of what might have been a very serious injury; our days spent 'lost' in the eastern Atlas nearly scuppered the whole film. In retrospect, the journey did follow a classical storyline, the inciting incident, the progressive complications;

the crisis; the climax and finally the resolution. It may have looked corny and melodramatic, but then just occasionally (thank goodness), so is life.

Yes, the trip was 'hare-brained', and yes, the bikes were a positive hindrance in climbing snowy mountains. So what! For me, such a frivolous, inconsequential adventure was a blast of fresh air. We were not testing a scientific thesis; we were just having plain, old-fashioned, self-indulgent fun. We did not want to be taken seriously; by serious travelling standards, it was not a 'difficult' journey. The motives for three thirty-year-olds embarking on a mountainbike jape could be seen as mildly childish, but then I (I cannot speak for Matt and Chris) have always found growing-up to be a spasmodic business. May the hiccups continue . . .

If there was one practical outcome of our little adventure, it was to have discovered empirically that mountainbikes and mule-tracks are not suited to each other. At least, not in the High Atlas Mountains. It was a disappointment to be forced to carry the bikes for so much of what should have been the most entertaining part of the route. If I was going to repeat the journey by mountainbike, I would avoid the Tessaout valley by using jeep tracks to the north, to link the valley of Bou Guemez with the village of Toufrine. Some of the mule tracks were worth all the suffering, for the scenery which they revealed; despite the agonies of the hike from Oulghazi to Zaouia Ahansal, I would not have missed the gorges and plateaux of the eastern Atlas for anything. And the abandoned road which leads from Toufrine to the crazy heights of the untrodden col above the Lake Tamda and so to the old Glaoua *kasbah* of Telouet was – despite the hours of carrying – one of the most exciting mountain crossings that I have ever tried. Mountainbikes were the quickest and most efficient form of self-propelled transport to travel from the Sahara Desert to the Atlantic Ocean by way of the High Atlas Mountains. They were fine for the tarmac roads, perfect for the jeep tracks and better valley mule-tracks. But the unusually steep, crumbling mountains of the Atlas range meant that away from the valleys, the mule tracks often deteriorated into rock-strewn scrambles.

'Atlas Biker' *did* prove (and this will apply anywhere in the world) is that for anywhere that a four-wheel drive vehicle can go, a mountainbike can go more quietly, more cleanly, more cheaply and often more quickly.

So, what of the cast? Nine months after the event, Alan Ravenscroft has recently completed a film profile of cricketer David Gower, and a video for the humanitarian organisation 'Medical Aid to Palestinians'. Current projects include a film series on transport in war, and a series of business programmes for the 'The Financial Times.' In 1990 he is returning with Jeremy West to film the marriage fair at Imilchil.

Shortly after returning to the UK, Graham Smith found himself on a plane to South America, where he spent three weeks in swamps and jungle filming the Camel Trophy car rally. At the time of writing, he is in Argentina filming Tom Vernon's latest 'Fat Man' cycling adventure.

Phil Millard completed the 1989 London to Brighton bike ride, and has worked on a natural history film in Saudi Arabia, and a pop video for 'Simple Minds' in Verona, Italy, which involved a crew of 80, and 18 cameras.

Stuart Bruce has worked as sound recordist on a rich variety of programmes ranging from 'The Victorian Kitchen Garden' for BBC Bristol, to 'The Burney Mob' for BBC2's 'Forty Minutes' programme, which followed a bunch of youngsters from Dundee through an SAS survival course on a remote Scottish island.

Matt Dickinson has been on film reconnaissance trips to the equatorial jungle of Gabon, and to the Yukon River in Alaska. He has been commissioned to write a trekking guide to the great ranges of north-west Africa, and has just started work on the second 'Voyager' series for John Gau Productions. The Zanzibar Aaton film camera is currently on the South Georgia islands being used to film a mountaineering expedition being led by Everest climber Stephen Venables. Zanzibar's next project is a documentary about Zimbabwe.

Chris Bradley's knee recovered over a period of six months but on the eve of his first marathon race he tore the ligaments in his ankle. In the meantime he led an adventure holiday group through Israel. Shortly he returns to Morocco, to make an extended trek through the mountains of the Anti-Atlas. (Bolton Wanderers did fight their way to Wembley, where they won the Sherpa Van Trophy in a 4-1 victory against Torquay United.)

Abedelilah Latmer joined three Frenchmen on a mountainbike trek into the High Atlas, and is currently studying English in Epsom, England, and working in the local Mcdonald's in the afternoons and evenings.

Annabel Huxley returned to her desk at the book publishers Viking Penguin, still under siege from the long-running Rushdie affair. She has since travelled in Ecuador by canoe, foot and steam train.

Jeremy West went off to Spain and followed in the footsteps of El Cid, before returning to the UK and resuming his new career as a sound recordist. He is planning to return to Imilchil to record the annual Berber marriage festival.

Andy Flanders finished building the rear/mid-engined Land Rover which he had begun three years earlier. On his second race he crashed, end-over-end and landed upside-down, but managed to finish the event after being turned the right way up.

Ahmed Echita – Mohammed – returned to his old job of ferrying tourists between Marrakesh airport and their hotels.

THE END

Appendices

Appendix 1: Atlas Biker Diary, 15 Jan – 3 Feb 1989

Day	Destination	kms covered	off-road kms	height climbed (metres)
1	Erg Chebbi – Plateau Camp (Meski)	106	38	300
2	Plateau Camp – Ziz Camp (Rich)	135	1	1306
3	Rich – Cold Camp (Outerbate)	90	65	880
4	Outerbate – Oudeddi	40	40	148
5	Oudeddi – woodcutters cottage	25	25	275
6	woodcutters cottage – bivouac	33	33	1365
7	bivouac – Zaouia Ahansal	39	39	478
8	Zaouia Ahansal – Tabant	63	63	1447
9	Tabant – Rouguelt	30	30	450
10	Rouguelt – Ichbakene	25	25	1010
11	Ichbakene – Toufrine	23	23	50
12	Toufrine – Telouet	55	43	1317
13	filming at Telouet			
14	Telouet – Ait Ourir	103	2	769
15	Ait Ourir – Asni	80	31	1142
16	Asni – Neltner Hut	28	20	1941
17	Neltner Hut – Toubkal – Neltner Hut	6	6	1061
18	Neltner Hut – Idni	103	20	786
19	Idni – Taroudant	110	6	522
20	Taroudant – Agadir	89	1	30

Total distance covered: 1,183km
Total distance off-road: 511km
Total height gain: 15,277m

Fastest day's cycling: Day 20, when we covered the 89 kilometres between Taroudant and Agadir, in 2 hours 40 minutes, an average speed of 33.4 kph. We had the benefit of a strong tailwind, and smooth tarmac.

Slowest day's cycling: Day 17, when we covered the 6 kilometres from the Neltner Hut to the summit of Toubkal, and back to the hut, in 9 hours 35 minutes, an average speed of 1.5 kph – slightly faster than snail's pace.

Appendix 2: Passes Climbed

To qualify as a separate entry, a *tizi* has to have a climb of at least 400 metres to its summit from the low point following the previous pass. Passes shown in brackets are adjuncts to the main pass listed on the same line. All heights are in metres.

		metres
Day 2	Tizi-n-Firest	1,700 (est)
Day 3	Tizi-n-Ali	2,000 (est)
Day 4	Tizi-n-Tioura	2,403
Day 6	un-named *tizi* after Oulghazi	2,750 (est)
Day 7	un-named *tizi* after Anergui	2,350 (est)
Day 8	Tizi-n-Ilissi	2,603
Day 8	Tizi-n-Tsalli-n-Imenain (Tizi-n-Tirghist)	2,763
Day 10	Tizi-n-Rouguelt	2,860
Day 12	(Tizi-n-Fedherat/Tizi-n-Timililt) Tizi-n-Tamda	2,850 (est)
Day 14	Tizi-n-Tichka (Tizi-n-Ait Imguer)	2,206
Day 15	Tizi-n-Tassaft	1,807
Day 17	Mount Toubkal	4,167
Day 19	Tizi-n-Test	2,092

Appendix 3: Equipment

FILM AND RECORDING EQUIPMENT: FIRST UNIT (Graham Smith, Phil Millard, Stuart Bruce)

Camera

Aaton 7 16mm camera
3 x 400-foot magazines
4 x 12 volt camera batteries

Lenses

1 x Zeiss 10-100mm zoom
1 x Agnenieux 16-44mm zoom
1 x Agnenieux 5.7mm fixed
1 x Zeiss Distagon 12mm fixed
1 x Zeiss Distagon 35mm fixed
1 x Canon 300mm fixed

Tripods
1 x Ronford Baker FL4 tripod head
1 x Ronford Baker tall and short tripod

Camera Accessories
Filters, including 85 ND Polar, ND Grads Star, Colour Grads
1 x Camera barney
1 x Lithium 12 volt battery
1 x Sekonic light meter
1 x Changing bag
1 x Clapper board
Camera tools
Battery chargers
1 x focus dolly, and tracks
1 x 1kw generator

Lights
2 x battery sun guns
1 x 800W red head and stands
4 x 25-foot extension cables

Film stock
25 x 400-foot rolls Kodak Eastman Colour, 7291 9½ mins filming per 400-ft roll
25 x 400-foot rolls Kodak Eastman Colour, 7202

2 GSAP (Zap) cameras with bike mounts
both cameras had 10mm and 5.7mm lenses
10 x 50-foot pre-loaded magazines of Kodak Eastman Colour 7291
10 x 50-foot pre-loaded magazines of Kodak Eastman Colour 7292

Sound Recording Equipment
1 x Nagra 4.2 recorder
3 x Micron radio-microphones
2 x Sennheiser rifle-microphones
1 x Panamic microphone boom with accessories
1 x SQN 4S mixer
1 x Sony Professional Walkman with crystal 'sync' unit
30 x reels of Agfa PER 368 recording tapes (20 minutes per reel)
10 x TDK 'Metal' cassettes

FILM AND RECORDING EQUIPMENT: SECOND UNIT (Matt Dickinson and Chris Bradley)
1 x Aaton 7 16mm film camera
2 x 400-ft rolls of Kodak Eastman 7291 colour
1 x magazine
1 x Zeiss 10-200 mm zoom lens with '85' filter
1 x Zeiss 10mm fixed lens
1 x re-chargeable on-board battery
1 x reserve Lithium 12 volt battery
1 x Sony Professional Walkman, with crystal 'sync' unit
1 x hand-held Sennheiser microphone
1 x Sekonic light-meter
1 x clapperboard
1 x air brush, lens cleaning tissues and fluid
1 x Maglite torch (for checking camera 'gate')

Total weight of Second Unit equipment approximately 15kg (after Chris' accident, Matt and Nick reduced the weight of the Second Unit equipment by leaving behind all sound gear, and the clapperboard.)

Film and recording equipment carried by Phil Millard and Stuart Bruce on Mount Toubkal
'Aaton 7' 16mm camera
1 x 400-foot magazine
2 x 400-foot rolls of Kodak Eastman Colour 7291
1 x Lithium 12 volt battery
1 x Polar filter
1 x camera barney
1 x changing bag
1 x Sony Professional Walkman
1 x Microphone
5 x TDK 'Metal' cassettes

Still camera equipment carried by Nick
1 x Olympus OM1
1 x 50mm lens
1 x 28mm lens
1 x 135mm lens
1 x Olympus AF-10 auto-focus, auto-exposure camera (with built-in flash)
10 x rolls of Kodachrome 64 film
2 x rolls of Kodachrome 25 film

BIKES AND EQUIPMENT

The Mountainbikes

2 x 22-inch Ridgeback 603 mountainbikes (Matt and Nick)
2 x 20-inch Ridgeback 603 mountainbikes (Chris and spare – not used)
Each of the Ridgebacks were standard specification and equipped thus:
Frames and forks: CroMoly butted tubing, with vertical drop-outs
Handlebars and stem: CroMoly
Wheels: Araya 26 x 1.75 alloy rims with stainless steel spokes. Shimano Deore Freehub
Tyres: Nutrak All Terrain 26 x 2.125; Matt and Nick changed to Ritchie Force 1.9 Racing tyres on Day 2
Brakes: Shimano Deore cantilever
Chainset: Shimano Deore Biopace triple, with 26-36-46 chainrings
Freewheel: Shimano Deore Cassette Freehub 7-speed, with sprockets from 12-28
Gears: Shimano Deore SIS ensemble (indexed, with thumb-shifters)
Pedals: Shimano Beartrap
Saddle: Madison Anatomic Mountain
Fittings: Water bottle and cage
To save weight, we removed the reflectors from the wheels and frames, and to carry our panniers, Madison Cycles fitted to each bike a light-weight Blackburn rear carrier. Each mountainbike weighed 13 kg.

Bicycle tools and spares carried by mountainbikers

1 x Mt Zefal Plus pump
1 x Nutrak puncture repair kit
2 x Madison plastic tyre levers
1 x Madison chain-link remover (lightened)
1 x Madison small adjustable spanner
3 x Madison Allen keys
1 x Madison 3-way spanner
1 x Madison inner tube
(A much larger tool-kit and spares supply – including tyres and inner-tubes, cables, spokes and so on – was carried with the support crew, though these proved unnecessary since the only bicycle breakdown we had on the entire trip was a broken rear brake cable on Nick's bike, caused by an overtight clamp-bolt. Between the three of us we had 9 punctures during 3,320 biker-kilometres of journey. More for entertainment than any practical reason, Nick and Matt switched at Rich from Nutrak 26 x 2.125 tyres to the lighter Ritchie Force 1.9 Racing tyres for the rest of the journey. Chris used the 2.125s for the entire ride.)

Personal clothing used by mountainbikers

1 x set each of thermal underwear ('Thermalite' made from Meraklon polypropylene)
1 x pair of salopettes (Nick); track-suit bottoms (Matt); Castelli 'Thermodress' wool cycling trousers (Chris)
1 x T-shirt
1 x Lowe 'Snap' Polarplus pullover and 'Lowe Polarplus sweater (Nick); 1 Karrimor Polarplus top (Matt and Chris)
1 x Caldo 'Cascade' Goretex overtrousers (Nick)
1 x Lowe Goretex jacket (Nick); Agusport breathable Outdoor Jacket made from 'PORAY-2000' (Matt and Chris)
1 x long thick 'Lakeland' 70% wool 30% nylon 'superloop' socks
1 x short thick 'Lakeland' socks (as above)
1 down hood (Nick), Lowe 'Wasa' polarplus hat (Chris), Karrimor Polarplus hat and anorak hood (Matt)
1 x pair of gloves
1 x pair of Goretex mittens
1 x pair Zamberlan 'Treklite' boots weighing 1.42kg, with Vibram 'Bimescol' sole (Nick); Axo Mountain shoes with Skywalk soles (Matt and Chris)
1 x detachable waterproof hood for jacket
1 x Hackett trilby hat

Personal equipment carried by mountainbikers

1 x Karrimor 30-litre Hot Ice rucksack weighing 900 grams (Nick);
1 x Karrimor 25-litre Hot Rock rucksack weighing 650 grams (Chris and Matt)
1 x Karrimor Kalahari pannier
1 x Karrimor 3-season sleeping bag
1 x notebook and biro (Nick)
1 x foil survival blanket
1 x watch
1 x pair sunglasses (Bollé Edge)

Medical kit carried by mountainbikers

1 x roll of sticky plaster
1 x tube of antiseptic cream

Communal equipment carried by mountainbikers

1 x map (1:100,000 IGN series for middle part of route only)
1 x Swiss Army knife
1 x compass
1 x whistle

1 x head-torch
2 x spare 'AA' Duracell batteries

Amendments to equipment carried by Matt and Nick from Tabant to Telouet
Left behind
Sony Professional Walkman
clapperboard
50mm lens for Olympus camera
bicycle panniers
Taken instead
Each of us carried a Karrimor 55-litre Para-Mont rucksack weighing 1.2kg empty

Additional equipment used while in contact with support crew
Wild Country 3-man 'Super Nova' tent, weighing 4.4kg
Karrimor 3-season sleeping mats

Additional equipment used by each of Matt and Nick for ascent of Toubkal
1 x Goretex 'Alpine pants'
1 x 'Best' Layerwear long thermal pants and woollen zipped polo-neck top
1 x ice axe
2 x 9mm ropes
1 x pair of crampons (Nick)
The support crew members and film crew who climbed Toubkal were equipped with full weather gear and an ice axe each.